Sir Richard Vernon, 1452.   Tong
Church, Shropshire

Frontispiece

BRITISH & CONTINENTAL
ARMS AND ARMOUR

by

Charles Henry Ashdown

DOVER PUBLICATIONS, INC.
NEW YORK

Published in Canada by General Publishing
Company, Ltd., 30 Lesmill Road, Don Mills,
Toronto, Ontario.
Published in the United Kingdom by Constable
and Company, Ltd., 10 Orange Street, London
WC 2.

This Dover edition, first published in 1970,
is an unabridged republication of the work originally published by T. C. & E. C. Jack, London
and Edinburgh, in 1909 with the title *British
and Foreign Arms and Armour.*

International Standard Book Number: 0-486-22490-2
Library of Congress Catalog Card Number: 74-113862

Manufactured in the United States of America
Dover Publications, Inc.
180 Varick Street
New York, N. Y. 10014

PREFACE

THE study of Arms and Armour is one of absorbing interest
to a large and ever increasing number of the community,
inasmuch as it appeals in a marked degree to the student
of history, the antiquarian, and to those who work in the
realms of art.   To the first it appeals as a concrete reminder
of the struggles of nations for liberty, independence, power,
or conquest; to the second it breathes of the age in which
it saw the light with all the feeling and tone which characterised it; to the third it is a source of delight by the
consummate beauty of its form or the exquisite details of
its adornment.   Unfortunately there are few books extant
which serve as a guide to the student, although there are
many which deal with the subject.   The great works of
Meyrick, with Skelton his illustrator, are standard only in
a sense that it is necessary to be thoroughly acquainted
with the subject in order to guard against the many errors
embodied in them.   Grose is hopelessly antiquated, while
Fosbroke, Stothard, Strutt, Shaw, Planché, Cotman,
and others who flourished before or about the sixties, only
deal pictorially or casually with the subject.   The Rev.

Charles Boutell by his translation of Lacombe did much to
foster the study, but it was from a French point of view, and
his epitome of English armour and arms, though excellent
in its way, is only superficial, and a digest of his great
works on Monumental Brasses.   In the latter he probably
did more to further the study than any preceding author ;
he was the first to rationally systematise the arrangement
of armour in periods in consonance with the salient features
it possessed, thus breaking through the previous methods
of classifying it by reigns, which was obviously absurd,
or by centuries, which was equally ridiculous.   I have
followed his method with but little variation in the pages
of this book, inasmuch as no better arrangement is extant.
It is a matter for great pride to myself that such standard
works should have emanated from a former Hon. Secretary
of the St. Albans and Herts Architectural and Archæo-
logical Society, and if the present volume should in any
degree further the good work of my predecessor it will
have achieved the height of my ambition.   Hewitt is de-
lightful reading, but his arrangement is unsystematic and
involved ; to the advanced student, however, he is invaluable.   The later works of Demmin, Clephan, Gardner, &c.,
are masterly monographs upon the subject, but hopelessly
out of place in the hands of a beginner.

It is with a view to rectifying this obvious requirement
that the following pages have been compiled, and it is confi-
dently anticipated that a careful reading and digest of each
separate period of armour, supplemented with the study of
local brasses, effigies, museums, private collections, &c., will
enable the average student to attack the more advanced
works upon the subject with equal profit and pleasure.   It

is perhaps necessary to caution the student of brasses against
many existing cases where the armour shown is not essentially that of the period when the person died, inasmuch
as many warriors in their old age requested that the armour
delineated upon their monumental slabs should be that in
which they achieved renown in youth or manhood. In other
examples the brass was not executed until some time after
the person represented had deceased, and details had under-
gone change in the interim; while cases are not unknown
where the brass of one person has been taken to record the
demise of another, perhaps many years later. A flagrant
example of this may be cited in the brass of Peter Rede, d.
1577, in St. Peter's, Mancroft, Norwich, who is represented
in complete plate of the years 1460 or 1470, with visored
salade, &c. Occasionally we find the artist exercising his
powers of recollection with startling results, as in the case
of the Wodehouse brass in Kimberley Church, Norfolk,
1465, but probably executed sixty years later. The knight
delineated has a skirt of mail of 1490 with three fluted tuilles,
very high pike-guards, a camail of 1405 or earlier, sabbatons
of 1500, and a breastplate with placcate of 1470. Fortunately
such vagaries are so apparent that the observer is placed
upon his guard at once.

The average Englishman is probably more unacquainted
with arms and armour than any other technical subject.
Beyond a general idea that the Crusaders fought in mail,
and the Wars of the Roses were waged by warriors clad in
plate, his knowledge does not extend, and he consequently
witnesses many startling incongruities upon the stage of a
theatre, or the arena of a pageant, with the most profound
indifference. He will perceive Richard III. in a camail and

Ivanhoe in a salade with the utmost complacency. The pity
of it is that those who are responsible for the historical
inaccuracies should be so ignorant, for no effort ought to
be spared in endeavouring to educate the nation, and especially the youth of it, in the fundamental principles of
rigid historical truthfulness. In our theatres recently we
have witnessed Bolingbroke in a fifteenth century tabard,
a waistbelt, and round-toed sabbatons, with the Duke of
Norfolk in an almost equally grotesque parody of the
Camail and Jupon Period; Pistol with a basket-hilted rapier;
Henry V. in a camail, late fifteenth century gauntlets, twen-
tieth century boots, and vambraces covering parts of his
coudières. Upon the arena knights of Richard II.'s period
have appeared in full plate armour of 1470; at Queen
Eleanor's funeral without ailettes; while bear's-paw sabbatons have figured conspicuously in many scenes previous to
1480. These are elementary details which even a cursory
knowledge of military equipment could avoid, but in the
illustrations of historical scenes in books and magazines
equal ignorance prevails, and a knight in pure mail and a
surcoat, making love to a maiden in a reticulated head-dress
seated under a two-centred Tudor archway, is only an
example of the incongruities which almost every day insult
the intelligence and offend the eyesight of the educated
reader. Unfortunately many illustrators go to the works
of Sir Walter Scott for details of mediæval military equipment, and are thereby led hopelessly astray.

It will be noticed in the following pages that continual
reference is made, respecting early armour and weapons,
to the MSS. which are preserved in our inimitable national
collection at the British Museum, and I cannot too earnestly

advise the student to utilise to the utmost extent possible the treasure-house of military detail preserved therein. The feeling which prompted early illuminators to represent Biblical and other personages in contemporary equipment, whereby Goliath was shown habited in Norman hauberk and helm, Moses appeared on horseback with couched lance in the mixed mail and plate of the thirteenth century, and Julius Cæsar crossed the Rubicon in a salade and complete Yorkist plate, is simply invaluable to the student, inasmuch as every detail, though at times almost microscopic, is faithfully delineated, and every new fashion recorded at once upon its adoption. I have drawn upon many manuscripts for illustrations, but there are scores still untouched which only need the student's attention to deliver up many valuable examples of details probably quite unknown at the present time.

There are collateral subjects connected with the study of Armour and Arms which the exigencies of space have compelled me to wholly or partially omit, such as heraldry, mantling and the changes it underwent, caparisoning and barding, the later development of weapons of precision, history and varieties of the sword, &c., some of which would require special monographs to deal with, and do full justice to, the subject.

One of the main ideas has been the simplification of those points upon which the majority of the books extant are either silent or deal with in a casual and unsatisfying manner. One period especially, which gave me infinite trouble as a student, is that between 1320 and 1360, while another feature, generally omitted or hurriedly glossed over, is the equipment of the common soldier.

In conclusion I must express my deep sense of obligation
to the authorities connected with the Tower of London, the
Wallace Collection, the British Museum Manuscript De-
partment, the South Kensington Museum, the Rotunda at
Woolwich, the Edinburgh Castle Museum, the United
Service Institution, the Armourers' Hall, &c., for the
kind facilities they have willingly and promptly afforded
for sketching, photographing, and examining the various
exhibits preserved in those institutions.

CHARLES HENRY ASHDOWN.

MONASTERY CLOSE,
ST. ALBANS, HERTS.

The Author gratefully acknowledges his indebtedness to Viscount
Dillon; the Marquis of Salisbury; the late Sir John Evans, K.C.B.;
The Very Rev. the Dean of Ely, D.D.; Sir Ralph Payne-Gallwey, Bart.;
H. J. Toulmin, Esq., J.P.; A. F. Calvert, Esq.; W. Page, Esq., F.S.A.;
E. J. Hunt, Esq., B.A.; H. R. Wilton-Hall, Esq.

CONTENTS

CHAPTER I

WEAPONS OF PREHISTORIC MAN

THE STONE AGE

THE prehistoric man of the Stone Age had undoubtedly one of the most difficult materials to deal with that can possibly be conceived, inasmuch as it was intensely hard, very brittle, and, so far as flint is concerned, occurred naturally only in comparatively small masses. Yet with this crude matter, and with implements of the same material, he succeeded in producing implements for husbandry and domestic use, weapons of war and for the chase, which excite our warmest admiration, both for the beauty of their proportions and the exquisite skill required in their manufacture. To the worker in flint the number of objects capable of being produced in that exceedingly refractory medium was limited, but these as the age progressed were eventually of a very high order of excellence, probably deemed unattainable by the earlier man. We will take the different weapons in the order of their importance, premising that in this chapter we shall have no armour to deal with, though doubtless the man of the very earliest age had some protection in the way of skins, plaited osier, or bark with which to ward off hostile blows, in addition to the shield, which is common to every race without exception when in the savage state.

FIG. 1.—Stone celt with cutting edge.

Celts.—The word " celt," said to be derived from a doubtful Latin word signifying a chisel, is the name by which a particularly large and widely distributed class of weapons or implements is known. The word has no connection with the Celtic people, and should be pronounced "selt" and not " kelt," as one frequently hears. The form of the celt is well known, inasmuch as many hundreds exist in our museums and private collections. They are found widely distributed in all parts of Europe, and generally throughout the known world, being regarded in many places in mediæval and even in modern times with superstitious reverence as thunderbolts with inherent mystical qualities.

The primitive celts occurring in England are simply flints roughly chipped into form with unsharpened edges, and are chiefly found in those counties where flint abounds. They are not,

FIG. 2.—Stone celt with cutting edge.

however, confined to them, but occur in other parts where flint is not abundant, being fabricated in a different material such as agate, quartz, granite, obsidian, clay-slate, greenstone, serpentine, and other rocks. These crude celts, being merely chipped out and very roughly formed, are at times difficult of recognition; they belong to

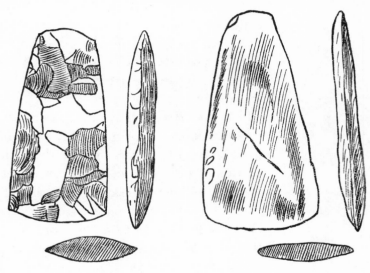

FIG. 3.—Celt with ground edge.   FIG. 4.—Stone celt with polished surface.

the Palæolithic or earlier period of the Stone Age. The second development of the celt appears in the grinding of one edge so as to produce a cutting portion (Figs. 1, 2), the ruder ones simply having a serrated edge produced by being chipped. This grinding was doubtless executed by means of sand and water, and in scores of examples a remarkably even result has been obtained (Fig. 3). The third form in which the celt is polished all over is the highest development and the most recent (Fig. 4), and is

classed in the Neolithic period. Some of these have ornamentation upon them in the form of ribs running longitudinally upon the sides, and some are bored with a circular
or oblong hole. For use these celts were fixed transversely
at the end of a haft of wood either by binding or by the
wood being cleft for their insertion; in peace they per-
formed all the offices which are asso-
ciated with a hatchet, and in war those
of a battle-axe.

FIG. 5.—Flint spear-
head.

Spear-heads. — The greater part of
these belong to the later period, and are
remarkable for the care and attention
which has been bestowed upon their
construction. They invariably present a
lance-like outline of symmetrical proportions with the edge in one plane,
and are chipped so as to be very thin
(Fig. 5); at times notches occur upon
either side to facilitate their fixing into
the end of the spear shaft and being
bound firmly in it. Others have been
found with the cutting edge carefully
ground and polished, but with the tang only chipped
and the edges serrated to afford a firm grip for the
sinews used to affix it to the shaft. They vary in length
from three to ten or more inches.

Arrow-heads and Javelin-heads.—The earliest forms
of these are simply elongated splinters of flint or other
stone, and undoubtedly were simply tied upon or inserted
in the end of the arrow shaft by a ligament. They show
but little work, simply as much as was necessary to give

a satisfactory point, and to provide a tang for fixing. These may be termed lozenge-shaped (Fig. 6), and side by side with them are those of a leaf-shape —these two being the designs presenting the least amount of work and skill in fabrication. Subsequently a barbed and tanged variety was evolved, showing the maximum amount of technical skill in the making, and having the most deadly properties by reason of the difficulty of extraction when once inserted under the skin (Figs. 7, 8). They are as a rule of symmetrical proportions, the barbs carefully chipped to offer the least amount of resistance to the penetrative force of the arrow, and even at times a certain amount of polishing and grinding was added to insure keenness to the point and edge.

Fig. 6. — Lozenge-shaped arrow-head.

The British Museum is in possession of a number of these arrow-heads, which may be considered almost as works of art, together with some of larger proportions which undoubtedly formed the heads of javelins (Fig. 9). Being fabricated of such imperishable material they have naturally been preserved in very large numbers, and hardly a museum exists without

Fig. 8.—Barbed arrow-head.

Fig. 7.—Barbed arrow-head.

at least a few specimens being contained in it. In the mediæval period many quaint superstitions were associated with them, and their preservation as amulets, charms, and general attributes of curative powers, &c., has led to the handing down to the present generation of scores which would probably have been broken up in the ordinary course of events.

Daggers.—The dagger is one of the commonest forms of weapon relating to the Stone Age, as might be supposed

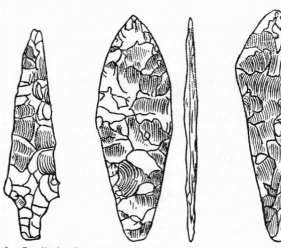

FIG. 9.—Javelin-head.   FIG. 10.—Dagger from   FIG. 11.—Dagger from
                            British Museum.   British Museum.

from its simple form and easy construction when compared with others. In its crudest and earliest condition it merely consisted of a flint rudely chipped to a point at one end; but subsequently it assumed a more definite form, and almost equal attention was paid to the handle and to the blade. The latter was invariably leaf-shaped, and broader towards the point than at the butt, where it is usually rounded or cut off square. The beautiful example, Fig. 10, is of white flint and may be seen in the British

Museum, while Fig. 11 from the same collection is of black flint and about eight inches in length. As this is thickened at the butt it may have been used without any handle, but undoubtedly most of these blades were so mounted, and in Fig. 12 we have an example of the notched variety, where two indentations are perceived on either side for the passage of the tendons fixing the blade to the handle. In a few cases a shaped handle having a pommel and a grip, and with the blade formed out of the same piece of flint, has been discovered ; the weapons in these instances have been ten or twelve inches in length, and modelled precisely the same as the bronze dagger which succeeded them. The highest type of flint weapons of the dagger class are those which have been discovered in Egypt ; they are provided with long thin blades, beautifully ground or chipped on one side to form an edge, and elaborately serrated upon the thicker side forming the back, with cross ripple

Fig. 12.—Dagger with notched edge.

markings for ornamentation, the whole forming a specimen of clever handicraft and skilful workmanship which can only be adequately appreciated by actual inspection.

Among the weapons of the Stone Age may be mentioned the sling-stones, which are found in considerable numbers in countries where flints abound ; they are of a lens-like shape and from two to three inches in diameter, being probably formed in this manner for insertion in a cleft stick which was used for throwing them. Balls of stone are also occasionally found with grooves in them, which suggest the presence at one time of string; these may have been used as weapons for throwing with the string attached, or wielded in the hand as a flail.

Battle-axes.—Although the celt may be regarded as fulfilling the functions of a battle-axe among its other

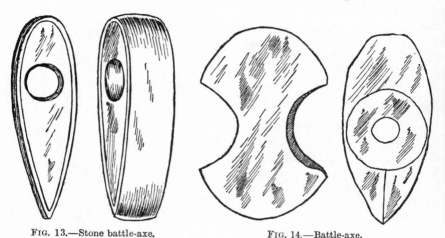

FIG. 13.—Stone battle-axe.   FIG. 14.—Battle-axe.

manifold duties, yet a true battle-axe was evolved by the Stone man towards the latter part of his existence. It was invariably perforated by a circular hole, effected by grinding, and as a rule assumed approximately the shape shown in Fig. 13. Examples of these battle-axes have been found with cutting projections upon each side of the shaft; this was probably the prototype of the bipennis subsequently made in bronze and finally in iron. An example is shown in Fig. 14.

THE BRONZE AGE

The term " Bronze Age," so generally used for the period immediately preceding the introduction of iron, conveys to most readers very scanty ideas as to the duration of time over which it extended. Indeed, to those thoroughly conversant with the subject, the chronological arrangements of the various periods of the age, and the grouping together of these into one comprehensive whole, is practically a case for individual calculation, and these tally but seldom. However, it may be taken that, speaking broadly, the bronze period commenced in Britain about 1500 B.C., and at a much earlier age upon the Continent, one authority placing it as early as 3000 B.C. Iron was in general use about three or four centuries before Christ on the Continent, and Cæsar makes no mention of bronze in his description of the weapons and accoutrements of the Britons.

Celts.—Of all the varying forms of bronze implements the celt is probably the most widely distributed and the best known, and there is every reason to believe it was the first of the articles to be manufactured. It is generally admitted to be both an implement for everyday use and also a weapon of war. Its general utility was that of a chisel, a wedge, or a wood-splitting hatchet; in war it was the prototype of the battle-axe. It is of very wide distribution, being found all over the Continent of Europe, and has many varieties. In order of development the flat celt is undoubtedly the earliest, and was derived from the celt of the Stone Age, the example shown in Fig. 15 differing but little from the flint proto-type. This pattern gradually developed until one similar

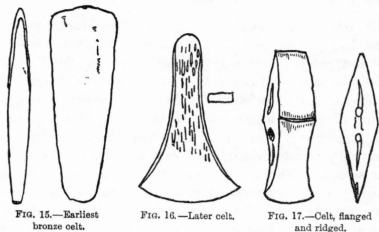

FIG. 15.—Earliest bronze celt.

FIG. 16.—Later celt.

FIG. 17.—Celt, flanged and ridged.

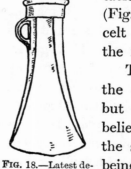

FIG. 18.—Latest de-velopment of celt.

to Fig. 16 was evolved. From this crude form the flanged variety was produced, giving an extra grip for the handle; then a transverse ridge was added, thus forming two receptacles to receive the split end of the handle (Fig. 17). The latest development of the celt is that in which a socket is made for the insertion of the handle (Fig. 18).

The relative form of the handle with the celt affixed has been much discussed, but the consensus of opinion leads one to believe that the handle was somewhat in the shape of a hockey-stick, the bent part being inserted in the socket of the celt. Before the evolution of the socketed celt the latter was inserted in a cleft stick and projected from

one side at right angles, being firmly bound in that
position by cross-lacing. This projection doubtless suggested the bent stick of a later period.

Daggers.—Of contemporary date with the celt, and
perhaps of even more remote antiquity, is the bronze
dagger, which in its original simple form
may have been used as a knife for
domestic purposes and a dagger for war,
though subsequently the two became
quite distinct. The general
form of the blade may be
gleaned from Figs. 19 and
20, where the ribs towards
the point may be readily
seen. This ribbing and
grooving of the blade are a
distinctive feature, and are
sometimes beautifully de-
veloped into a pattern more
or less intricate. The
handles were made of ivory,
bone, or wood, and are very
seldom found entire. The
method of adjusting the haft

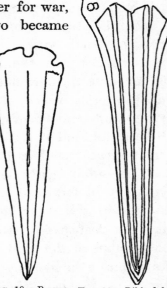

FIG. 19.—Bronze   FIG. 20.—Ribbed bronze
dagger.   dagger.

will be gleaned from the position of the rivets; the handle
was evidently either split into two pieces and then placed
on either side, or a cut was made for the insertion of the
tang or lower part of the blade. In some cases the pommel
of bronze has been found accompanying the dagger, and
also traces of what may have been the sheath. That
variety of dagger having a tang to fit into the shaft seems

to be peculiar to our islands, as those found on the Continent invariably possess a socket into which the handle
could be fitted. Some very small and thin daggers have
been found side by side with flint weapons, which appears
to point to a time when the metal was very scarce, in the
earliest part of the Bronze Age; subsequently the stouter
form of weapon shows analogies with continental forms,
and so points to intercommunication between the main-
land and this island at that early date.

Swords.—The sword does not appear to have been
contemporaneous with the early thin dagger, but was no
doubt a subsequent evolution based upon the dagger.
Of all the forms which have been handed down to us
from the most remote antiquity the bronze sword is the
most beautiful, and it is very questionable if any of the
hundreds of shapes of lethal weapons of that description
which have subsequently seen the light can vie with it
in symmetry of form and general gracefulness. Only one
other class of weapon of this period attempts to rival in
beauty the leaf-shaped sword, and that is the spear,
which is often of the most graceful lines. The beautiful
workmanship exhibited by these weapons raised doubt
at times as to their real origin, many asserting that
they were of Roman fabrication, but it has been
definitely settled that they antedated the Italian historical
period. Iron and steel were substituted for bronze at a
very early period in the Roman army, the shape, however, being unaltered. The fact that the majority of
finds of bronze swords occurs in countries where the
Romans never penetrated militates against the supposition of their Roman origin. The length of the blade

averages about two feet, though some are as short as one and a half feet, and some as long as two and a half. The hilt plate alters much in form, and there are many varieties: the handle was of wood, bone, or horn, split into two plates and riveted on either side (Figs. 21, 22). The blade was apparently cast in a mould so carefully made that there was no necessity for file-work or hammering afterwards, the edges being formed by the uniform reduction all round of the thickness of the metal (Fig. 23). Blade and tang were cast in one piece, although one variety which appears to be common to the British Isles has a handle affixed to the blade by rivets, after the manner of the dagger (Fig. 24). The rivet heads occasionally show signs of having depressions in them, as though they were splayed by a punch, while some have been closed by a hollow punch so as to leave a small stud. Occasionally swords are found having the hilt and finished blade cast in one piece,

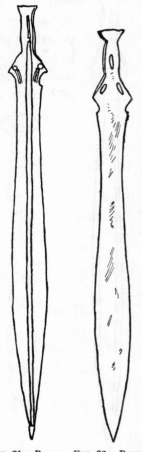

FIG. 21.—Bronze sword.

FIG. 22.—Bronze sword showing rivet-holes.

while others occur bearing signs of the hilt being cast upon the blade. A few swords have been found with gold ornamentation upon the hilts, and many in which the blade is decorated with a pattern produced in the casting. Although of bronze, and therefore not subject in any great degree to aerial oxidation, the sword appears to have been universally protected by enclosure in a scabbard. These in some instances were of bronze, but more often of leather or wood, with fittings of bronze, and in all cases the scabbard was of greater length than the blade it contained. Some scabbards even appear of fantastic forms, as though the man of the Bronze Age, like his successor of the Iron Period, was not averse to the occasional outshining of his fellow-man.

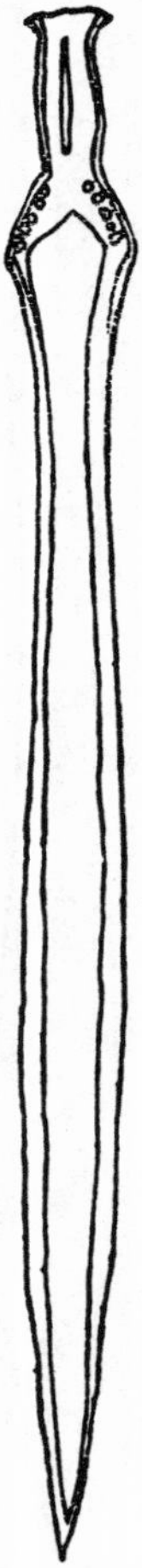

The Spear.—The spear is undoubtedly of the most remote antiquity, and dates far back into the Stone Period; its inception seems to be inherent in all savage tribes, and is a natural evolution of the idea of inflicting injury upon a foe at a distance, and again of preventing his approach to do personal harm. The primitive man probably pointed a long stick by attrition on a rock, and subsequently hardened it by fire: a splint of bone, being harder than the wood, occurred next, and probably

Fig. 23.—Bronze sword with cast edge.

Fig. 24.—British sword with riveted handle.

the flint succeeded, to be followed in due time by the bronze head. The difficulty of affixing the head, however, seems to have hindered progress at first in this direction, for the bronze dagger undoubtedly antedated the spear-head, which continued to be of flint for a long period after the dagger was introduced. It is highly probable that the first spear-head was not constructed until the Bronze man discovered the secret of making the socketed celt by means of a core placed within the mould ; with the advent of this invention spear-heads became possible. Of course it may be open to question whether any of the blades with tangs were really spear-heads and not daggers, or incipient sword-blades. Some spear-heads have been found which are un-doubtedly of the tanged description, but they are not of British, and possibly not even of European origin. The general form of the head tends towards the leaf-shape, though this is not so pronounced as it is in the sword (Fig. 25). The advent of the spear - head occurred when man had de-veloped considerable skill in the casting of bronze and its manipulation under the hammer, and the really extraordinary deft-

Fig. 25. — Bronze spear-head, leaf-shaped.

ness shown in making the core, so that the minimum of metal was used with the maximum of effect and strength, calls forth the warmest admiration. Some of these cores are prolonged through the centre of the blade, so that the metal is really attenuated, but at the same time of uniform thickness, the inserted staff providing the necessary rigidity. Respecting the sizes of those found there can be no question but that the larger heads (and some have been found nearly a yard in length) were intended for use only in the hand as spears, while some of the smaller are the heads of javelins, or possibly of arrows. The blades are at times of remarkable beauty of design and of excellent workmanship. The sage-leaf form is of very common occurrence, the central core reaching to the point, and ornamented with subordinate ribs which also strengthen the blade. In these forms a hole is punched in the socket for the insertion of a rivet to fix it to the lance shaft. Others show two small loops cast upon the socket for a thong to pass through, which was afterwards brought down to the shaft and securely fastened (Fig. 26). This variety shows no rivet-hole. Ornamentation is by no means rare upon these spear-heads ; it generally takes the form of open work, such as circles and ovals perforating the blade, and of filed or cast patterns upon the sockets, some even showing traces of gold inlaying. Barbed spear-heads are extremely rare, and were probably only used in the chase.

Fig. 26.—Spear-head with apertures for thongs.

Arrow-heads.—Arrow-heads in bronze practically do not exist in this country, although they occur on the Continent and in Egypt, where they are generally of the types shown in Figs. 27 and 28. It is highly probable that

A. F. Calvert

PLATE I*

Shield of Italian Workmanship, Sixteenth Century

the flint arrow-head was in use through the whole, or nearly the whole, of the Bronze Age, being retained because of its efficiency and cheapness.   Bronze must have been a comparatively rare and dear alloy, and the weapons exhibit as a rule the minimum of metal in their construction compatible with efficiency; arrows from their very nature are continually being lost, and this fact alone would render their use expensive.

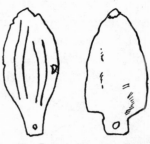

FIG. 27.—Bronze arrow-head.   FIG. 28.—Bronze arrow-head.

Shields. — Among primitive races the shield was invariably of wicker-work or of wood, and as the examples in bronze which have been unearthed are of a high order of skill in workmanship and design we may naturally infer that they were of comparatively late introduction, and only

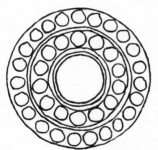
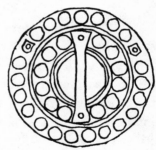

FIG. 29.—Bronze shield.   (British Museum.)

appeared when the expert artizan of the age was capable of producing plates of considerable area and of uniform thickness.   In the British Museum are several very fine examples of shields, one of which we illustrate to show the general form and shape (Fig. 29).   It was dug up not far from the river Isis, in the vicinity of the Dyke Hills, near Dorchester in Oxfordshire. It is circular in form, about 13 inches in diameter, and ornamented with two concentric rings of bosses which encircle an umbo. All these bosses have been repoussé in the metal except four, which are used in two instances as rivet heads to fix the handle in position, and in two others to fasten buttons to the interior of the outer rim. It is probable that a guige was fastened to these buttons. So thin is the metal that it can hardly have served as a shield without some auxiliary strengthening, and this was conjecturally afforded by a lining of leather moulded into the depressions of the shield when wet. There is no reason for supposing that the metal now seen was the size of the original shield; in fact there is a probability that it was larger, and that the metal merely formed the centre. A bronze buckler found near Aberystwith was formerly in the Meyrick Collection and preserved at Goodrich Court, whence it was transferred to the British Museum. It is about 26 inches in diameter, with no less than twenty concentric circles of knobs and ribs, with the usual buttons for fixing the guige. The general type of shield is that having a series of concentric rings raised in the metal with studs between the ribs. The ornamentation is in all cases raised by hand with hammer and punch, and doubtless the metal was much thicker and the diameter much less in the early stages of making.

FIG. 30.—Bronze mace-head.

A considerable number of bronze weapon-like forms

have been from time to time discovered, the uses of which are only conjectural. Thus long blades of a triangular bayonet-like section occur, which may either have been a sword or rather rapier for thrusting only, or have been attached to a shaft and served as a spear. Others, again, have a socketed head from the side of which projects a cutting blade of various sizes and forms which might be the halberd in an incipient stage. There also exist short, thick, scythe-like blades of great strength, with strong rivets for attachment to some shaft, which may have been constructed to fit upon the wheels of chariots. Knobs of bronze occur having a socketed centre and projecting spikes upon the sides which undoubtedly when fitted to suitable handles formed the maces of the Bronze Age (Fig. 30), or possibly were portions of early "morning stars" or military flails.

CHAPTER II

THE ASSYRIANS

The bas-reliefs of Assyria afford us ample materials for becoming acquainted with the arms and armour of that great and warlike empire, and our own national collection probably contains the richest store of detail.

The Tunic.—This appears to have been of thick quilted linen or of leather, as sometimes long hair is shown upon it. It reached to the knees and had half-sleeves : at times a pectoral is shown of large proportions. Another, and much more military style, consisted of rope fastened side by side, and so bound round the body that it had the appearance of a tight-fitting cuirass. This would be much more efficacious against the sword and the arrow than the tunic. It generally terminated at the waist. In the earlier sculptures there are no indications of the metal cuirass or of greaves, but the latter subsequently came into vogue ; they were of metal and reached to the knees.

In the invasion of Greece by Xerxes the Assyrians are described as having defensive tunics of flax, which were stuck together surface to surface by a soft mucilage to the number of over a dozen, and formed an excellent defence against a sword-cut. All the varieties of armour are faithfully shown upon the sculptures, some exhibiting the scale-like nature of a few cuirasses, from which we may infer that mascled armour was known to them as to most Oriental nations.

The Helmet.—This was generally the hemispherical skull cap so much affected by Asiatic races then and now; it was made either in iron or leather, furnished with a chin-strap, and decorated at times with a horse-hair crest. A design is sometimes seen which strongly approaches the Phrygian in shape, having a portion of the crest curving over towards the front, while another variety is that of a truncated cone curved backwards. Defences for the neck and sides of the neck are common.

At Marathon the helmets worn were "interlaced or interwoven," from which we may infer that chain mail was not unknown to the Assyrians; it may, however, refer to bands of metal plaited together.

The Shield.—This was circular and concave and, if we may credit Herodotus, made of cane. The representations of this defence bear out the assertion, however, for the front is generally marked out in concentric circles, and wherever the back is exhibited the same circles invariably appear. The light and tough nature of the material would strongly commend itself for this purpose. Occasionally shields are shown covered with leather, or one plate of metal, while others have a surface covered with lozenges, which doubtless represents a kind of pourpoint or quilted material stretched over the framework.

The Sword.—The Assyrian sword as delineated upon the sculptures was slung at the left side, and passed through two notches in the belt so as to make it assume a horizontal position.

The sculptures in the British Museum show the general

character of the sword (or rather of the scabbard, for they are all sheathed) with great minuteness. The pommel is very elegant in form and generally carved; the grip is of peculiar formation, and there is no guard; from actual examples which have been found we know that the broad blade has two edges and terminates in a point. The scabbard is extremely artistic in form, and the whole weapon partakes more of the nature of the dagger or anelace than of the sword.

The Bow was a favourite weapon and of the usual Oriental pattern, being composed of horn, wood, and the large sinews of certain animals firmly glued together. It was carried partly unstrung over the shoulder when not in use ; the total unstringing was not advisable because of the time occupied in getting it ready, most Asiatic bows bending backwards into an oval shape when unstrung, and requiring much physical exertion and time to replace the string. The quiver was also suspended in the same position, containing arrows of some length made of cane.

The Lance was of short proportions, with oblong and leaf-shaped heads, often unbarbed ; it could be thrown, if desired, like a javelin. The mace is also shown upon the sculptures, but rarely.

THE EGYPTIANS

The Tunic.—This was invariably of a quilted material, thickly padded, and generally composed of linen several times folded ; it could resist a cutting weapon but not the point of a sword or lance. Over it was placed the pectoral, which covered the shoulders as well as the chest, and was very similar to the mediæval camail.

The Helmet was of the semi-globular form as a basis with various additions, none, however, of a distinctive national character. The material used was quilted linen of many thicknesses glued together.

The Shield was used only by the spearmen, and was about a yard in height; it was of peculiar shape, being rectangular in the lower part and semi-circular in the upper, where a round opening was pierced, through which the approach of the enemy could be viewed with safety. The outer parts were covered with leather strengthened with rings and studs.

The Bow.—The main strength of the Egyptian armies lay in their bowmen, who fought from chariots or on foot. The bow more nearly approached the dimensions of the English pattern than the Oriental, as also did the arrow, which was at times over 30 inches in length. The latter was made of cane or reed, feathered and barbed, the heads being of bronze.

The Spearmen or heavily-armed troops were accoutred in cuirasses of bronze scales overlapping, and supported on the shoulders by straps; or else in short tunics of heavily-quilted material with bronze plates sewn on in a pattern. Their helmets were quilted like the tunics.

Various weapons appear to have been used by the Egyptians, but they were all secondary to the bow and spear. The sword was straight, double-edged, tapering from the hilt to the point, and constructed of bronze. Scimitars, daggers, battle-axes of various shapes, and slings were in use, while a speciality seems to have been made of the javelin, which was hurled by means of a stick.

THE GREEKS

For the better understanding of the arms of the Greeks it is desirable to consider those of the two distinct ages into which their history naturally falls, viz. the Heroic and the Historic.

THE HEROIC AGE

This period is approximately 1000 years B.C., of the time of Homer, from whom we obtain all, or nearly all, of the particulars respecting arms and armour.

The Cuirass.—This was made of bronze, as was the whole of the defensive armour at that time. It was worn over a linen tunic, and apparently consisted of a breastplate guarded round the arms and neck with lames. That of Agamemnon is stated to have had ten bands of bronze, twelve of gold, twenty of tin, and six of bronze round the neck. We have mention of the defensive equipment of Menelaus which was pierced by the arrow of Pandarus. It first passed through the golden clasps of the waist-belt, then the breastplate, and finally through a coat of mail which was worn underneath. The cuirass was often very highly ornamented by repoussé work and also inlaid with gold.

The Helmet.—The most elaborate helms were those fitting lightly to the head and adorned with a crest which projected before and behind, and was also furnished with plumes. The simpler forms were of leather or bronze, fitting closely to the head, and without peak or plume.

A. F. Calvert

PLATE II *
Shield of Philip II.

The Greaves covered the legs from the knee to the instep, and from their form must have been constructed of bronze or some alloy possessing a large amount of pliability, inasmuch as they were in one piece, and yet nearly met behind the legs, where they were fastened with clasps. Homer frequently alludes to the excellent way in which these defences were made, whereby they in no way hindered the wearer (Fig. 31). It is conjectured that the bronze used in the construction of the greaves resembled in some respects the hardened brass or " latten "

FIG. 31.—Greek greaves (front and back view).

FIG. 32.—Greek shield.

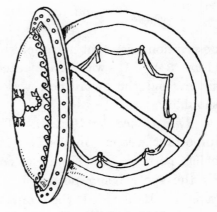

FIG. 33.—Greek shield (front and back).

of the mediæval ages, and that they were carefully moulded to the limbs of the wearer.

The Shield, by far the most important part of the defence, was either round or oval in form and made of bronze, protected at the back with hide, and at times covered with it. Strengthening discs of metal, bosses, and rings of metal were also added (Figs. 32, 33). It appears to have been of very great weight, even Ajax on one occasion being embarrassed by the weight of his

own shield, which we are told was of bronze backed by seven tough bulls' hides. They reached from the neck to the ankle, and were often elaborately decorated. A guige appears to have been fitted at times, which passed over the right shoulder.

The Sword. — Homer applies the terms "long, large, sharp, trenchant, and two-edged" to the sword, and it is evident that it was of the same description as that characteristic of the Bronze Age (Fig. 34). It was ornamented with studs of gold or silver, and the sword-belt was apparently worn over the shoulder.

FIG. 34.—Greek sword in scabbard.

The Lance or Javelin.—This was by far the most important weapon in the Grecian armoury, and plays the chief part in all Homeric combats, which commence by the spear being poised in the hand and hurled as a javelin. It decided the contest as a rule, and it was only upon its failing to do so that the combatants had recourse to the sword. The lance was made of ash— long, tough, and ponderous; the head was of bronze and unbarbed.

The Bow.—Only one description of a bow is given to us—that of Pandarus, which is said to be of ibex horn, strung with sinews (Fig. 35). The arrow-head is of iron ; the only mention of that metal in the warrior's equipment, and the arrows were kept in a quiver fitted with a lid. The sling appears to have been relegated to the lowest order of combatants, who occupied the rear of the army, and sent their missiles over the heads of those in front. The great chiefs and the spearmen did not disdain to use the stone upon occasion, and we have graphic descriptions of the huge rocky pieces the combatants hurled at one another.

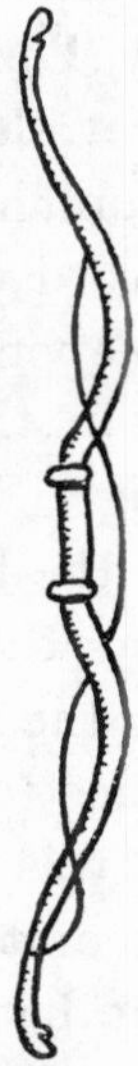

THE HISTORIC AGE

The equipment described by Homer had not particularly altered in the Iron Age except in certain details and modifications necessitated by the changed order of combat. The heavily-armed soldier, having already a tunic as a *just-au-corps*, put on greaves, cuirass, sword (hung upon the left side by a belt passing over the right shoulder); the large round shield, supported in the same manner, helmet, and spear, or two spears, as occasion required. Men thus equipped were termed Hoplites, the term " hopla " more especially denoting the defensive armour, the shield and breastplate, or cuirass. The mode of combat by the Greek phalanx necessitated the adoption of a long and heavy spear ; the ranks were sixteen deep, and each rank consisted of the men standing close together with shield touching shield, while the spears or pikes, each

FIG. 35.—
Greek bow.

24 feet in length, reached 18 feet in front of the nearest
rank when couched. As a space of about 2 feet was
allowed between each rank, the spears of the five files
behind him projected in advance of each front-rank man.

The sword continued to be of the leaf-like form which
prevailed in the Bronze Age, and was longer than the
Roman sword of the following era. At the same time a
sword was in use which was the prototype of the subsequent
weapon : it had a long, straight blade slightly tapering
from the hilt to the point, where it was cut to an acute
angle for thrusting. A central ridge traversed both sides
of the blade, and it was double-edged. Upon these swords
and their scabbards a wealth of decoration was lavished
by the Greeks. The great shield of the Heroic Age gave
place to a round or oblong shield reaching only to the knee ;
it was concave to the body, and appears to have been
decorated as a general rule : one invariable ornament was a
flat band or border round the circumference. This shield
was the true battle-shield of the heavily-armed hoplites. A
much smaller and lighter one was used by the cavalry and
the light infantry, being made of hide with the hair on. A
cross-piece was affixed at the back for a handle, and a cord
was looped round the inside of the shield, which afforded
a grasp for the hand.

The helms all appear with characteristic neck-guards
and pendent guards for the face, which were free to move
upon simple attachments at the side ; the front is shown
to be protected by a more or less ornamental visor or nasal.
The crest, of which three distinct varieties are shown,
assumed many modifications of those varieties, but the
general arrangement was to lengthen it so as to extend from

the front portion of the helmet to the neck-guard, and the upper portion spreading like a fan. The body of the helm in nearly every instance was made the ground for elaborate decoration. To the crest was added at times one or two plumes, the whole producing a striking military effect (Figs. 36 and 37). The true Greek war-helm, however, had very little exterior ornamentation, but was in every respect

FIG. 36.—Greek helmet with cheek-guards.   FIG. 37.—Greek helmet.

a most serviceable and business-like head-piece. It was known as the Bœotian helm (Fig. 38), and the general shape may be gathered from an examination of the Italian " barbuta " of the fourteenth century, its lineal descendant. A fine helmet of this character is preserved in Case 24 at the Tower of London ; it is of bronze, and was excavated at Cumæ, an ancient Greek colony near Naples. It is shown in Fig. 39. Fitting closely to the head and neck, the lower part reached to the shoulders ; in front two openings for the eyes, with a drooping nasal between and a narrow vertical opening opposite the chin and neck, gave a general protection which was most effectual, and only exposed the

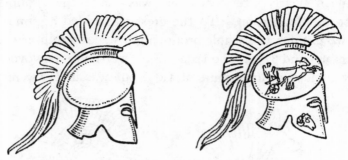

FIG. 38.—Greek helmets of the Bœotian shape.

absolute minimum to chance of injury. Its efficacy was soon recognised, and it was eagerly assumed by the hoplites and the leading Greek warriors. The greaves now appear without straps behind, and were retained in their place solely by the elasticity of the metal; they are represented as adhering closely to the limb, and were probably moulded from casts taken direct from the wearer. About 400 B.C. the heavy bronze cuirass of the Greek soldier, which had been transmitted from the Heroic Period, gave way to a lighter but equally efficacious defence, made of linen crossed many times in folds and glued together, such as we have seen used by the Egyptians, and, in fact, by nearly all Asiatic races. The mounted soldiers wore a shorter cuirass than the hoplites; it was moulded to the figure, and from the lower edge pendent straps of leather were affixed for

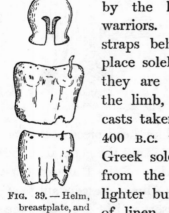

FIG. 39.—Helm, breastplate, and backplate from Cumæ. (Tower of London.)

the protection of the lower part of the body and the thighs. These "lambrequins," as they were termed, were very numerous, and at times ornamented with metal plaques; they were longer than the Roman lambrequins of a subsequent period by reason of the Greek cuirass terminating at the waist (Figs. 40 and 41). The javelin or throwing-spear of the light-armed troops was furnished with a strap to aid in propelling it. A pair of Greek greaves are pre-

FIGS. 40 and 41.—Greek cuirasses.

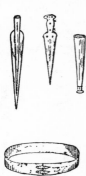

FIG. 42.—Spear-head, dagger and sheath, and bronze belt from Cumæ. (Tower of London.)

served in Case 24, Tower of London, which are probably of the Heroic Age, as they are furnished with rings for the attachment of fastening straps. From the same case we have examples of the bronze cuirass, back-plate, and breast-plate, with a bronze attachment at one shoulder for fastening the two together. An outline of the chief muscles and prominences upon the human form are crudely imitated in repoussé work, and indications exist upon the back-plate of the fastenings by which it was attached to the front (Fig. 39). The bronze belt or zone which was worn by many warriors below the cuirass is also exemplified and shown in Fig. 42. The fastenings in front show a considerable amount of artistic skill. To this zone were attached the lower defences for body and limbs.

The shape of the spear-head is similar to that shown in Fig. 42. It has a central ridge strengthening the blade, and is furnished with a hollow socket for receiving the head of the shaft.

The Greek dagger was termed the "parazonium," and

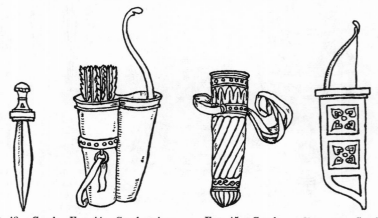

FIG. 43.—Greek parazonium.　FIG. 44.—Greek quiver bow-case.　FIG. 45.—Greek quiver.　FIG. 46.—Greek bow in case.

was common to all the troops (Fig. 43): it was broad in the blade and came to an acute point, the general shape of the blade being of a leaf-like outline similar to the sword. This shape was subsequently adopted by the Romans. A dagger and sheath from Cumæ differs in form from the foregoing (Fig. 42), and partakes more of the character of the anelace of the mediæval period. The holes are shown for rivets by which the wooden or bone handle was fastened, and the sheath, which is very

A. F. Calvert

PLATE III *
German Shield, Sixteenth Century, by Desiderius Colman

plain, terminates in a small knob. The dagger had a small shoulder-strap of its own, by which it was suspended at the right side in a sloping position much higher than the waist.

The bow was of the short form, and made of the same materials as those used in the Heroic Age. A quiver was in general use by the Greek archers, which contained both bow and arrows, as in Fig. 44, which is shown with its accompanying

FIG. 47.—Etruscan helmet.

strap. This, however, was not always the case, as quivers are shown for arrows alone, as in Fig. 45, and also bow-cases which are not adapted for arrows as well (Fig. 46).

THE ETRUSCANS

With regard to the arms and armour of the Etruscans we find but little difference existing from those of the Greeks, but certain developments occurred which distinguished them from those of the parent country and were subsequently adopted by the Romans, thus laying the foundation for a separate and distinct style of equipment. The helmet in general followed the Greek lines but had a tendency towards the formation of a deep bowl-shape for the head; also wings were adopted, at times, which projected to a considerable extent and gave a distinctly Asiatic character to the head-

FIG. 48.—Etruscan soldier's helmet.

piece (Fig. 47). For the ordinary soldier a skull-cap
was in use with a truncated point upon the summit, and
ornamented bosses round the rim (Fig. 48).

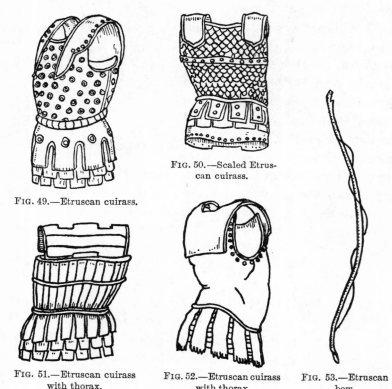

FIG. 49.—Etruscan cuirass.

FIG. 50.—Scaled Etrus-
can cuirass.

FIG. 51.—Etruscan cuirass
with thorax.

FIG. 52.—Etruscan cuirass
with thorax.

FIG. 53.—Etruscan
bow.

The cuirass with its dependent lambrequins was formed,
like that of the Greeks, by joining a back- and breastplate, but the overlapping shoulder-guards, with a tendency
to meet in front, so often observed upon Etruscan pottery,
are quite distinct from the Greek model (Fig. 49).
Cuirasses are also shown made of overlapping plates of

metal (Fig. 50); of discs or lames of plate sewn on a padded base (Fig. 51); and one quilted throughout apparently without any metallic defence (Fig. 52). It has the thorax attached to it, and being viewed from behind exhibits that protection, as is also the case in Fig. 51. As a rule greaves were not worn, the limbs being entirely unprotected. The archers had a cap similar to Fig. 48, together with a tunic of leather. The bow in

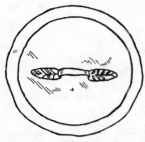

FIG. 54.—Etruscan shield. (Inside.)

use was of a very simple form, as shown in Fig. 53. The shield was circular, and similar in outline to that of the Greek, but differed in its great convexity; the one shown in Fig. 54 exhibits the interior, with the method of affixing the handle.

CHAPTER III

THE ROMANS

THE defensive armour of the Romans differed essentially in the early form from the later, or, broadly speaking, between the Republican Period and the Imperial Period; though it overlapped considerably it may be as well to accept these periods for differentiation.

REPUBLICAN ARMOUR

Cuirass or Lorica.—This was formed upon the Greek style of armour based upon the Etruscan model, and consisted of a back- and breast-plate, strapped together at the sides and fastened by broad epaulette - like belts upon the shoulders (Fig. 55). These belts fastened in front to a ring attached to the breast-plate, and were permanently fixed, low down over the shoulder-blades behind. The lorica was of bronze, and modelled to the shape of the figure; short straps of leather were fixed at the arm-openings, which fell over the shoulders; at the lower part of the cuirass there were two bands of leather, one showing underneath the other, and both generally dagged at the edges; below this again

FIG. 55.—Lorica of Roman General (Republican).

36

depended the lambrequins, often covered with metal studs or plates, and sometimes curled and plaited. They were of the same shape as the shoulder-pieces, but much broader, and always of leather. The tunic worn under the cuirass had half sleeves, and its lower border reached nearly as low as the lambrequins.

The military cloak or paludamentum was draped over the cuirass in picturesque folds, varying according to the taste of the individual wearer.

FIG. 56.—Roman helmet (Imperial Period).

The Helmet was very similar to the Greek model, and had a crest and cheek-pieces (Fig. 56).

The Roman leaders often affected the laminated cuirass, or else that composed of overlapping scales of bronze (Fig. 57). The shield was made upon the Greek model, and the weapons consisted of the lance, javelin, and sword.

FIG. 57.—Officer's lorica (Republican Period).

THE IMPERIAL PERIOD

With the advent of the emperors our knowledge becomes of a more definite character. The admission of foreigners into the Roman army, although it had proved disastrous to the republic, was continued by the emperors, and not only were the natives of the conquered countries enlisted but also mercenaries were employed.

Consequently a great variety of armour and arms

existed in the Roman armies, but the essential ones stand out prominently in sculptures, painting, and upon coins, &c., and with these only will we deal.

The Cuirass.—The heavily-armed troops bore the laminated cuirass (Fig. 58), which consisted of about seven lames of steel encircling the trunk, each lame being divided into two portions, which joined in the middle of

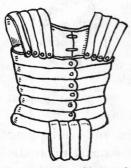

the back and in front. Affixed to the top lame, back and front, were four or more bowed lames passing over the shoulders and working freely upon the pivots which secured them. In front, and fixed to the lower part of the second lame from the bottom, were three or four short lames pendent and hanging vertically so as to protect the middle of the body below the waist.

FIG. 58.—Roman laminated cuirass.

The lames encircling the body were sewn down to a tightly-fitting leather garment, the true cuirass, which was continued upwards before and behind in order to protect the chest and throat and passed over the shoulders under the curved lames. The whole cuirass opened down the front, the iron bands being hinged behind, fastening with a clasp in front. To the lowest lame was generally affixed two rows of leather, dagged at their edges, and the lambrequins descended beneath them, one row of the straps being shorter than those beneath, which fell lower than those used in the earlier age.

The officer of the Imperial Period affected the lorica modelled to the figure as worn by the soldiers in the

Republican Period, but considerably shortened and seldom reaching below the waist, but the scaled cuirass was also a favourite.

The Helmet of the soldier was simply a skull-cap with a peak and pendent cheek-guards (Fig. 59), but subsequently was furnished with a descending hollowed neck-guard, a bar across the forehead acting as a visor, and two cheek-pieces, hinged, which could be fastened together beneath the chin (Fig. 60). During the later days of the empire the helmet became deeper. A common form of ornament for the crest was simply a round knob.

FIG. 59.—Roman helmet.   FIG. 60.—Roman helmet.

The Shield.—This was of two distinct kinds, a long, rectangular, and very concave shield borne only by the legionaries, and an oval, flattened form carried by the horsemen. The rectangular shield was about two feet six inches long, and composed of two plates of metal overlapping, with bands of metal strengthening it at the top and also at the lower edge, where it often rested on the ground. With this shield the well-known testudo was formed. The cognisance of the legion appeared upon the outer face, and on the column of Trajan, where members of the " thundering legion " are depicted, the device is that of a conventional thunderbolt of the usual zigzag description. The oval shield carried by the cavalry (the equites) and the light-armed troops (the velites) was a much-flattened variety of the old shield, and in the later years of the empire was adopted by the legionaries when the rectangular shield was discarded; it was, however, considerably enlarged in its later form.

The Sword.—The early sword, like that of most nations, was of bronze of the well-known leaf shape, and, compared with those of other nations, comparatively short. In the first century B.C. it had become modified into a weapon about two feet in length, having a two-edged blade with parallel sides, and the point at an obtuse angle

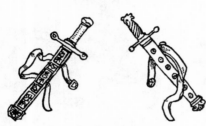

FIG. 61.—Roman swords.

(Fig. 61). A short cross-guard, thin grip, and swelling pommel completed this remarkable weapon, which when used against adversaries armed with lance, javelin, or a long sword must have necessitated the Roman legionary getting within the guard of his adversary before being able to use his weapon, thus implying a high degree of personal bravery. It was worn upon the right side, suspended from a shoulder-belt. Upon the Trajan column, dating from 114 A.D., the sword appears much longer than in earlier representations, and shortly afterwards a long single-edged sword called the "spatha" was in use side by side with the short sword.

The Spear.—"The spear that conquered the world," as a French author defines it, was the redoubtable *pilum*, concerning which much has been written and much disputation has arisen. It is most remarkable that a weapon which is constantly alluded to as the essential arm of the Roman warrior, and which has been fully described by a writer, should be of such extreme rarity that

A. F. Calvert

PLATE IV *

Shield of Augsburg make, Sixteenth Century

its very form has provided matter for discussion and dispute. The description of the pilum by Polybius, who flourished in the second century before Christ, is comprehensive and distinct, but owing to the lack of representations and of actual models, much misconception has arisen concerning the exact meaning of his words. He describes it as a weapon having a very large iron head, which was furnished with a socket to receive the wooden shafts. The socket was about a third of the length of the weapon, and the barbed head of the same length. In the Museum at Wiesbaden there is a reputed pilum, but the marvel is that there do not exist hundreds of examples of a weapon with which combats without number have been fought over an area equal to the half of Europe.

The large iron head mentioned by Polybius is an obtusely pointed pike-head with three or four barbs projecting backwards to a short distance from the head; behind the head is the neck, which, though long and slender, is capable of resisting a considerable amount of violent usage. This neck is about twenty inches in length, and at its base swells into a socket for the shaft, and encases the latter for a good portion of its length, being fitted with extreme care. The whole weapon was about six feet nine inches to seven feet in length, and may be described as one-third visible shaft, one-third shaft in iron socket, and the remainder a slender iron rod bearing a large head. It will readily be seen that, owing to the uncased shaft at the base, the centre of gravity would lie between the middle portion of the weapon and the head, thus adapting it for throwing purposes.

The particular purpose of the pilum was to deprive an adversary of his shield. The method adopted was to approach within throwing distance and hurl the massive weapon at an opponent, who would naturally interpose his shield in defence; if the head crashed through the shield the object was accomplished, for owing to its form withdrawal was impossible, while the heavy shaft prevented any advance, and at the same time hindered retreat. To prevent the probability of either, however, the legionary with sword and shield promptly fell upon his embarrassed adversary, and there could be but one ending to such an unequal combat. For use at close quarters it was also equally efficacious, for, wielded with both hands like a mediæval pike, it could resist with ease the sword-cuts of the enemy; indeed Polybius tells us that the legionary received the sword-cuts of the enemy with calm confidence on his pilum, which resisted them with ease, while the adversary's weapon was cut and hacked into the mere semblance of a strigil, or skin-scraper. This weapon was essentially Roman, and the troops wielding it were known as *pilani*. The cavalry carried a long and slender lance furnished with the *amentum*, a leather thong fitted nearly two-thirds of the length of the spear from the butt, being the centre of gravity of the shaft. This thong was of great use in propelling the spear when used as a javelin. The Roman dart was about three feet in length, and fitted with an extremely thin point about six inches long; upon striking any obstacle the point became so bent and distorted that it was of no use for hurling back again at the enemy. The light-armed troops also possessed a spear which was about four and a half feet in length.

THE FRANKS

were a nation of Germanic origin, and originally occupied the land lying upon the north bank of the Rhine, stretching from Mayence almost to the sea. They successfully resisted the advance of the Romans in the second and third centuries, and eventually began an aggressive migration southwards, which finally resulted in the subjugation of the modern countries of Holland, Belgium, France, and partly of Germany and Italy. Long before this consummation, however, we find that the Franks freely enlisted in the Roman armies, and eventually formed the bulwark between the western dominions of the Romans and the fierce barbarian hordes who poured down from the north in almost overwhelming numbers. History teems with examples of their prowess as a military nation; their large stature, bold and wild aspect, and utter fearlessness, rendering them at first most formidable opponents of the comparatively little men of the native Roman armies, and equally valuable allies afterwards. As a Teutonic race we naturally expect to find them armed with the weapons characteristic of the northern tribes.

The Francisca.—Under the Merovingian dynasty, from the fifth to the eighth century A.D., the Franks used a weapon in their warfare which has become associated with their name. The *francisca*, or battle-axe, was a heavy missile weapon which has been described by Procopius as having a very broad blade and a short handle, but so many varieties have been found that we must infer that his description was simply a broad and general one. Thus some are long and narrow in the blade and only slightly curved, and some have a cutting projection of various shapes upon the back portion of the axe-head.   In use it was thrown with tremendous force and unerring aim at an enemy, the Frank being able to accomplish this because of the freedom from embarrassing armour or clinging garments which he enjoyed, and also, owing to constant practice, the distance to which it was hurled was a very remarkable feature.   So heavy and strong was this formidable missile that a shield was invariably crushed in or cut through, if interposed, whilst a blow received upon the person inevitably ended in death.   If used in the hand the weapon was of the same terrible character.   It is questionable whether the bipennis, or double-headed axe, ever found great favour with the Franks, although it has been attributed to them.

The Lance, sometimes termed the *framea*, appears to have been a weapon chiefly associated with the cavalry, and not differing in any essential points from that generally carried by horsemen at the time.   The head was of many forms, and the socket always an integral part of it ; the latter extended to a distance of eighteen inches or more from the head, and was hollowed to receive the shaft, being fixed in position by a rivet which passed through the wood and also through two holes in opposite sides of the socket.

The Angon.—The angon was both in form and in use similar to the pilum of the Romans.   It had a barbed head and a long, slender neck of iron, one found in Germany being over a yard in length.   A socket fitted over a heavy shaft, and the whole weapon had a length of about six feet. In use the angon was hurled at the enemy in order to pierce his body or his shield; if the latter occurred the soldier was practically deprived of his defence, as he could neither advance nor retreat with such an incubus fixed in it. The Frankish warrior, however, quickly seized the advantage thus gained, and rushing forward deliberately trod upon his weapon, thus dragging the shield out of the hands of his opponent who, being left comparatively defenceless, was easily overcome with axe or sword.

The Sword.—The Frankish sword was about thirty inches in length; the blade was broad, straight, and double-edged, with parallel sides ending abruptly in a somewhat obtuse point. It had a very short cross-bar as a guard, a straight grip, and a small, slightly swelling pommel. The scabbard, constructed of either wood or iron, was decorated with plates of inlaid work, generally in copper. This sword does not appear to have been universal in the army, but to have been appropriated by those having an official position. What may be termed a large knife, or a long and heavy dagger, also formed a characteristic Frankish weapon.

With regard to the defensive equipment of the Franks we are in some degree of doubt, inasmuch as no national armour was evolved. In the earlier part of their history they appeared to have disdained any defence but the shield, but in the time of Charlemagne a simple hauberk of pourpoint was worn, covered more or less with metal plates, and a leathern cap upon the head. The shield was of metal and circular, with a central projecting boss or umbo similar to that of the Saxons. The soldiers forming the élite of the army were provided with an equipment which was a modified form of that worn by the Roman legionaries.

The earlier Franks appear to have been a nation of infantry, but in the Carlovingian period they developed qualities of horsemanship which eventually led to their army being exceptionally rich in cavalry, almost one half of their force subsequently being classed under this heading.

CHAPTER IV

SAXONS AND DANES

THE military equipment of our Saxon and Danish forefathers is of much interest to us as a nation, inasmuch as we are curious to ascertain with what weapons and with what personal defences our ancestors were able, apart from personal courage, to overcome the fierce opposition of the Romanised Britons. That this resistance was of a formidable character we may judge from the extended time occupied in the conquest of England, running into hundreds of years and necessitating waves of invasion. They won the country bit by bit, and the conquered were effectually displaced by the invaders; so thorough was this that practically the Britons disappeared before the warlike Teutons, whereby all their traces of occupation were wiped out and only the great works of engineering or building skill of those "who built for eternity, and not for time," resisted their devastating march. It is probable that during the many centuries of Roman occupation many of the Britons had learned the method of warfare and the use of the weapons of their conquerors; and we know that British recruits for the Roman armies were in considerable demand. Consequently we may fairly assume that the Saxons were opposed by Roman swords, spears, and javelins, and that a certain amount of Roman armour protected the defenders. To this equipment we may ascribe the fierce and prolonged resistance

offered to the invaders, who were only able to found their
first petty kingdom, that of Kent, after a struggle of nearly
forty years' duration.

The Saxon Spear.—The chief weapon of offence among
the Saxons was undoubtedly the spear, which was of two
kinds—the longer, used by the cavalry, or in certain cases
to be employed against them, and the shorter, which partook
of the dual nature of a spear and of a javelin.

The chief authorities for Saxon arms and armour are (*a*)
the illuminated manuscripts preserved in the British Museum,
the Bodleian Library, &c., some of which date back to the
eighth century or even earlier ; (*b*) the written description of
the equipment of certain warriors of a still more remote
period ; and (*c*) the sagas, most of them of a warlike nature,
which not only laud the heroic deeds of warriors but
constantly refer to the weapons and armour borne by them.
But these details, necessarily crude and by themselves to a
certain extent unreliable, are fortunately supplemented by
actual examples which have been found in Saxon barrows
all over the country and preserved in many museums, from
which we are enabled to verify the illuminations and
descriptions.

A spear is found as a rule in all Saxon interments, or
more strictly speaking the iron head, the wooden portion
having generally decayed. From numberless references to
the latter we find that it was invariably made of ash, and
the warrior is often poetically referred to as the " ash-bearer."
The shorter kind is found in barrows, doubtless because of
limitation of space, and so commonly do they occur, that
probably every Saxon, from freeman upwards, was interred
with one. They are sometimes found reversed, with the

A. F. Calvert

PLATE V *

Italian Rondache, Sixteenth Century

iron head near the feet, and the hollow shoe or button which
protected the end of the shaft near the skull. From many
measurements taken from the head of the spear to the
shoe, the total length of the shorter kind has been found
to be about six feet.

In some places portions of the wood have been found
still preserved; these have been tested and proved to be of
ash wood, but in no case have these remains demonstrated
that the shaft was excessively thin as is represented in illuminations, where as a rule only a narrow ruled line is drawn
for the shaft. Judging from the numerous illustrations of
mounted horsemen with which the MSS. abound, the length
of the longer variety was about nine or ten feet. The
accompanying illustration (Fig. 62) represents various forms
of spear-heads copied from Saxon MSS. in the British
Museum, from which it will be seen that no stereotyped
pattern was in vogue, but that almost every variety of
possible form was brought into use. That which at once
attracts the attention is the form of guard invariably used
below the spear-head, and which was doubtless intended to
ward off sword-cuts which might possibly sever the shaft.
They were of iron, and sometimes as many as three were
in use. In two of these examples the barbed form of head
is shown, which is the most uncommon, both in illustrations
and also in actual finds in barrows. Probably this form
was generally in use for javelins, the other variety being
easily withdrawn after inflicting a wound. In Fig. 63,
which presents examples of actual spear-heads found in
Great Britain, we notice that the shaft is fixed in a socket
which is always furnished with a longitudinal slit. Nails or
rivets were used to fasten it to the shaft. The absence of

the cross guards should be noticed; probably they were inserted in the shaft and formed no integral part of the spear-head. In the Tower Collection, however, is a spear-head, with a cross-piece similar to the guards shown in illustrations, which was discovered some time since near

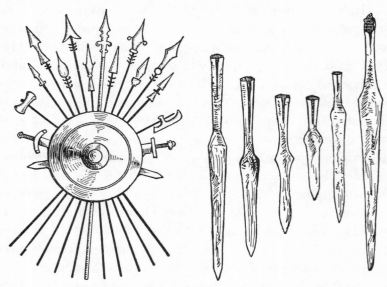

FIG. 62.—Anglo-Saxon spears, &c.
(Add. MS. 11695; Tib. c. vi. &c.)

FIG. 63.—Saxon spear-heads.

Nottingham. The short spear was not carried singly but generally in pairs, and at times three are represented; for instance, in a British Museum MS. the destroying angel is shown with three javelins, one in flight, one poised for throwing in the right hand, and one grasped in the left.

The Sword.—Swords were essentially cavalry weapons among the Anglo-Saxons, and were not carried by any person beneath the rank of thane. The earliest of those found in England have no quillons or cross-pieces, but merely pommel, grip, and blade. The latter was long, straight, rounded at the point, and double-edged, 30 inches long and 2 inches wide at the hilt; the grip was of wood and with but little swell. The total length is generally about three feet. Irish swords of the same period are about six inches shorter; both kinds were provided with wooden scabbards. Undoubtedly this sword was fashioned from classical models. During the later Saxon occupation a cross-piece was added to the weapon; it became more acutely pointed, and the pommel occasionally showed signs of ornamentation. No. 2 of Fig. 64 is a sword found in Cambridgeshire, and shows the quillons in an incipient form, while the addition of a knob to the pommel relieves the monotony seen in No. 1. No. 3, from the same find, has the cross-piece enlarged, while the other swords show various stages of development. The two swords, Nos. 5 and 6, are from MSS. of the eighth century. A rare example of the sword of this period is preserved in the Wallace Collection, and is shown in Fig. 65. It has a flat, crown-shaped pommel, with five small lobes and short, straight quillons rounded at the ends, the grip being missing. The blade is grooved, measures $30\frac{1}{4}$ inches in length, and shows traces of an inscription or ornament.

The sword preserved in the British Museum, which was obtained from the bed of the River Witham, is very similar to this and is probably contemporary, while another weapon has recently been found in the Thames with the hilt upwards which is almost identical with that found in the Witham. The blades of all three examples are about thirty inches in length. The grip of the swords appears to have

been made of pine-wood, judging from a few remains which
have been found.   It is more than probable that the wood
was covered with leather, bone, or horn.   That the sword-
hilts were at times of a costly character and richly ornamented we may infer from the Wallace sword, which has

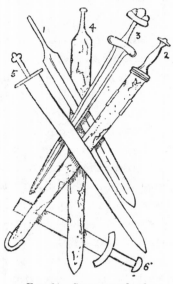

FIG. 64.—Saxon swords of
various dates.

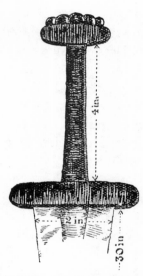

FIG. 65.—Sword, 9th century,
traces of ornamentation
very rare.   (Wall. Coll.)

traces of silver work upon the quillons; the British Museum
sword, which has the pommel and quillons inlaid with gold
and copper in a lozenge pattern; and from numerous
references in the MSS. to weapons with hilts of gold or
silver, inlaid work, setting of precious stones, &c., the
illuminations invariably showing the hilts and mountings
of a yellow colour, thus implying gold, or gold plating.
The sheaths were invariably of wood covered with leather,

with ornamental designs painted or stamped upon them, and mountings of bronze or more costly metal. The sword is less often found in Saxon graves than the spear, as might

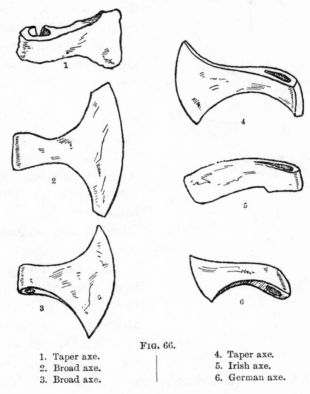

FIG. 66.

1. Taper axe.   4. Taper axe.
2. Broad axe.   5. Irish axe.
3. Broad axe.   6. German axe.

be expected, seeing that its use was confined to the upper classes.

The Axe.—The axe was a distinctive and characteristic weapon of the northern nations, and its use by the Anglo-Saxons is proved by references and illustrations in a few late MSS. It is therefore possible that the Danes introduced its extensive use.

Its occurrence in interments in this country is extremely rare, and but very few examples have come to light. There appears to have been three varieties in use, the taper, the broad, and the double. Examples of the taper axe, found in Kent, are engraved in Fig. 66, Nos. 1 and 4; the broad axe is shown in Nos. 2 and 3, while a few other varieties are drawn. The double axe, or bipennis very rarely occurs in illuminations, and has not been found in any Anglo-Saxon grave. Its form is shown in Fig. 62. The pole-axe is a variety, and appears in the hands of the Saxons at the battle of Hastings.

FIG. 67.—Saxon knives.

The Dagger or knife was a weapon in common use, and has been found in many Saxon graves. They are of various sizes, but probably only those of large dimensions were weapons, the smaller being used for domestic purposes A fine example from Kent is No. 1 in Fig. 67. It is 16 inches in length, and provided with a small cross-piece. No. 2 is

FIG. 68.—From an Anglo-Saxon Psalter.

also from a Kentish find; Nos. 3 and 4, Irish. No. 4 is remarkable by reason of the preservation of the wooden handle, which shows traces of carving.

The use of the dagger is shown in a very spirited little sketch taken from an Anglo-Saxon Psalter of the Duc de Berri (Fig. 68), where the spearman has been assailed by a dagger of the form shown in Fig. 67, No. 3. The head of the javelin is barbed in contradistinction to that of the spear, as previously mentioned. Both of the combatants appear to be emerging from the encounter second best. The long-bow was used by the Anglo-Saxons, but not extensively, and but few illustrations are found in MSS., while examples of

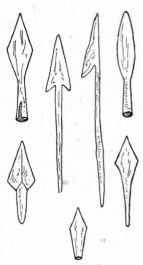

FIG. 69.—Saxon arrow-heads.

arrow-heads in graves are uncommon; those illustrated in Fig. 69 are from MSS. chiefly, and but few from finds in graves. The sling was not extensively used, although it is occasionally shown in MSS. The accompanying cut (Fig. 70) is from the Anglo-Saxon and Latin Psalter of Boulogne. Other examples occur in Cott. MS., Claudius B. IV., and on the Bayeux Tapestry. Fairly numerous weapons may be cited

FIG. 70—Saxon slinger.

as being occasionally in use, such as the bill, the mace, the pike, the "morning star," &c., but they were in their incipient stage, and individual not universal favourites.

Respecting the defensive equipment of the Anglo-Saxons we are forced to the conclusion that the helmet and the shield were the principal portions, and that in numberless cases these only were adopted, others being considered subsidiary or superfluous. Indeed in the earlier periods of the Saxon occupation they are invariably represented with these defences only, the byrnie, &c., being essentially reserved for the leaders; but as the nation increased in prosperity so the additional defences were slowly added.

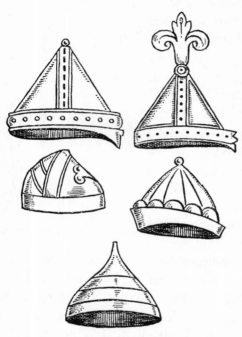

FIG. 71.—Saxon helmets.

The Saxon Helmet was commonly of the Phrygian shape, but examples are plentiful of the hemispherical, the conical, and the combed hemispherical, side by side with the Phrygian. The foundation of the helmet was a framework of bronze or iron bands riveted together, of which the principal was the piece passing round the head, and that reaching from the forehead over the head to its junction with

A. F. Calvert

PLATE VI *
Italian Rondache, Sixteenth Century

the plate at the back. These two were of thicker material than the rest. Occasionally the latter band was produced so as to form a nasal which became universal at the end of the tenth century. Upon this substructure a leather cap of varying forms was fixed, sometimes with ornamental additions in leather crowning it. The commonest form is seen in Fig. 75, while other varieties are perceived in Figs. 71, 76, and 77.

The Shield.—The shield was of wood covered with leather, invariably round in shape, but at times oval and convex. The lime was the favourite wood used in its construction, the "yellow linden" being often mentioned by Saxon poets. The

FIG. 72.—Saxon helmet with comb. (Add. MS., 18043.)

distinguishing characteristic of this defence was the central boss or umbo, of which such a large number

FIG. 73.—Saxon umbos.

have been found in Saxon interments (Fig. 73). It was a hollow boss of varying form and dimensions, but generally about six inches in diameter, and projecting three or four inches from the outer surface of the shield; the wood was cut away to allow of its being fixed, and across the hollow at the back a piece of metal was carried, riveted at both ends to the boss.

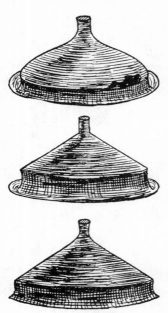

This formed a grasp for the left hand by which the shield was carried, the umbo protecting the hand from injury. As it was often spiked there is reason to suppose that at times the shield was used as an offensive weapon (Fig. 75). To strengthen it, radiating strips of iron or bronze were occasionally carried from the umbo to the edges of the shield, the simplest being a prolongation of the grip. It was not a heavy shield, in no way comparable to those of some other nations. The mode of carrying the shield when not in use is seen in Fig. 76.

FIG. 74.—Saxon umbos, from the Herts County Museum, St. Albans.

The Byrnie or Battle-Sark was at times made of leather. In the figure reproduced from a British Museum MS. (Fig. 77) the coat appears to be of hide with much of the hair apparently left upon it; its lower edges are dagged, and it defends the body and a part of the legs, whereas in Fig. 78 the defensive covering appears only upon the upper part of the body. The byrnie was also made of padded stuff judging from the illustrations, but the earlier examples are so excessively crude and inartistic that it is rash to

make authoritative statements. When a forest is indicated
by four leaves and a twig, a mountain pass by a bulbous
mole-hill, and elaborate Saxon embroidery by half-a-dozen

FIG. 75.—Saxon king and shield bearer.
(MS., end of 10th century.)

scattered dots, it will readily be perceived that such a
technical detail as body armour cannot be definitely settled
by these rude drawings. Hence a controversy has arisen,

which can by no means be considered as definitely decided, upon the question as to whether the Anglo-Saxons possessed byrnies of true interlinked chain mail.

FIG. 76.—Anglo-Saxon horseman.
(Cott. MS., Cleop. C. 8.)

FIG. 77.—Saxon byrnie of leather.
(Cott. MS., Cleop. C. 8.)

Hewitt in his "Ancient Armour" maintains the affirmative, and contends that the references in the poem of

FIG. 78.—Leather armour, 10th century.

"Beowulf" to the "twisted breast-net," the "hard battle-net," the "locked battle-shirt," the "byrnie twisted with hands," the "war byrnie, hard and hand-locked," can only mean chain-mail. He further refers to the Bayeux Tapestry where a body is being stripped, and the links show inside the hauberk as they are represented on the outside. These arguments certainly carry weight,

but until a *bonâ-fide* example of Anglo-Saxon manufacture is brought to light the question must apparently be left in abeyance. One of the modes of defence concerning which there is no doubt was the sewing on of separate flat

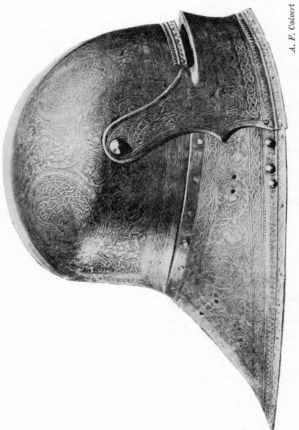

PLATE VII *

Milanese Salade, Fifteenth Century

rings of iron to a tunic of woven material or leather, and
also the covering of the same with metal or leather plates,
either cut into the form of scales and overlapping, or
square or oblong.

A very interesting little group is shown in Fig. 79

FIG. 79.—Group from Cott. MS., Cleop. B. 4. c. 1000.

from a Saxon MS., Cleopatra B. 4, in the British Museum.
The book is Ælfric's Paraphrase of the Pentateuch and
Joshua, and the subject of the drawing is the battle of
the three kings against the cities of the plain. One
king is habited in a ringed byrnie which extends to the
knees and half way down the arms; he wields a sword

with a trilobed pommel and short quillons, and defends himself with a shield having a spiked umbo. His armour-bearer carries another shield, but is quite unarmed, his duty merely being to defend his master. The Phrygian cap and simple tunic he wears are probably those of everyday life. The second king has no defensive armour and no armour-bearer, unless the figure seen behind him in a grotesque attitude fulfils that office. The bifid beards and the characteristic Saxon wrinkling of the sleeves should be noticed, as also that the legs of the group appear to be bare.

FIG. 80. — From Anglo-Saxon MS., Prudentius, 11th century.

The leg-bands seen upon the Saxon soldiery were similar to those worn by all civilians, and adjusted in the same manner; if, however, they were of leather instead of the usual textile fabric a certain amount of defence could be obtained (Figs. 77 and 80). It is curious to observe that a number of soldiers are habited precisely as the civilians, with no other defences than the helmet and the shield, from which we conclude that the Anglo-Saxon of an early period simply dropped his implements of husbandry at the call to arms and took up the shield, helmet, and the spear.

Towards the latter end of the Saxon period the arms and armour became almost identical with that in use on the Continent owing to the constant intercourse which occurred in the reign of Edward the Confessor, so that in 1066 the difference in accoutrement was simply small matters of detail.

THE DANES

The military equipment of the Danes was very similar to that of other northern Teutonic nations, and no single piece of their arms and armour has been immortalised as of special significance with the single exception of the Danish axe. Upon their first appearance in England the only armour worn was a defence for the chest, consisting of a broad collar encircling the neck, with depending pieces upon which were sewn flat rings, plates of metal, horn, &c. In addition to this pectoral, if it may be so termed, greaves were used, consisting of

Fig. 81.—Danish helmet, shield, and sword.

stout pieces of leather affixed after the form of shin-pieces, and, judging by representations in illuminated MSS., carefully moulded to the limb, inasmuch as the prominent muscles are shown upon them. This was probably effected by boiling the leather and subsequently pressing it into shape. After their settlement in England they gradually adopted other defences in imitation of the Saxons, but more especially of the Normans, until their equipment in the first half of the eleventh century became in every respect a replica of that of the latter nation.

The Danish helmet in its early form was a close-fitting skull-cap fitting well down into the back of the neck; upon this as a foundation the chiefs wore protruding horns, and at times wings of metal, imparting a highly-ornamental aspect to the head-piece. Later a conical helmet having a knob upon the top and being made of metal or leather, or a mixture of both, was adopted ; this in its fully-developed state was fitted with a nasal (Fig. 81).

The shield is reputed to have been of the shape shown in Fig. 81, which is taken from the prayer-book of King

Canute, MSS., Cal. A. 7, in the British Museum. Presuming that the illuminator has not allowed his imagination to run riot we must admire the highly ornamental form there delineated, evidently founded upon the universal circular shield of the Teutonic nations.

Fig. 82.—Danish weapons.

The Danish sword was similar to that of the Anglo-Saxons, and differed only in the scabbard, upon which more labour was spent in ornamentation.

The spear illustrated (Fig. 82, No. 2) is that of Canute as shown upon his coins, while the companion weapon is that of the ordinary soldiery.

The Danish axe (Fig. 82, No. 3) was the famed bipennis, consisting of two axe-blades of similar form on either side of the shaft, which latter in a few cases was furnished with a spike. The axe could be used as a pole-axe for close combat, or, if furnished with a shorter handle, be hurled in a similar way to the francisca. A variation of the bipennis is seen in the companion axe, which is furnished upon one side with a diamond-pointed cutting blade of steel in substitution for the axe-blade.

PLATE VIII

The Bayard Armour in the Rotunda, Woolwich

CHAPTER V

THE NORMAN PERIOD TO 1180

With the advent of the Normans in 1066 the subject of arms and armour in England becomes more definite and exact. This is chiefly owing to the Bayeux Tapestry, to the multiplication of MSS., carvings in ivory and metal, and the records preserved upon seals. The date of the famous tapestry has long been a matter of dispute, but it is universally agreed that if it was not woven by Matilda and her handmaidens it was certainly begun and completed within fifty years of the Conquest. Hence its reliability is undoubted upon contemporaneous arms and armour.

The Lance. — The head of the lance was commonly of the leaf form, and sometimes approached that of the lozenge; it was very seldom barbed, although this variety, together with the others, appears upon the Bayeux Tapestry. The horizontal bar-guards,

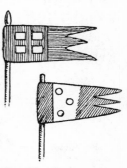

Fig. 83.—Norman pennons (Bayeux Tapestry).

so characteristic of the Anglo-Saxon spear, are very rarely pictured; they were not, however, relinquished by the conquered nation, but are seen at times in MSS. written subsequently to the Conquest. Nearly all the Norman spears were embellished with pennons of from two to five points (Fig. 83). The length of the spear appears to have differed little from that of the Anglo-Saxon, and like that weapon they were of uniform thickness throughout (Figs. 88, 91, 92, 93, &c.).

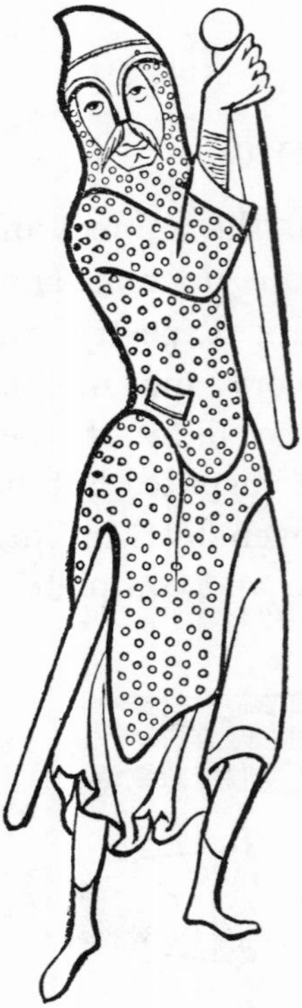

The Sword.—Remembering that the Normans were essentially a Scandinavian nation, we might fairly expect to discover traces of their origin in the sword of the period, and this we find to be the case. It was still straight, long, and double-edged, slightly tapering towards the acute-angled point. The quillons were straight at the time of the Conquest, but became bent in a small degree towards the close of the period; the grip was without swell, and a spherical knob formed the pommel. The scabbard was suspended upon the left side by a small cord round the waist, but occasionally was supported by the hauberk by being passed through a hole in the garment, which thus concealed a portion of it. See Fig. 84, which dates from *c.* 1125, and exhibits this peculiarity.

FIG. 84.—Figure from "Massacre of the Innocents." (Cott. MS., Nero, C. 4, *c.* 1125.)

The Bow.—At the battle of Hastings the Normans appear to have been extremely well provided with bowmen, in contradistinction to the Saxons. The Conqueror is said to have reproached the latter for this omission, but archers appear in the ranks of the Saxons on the Bayeux Tapestry, grouped in small numbers among the axemen, and arrow-heads of iron are occasionally found in Saxon graves. It would appear that all the Norman foot soldiers carried bows, and we know that the rain of arrows from the sky had a marked effect upon the fortunes of the day at Hastings. The bow was of very simple construction at that time, and the quivers were without covers, and at times slung upon the back, so that the arrows are seen over the right shoulder.

The Mace.—At Hastings the Saxons appear to have used the stone hammer and the Normans a mace having the head heart-shaped ; they had recourse to this after the lance had been splintered. The axe is not seen in the hands of the Normans, though it subsequently came into high favour with them, but many of the Saxons wield the weapon which, from its handle being four or five feet in length, may justly be termed the pole-axe.

The body armour of this period is of great interest by reason of its complexity and variety. Upon the Bayeux Tapestry there are delineated seven different kinds, which are reproduced in Fig. 85. No. 1 is undoubtedly the ringed byrnie which we have noted during the Saxon period, and No. 2 is either intended to represent inter-linked chain mail or, what is more probable, scale armour, as it is invariably represented with the points of the scales downwards. These scales were of various materials, such as iron, bronze, leather, cuir-bouilli, and horn. Cuir-bouilli was leather softened by boiling (generally in oil), and stamped or moulded into a definite form when in that condition ; upon drying it became intensely hard and tough. It was a favourite agent for defence for centuries, and did not eventually disappear in England as such until the close of the fourteenth century. Nos. 3 and 4 may possibly be composed of iron rings or discs of metal lying upon leather or padded material, with strips of leather sewn on between the rings. Some authorities profess to discover jazeraint work in this representation, which was a method of defence much used in later centuries for archers' jacques and various other garments, but we have no right to assume that the Normans at

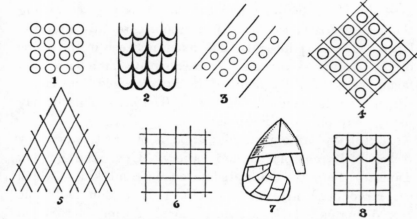

FIG. 85.—Details of armour (Bayeux Tapestry).

that period carried such a heavy weight of armour as this would necessitate, or were acquainted with such a technical and complicated manufacture as jazeraint work implies. The circles, moreover, are too large to represent studs. Nos. 5 and 6 are the ordinary markings used for the Gambeson (or Wambeys), the plain quilted defence which is perhaps the most ancient of all armours and was known to the early Egyptians. It was padded with a soft material such as wool, or tow, or cloth reduced to shreds, which was enclosed between two layers of material and then sewn together. Although offering but little opposition to a lance-thrust it was highly efficacious in warding off a sword-cut, or stopping arrows when not delivered at short range. Against the mace, or a stone from a sling, it was of little use in preventing bones from being broken. This defence, with various styles of quilting and varieties of stuffing materials, was in use for many centuries in England as an under garment, to prevent the chafing of chain mail and plate, besides affording additional protection, while among the rank and file of our English armies it was often the only defence worn. In MSS. it is shown in different tints, invariably self-colours, but occasionally in stripes, chequers, &c., and this serves to prove, if proof were needed, that the surface exposed to view was not metal but material. No. 7 is a crude representation of the ordinary conical helmet, furnished with a nasal, to which is attached a coif or camail of quilted material, defending the back and sides of the head and falling upon the shoulders. As a rule, this quilting was continued over the head, and protected the wearer from the chafing of the helmet, while at the same time it distributed its weight. At times, however, this method was not in use, but a separate covering of soft or padded material was adopted; in Fig. 86 it is represented cut into the shape of a coif and tied under the chin. No. 8 is an example of different markings upon the same dress which is very common in MSS.; it is invariably introduced in those places where additional defence was required or desirable, and probably consisted of metal reinforcing the under garment.

It may not be out of place to deal at this point with

various armours, quite apart from plate, which will be referred to or illustrated in this work. Hewitt has dealt

with this subject perhaps more fully and lucidly than any other author, and the woodcut on opposite page (Fig. 87) is taken from his work. No. 1 is perhaps the commonest of all, and will be referred to as " banded mail." Its construction is fully dealt with in Chapter VII. Occasionally the lines between the alternate crescents are shown double, but probably that is only a modification of this style of defence. During the thirteenth and fourteenth centuries it was in constant use, and did not altogether die out for some considerable time afterwards. It is interesting to compare the variations in this style either of the actual defence or of the modes of delineation by the artists; the brasses of

FIG. 86.—Figure showing coif worn under mail.

Bacon, Creke, d'Aubernoun, Northwode, Raven, Cheyne, &c., may be cited as examples worthy of interest in this respect, though many more may be found upon careful inspection. No. 2 is very common in illuminated MSS., and is occasionally found chiselled upon effigies; the

Trumpington brass is an example of its incision in metal. No. 3 is generally found exemplified in brasses and effigies of the thirteenth to the fifteenth centuries, and is by far the finest method for representing interlinked chain

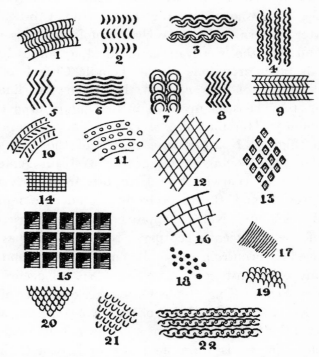

FIG. 87.—Methods of representing different kinds of defences, other than plate.

armour. It has a richness and reality which is unsurpassed by any other method. On the brass of Sir Thomas Burton it is shown in perpendicular chains; horizontal on that of Sir William Bagot; large rings are engraved in the case of Sir John Hanley, and there are many examples of small rings. On the brass of Sir

Robert Russell there is a remarkable width between the parallel rows of chains, from which it may be inferred that although the chain - mail proper linked laterally, and also above and below, occasionally parallel chains linked at the sides only were in vogue. It is probable that the mail shown on the D'Aubernoun brass is of the latter pattern. No. 4: early examples of this are to be found on the Septvans and Buslingthorpe brasses. No. 5 is taken from one of the Temple Church effigies; a modification of this method, in which the lines are straight, may be seen upon an incised figure of a knight at Avenbury, Herefordshire, c. 1260. No. 6 occurs upon foreign effigies. No. 7 is an example of the mail shown upon the monumental statue of Sir William Arden, in Aston Church, Warwickshire. No. 8 is from early wood-cuts. Nos. 9 and 10 are probably intended to represent banded mail, and No. 11 appears upon an ivory chess-man of the thirteenth century. No. 12: this has been mentioned as occurring in the Bayeux Tapestry, and there are many other instances of its use. No. 13 occurs upon the Great Seal of King Stephen and other examples of early seals. No. 14, a variety of No. 12. No. 15, from a steel statuette; the indentations appear to have been made with a punch. No. 16 is from an effigy in Bristol Cathedral. No. 17, from Roy. MS. 14, E. IV., a manuscript written and illuminated for King Edward IV. No. 18 is much used upon seals—one of King Stephen, for example. Nos. 19 and 20, from Add. MSS. 15295 and 15297. No. 21, from two MSS. of the twelfth and thirteenth centuries (Egerton MS. 809; Add. MS. 15268). No. 22, from Harl. MS. 2803.

PLATE IX

The "Rhodes" Suit at the Rotunda, Woolwich

Under the gambeson or the hauberk or both was worn a tunic reaching nearly to the knees, and as a rule a little longer than the defensive garments.   It is well shown in the accompanying figure (Fig. 88, from Harleian Roll, Y 6, "The Life of St. Guthlac," a work of the close of the twelfth century).

The Hauberk.—The hauberk was to the Norman what the byrnie was to the Saxon, the chief method of bodily defence.   The coif for the head was generally a part of it, with only a small opening for the face, but at times it is shown made in two pieces, the lower extending upwards to the neck and the coif falling over it.   This was doubtless to afford better means of adjustment for the gorget, plastron-de-fer, or other reinforcement which was undoubtedly worn under it upon the breast.   The lower part of the garment was generally

FIG. 88.—Armour, *c.* 1190.

made to open up the front in order to afford convenience in riding, but occasionally examples are met with where openings are made upon both sides.   For foot soldiers no opening was, as a rule, necessary.   In some cases the reinforcement for the breast appears upon the outside of the hauberk in the shape of a square or oblong pectoral; when worn thus it was possibly of metal plates or studs attached to leather (Fig. 89).

FIG. 89. — Norman hauberk, 1066.

Towards the end of the eleventh century the different distinct styles of armour became more numerous, and do not present such uniformity as at the time of the Conquest. Hefner gives an illustration of tegulated armour (Fig. 90) from a painting on vellum dating from *c.* 1090, when this system appears to have been introduced.　In the original the plates are silvered, and some bosses on pendant scales of a figure shown upon the right are gilded. The square or oblong scales are shown as overlapping like slates upon a roof, and being probably sewn upon leather would afford a good protection to the wearer. Two soldiers also in the same group have chausses of mail of the same description,

FIG. 90.—Tegulated armour, *c.* 1090.

FIG. 91.—Scale armour. (Harl. MS., 603.)

and the coif is continuous with the body portions of the hauberk.

Fig. 92.—Armour, 1148.   (Add MS., 14789.)

Chausses of mail of various patterns apparently came into general use about the commencement of the twelfth century. They are mentioned above, and apparently in the figure referred to (No. 90) are continuous scale work round

FIG. 93.—Goliath. (Harl. MS., 2803.)

the limbs; in other examples they partake of the character of half-leggings protecting only the knees and shins of the wearer (Fig. 86). An excellent example of this (Fig. 92) is afforded by a small representation in an illuminated manuscript Bible of the date 1148, where, in a capital letter F, the figures of David and Goliath are introduced, the giant lying prone upon the central projection of the letter with a stone in his forehead and the neck of the hauberk partly cut through. This is beautifully illustrated in Shaw's "Dresses and Decorations." The hauberk is shown continuous with the coif; the legs are protected by chausses of some pliable material, thickly covered with protective studs. These evidently fasten down the back, and are drawn over the feet by bands or straps meeting underneath. Later still, in a MS. written about 1170 (Fig. 93), we have an example of Goliath wearing chausses consisting of a thin material which creases near the calf, and only a single row of the protective studs down the shin. The short boot is analogous with those worn in Fig. 88, though here defended, or ornamented, with a few studs.

The Norman Shield.—The shield generally adopted by the Norman cavalry was kite-shaped and probably of Sicilian origin; it was either flat, or round so as to encircle the body to some extent. The protection afforded by such a shield is obvious, inasmuch as it guarded the upper part of the body where it was the broadest, and by tapering downwards defended the left leg. It was invariably made of wood and covered on both sides with leather, in addition to which extra defences of metal were added. Shields of this description

FIG. 94.—Great Seal of Alexander I., King of Scotland.

are referred to which intimate that the whole of the exterior was of polished metal, though they seem to be exceptional. On the great seal of Alexander I., King of Scotland (Fig. 94), the rivet, heads are shown upon the reverse of the shield, which fastened the plates in position. It was held in the left hand by a bar or strap near the inside upper portion as shown in the figure. The length varied, but may be taken as approximately four feet in height with a maximum width of two feet. The shield for foot soldiers was somewhat small, as may be seen in

Fig. 88. At the time of the Conquest flat shields were frequently used, but all were eventually bowed. The umbo occasionally appears in illuminated MSS., but its use was exceptional. In nearly every case a guige, which is very plainly shown in many of the engravings, is provided for suspending the shield round the neck. The round shield (Fig. 95) is of much rarer occurrence. It is shown in Harl. MS. 603 and other MSS. of the close of the eleventh century, and was very probably confined entirely to foot soldiers.

FIG. 95.—Circular shield, c. 1090. (Harl. MS., 603.)

The Helmet.—The characteristic defence for the head at this period is the conical helmet fitted with a nasal, thus distinguishing it from the Saxon type, which did not possess this extra defence for the face until a few years previous to the Conquest, when Norman influence began to prevail in England. In the Bayeux Tapestry the nasal is shown upon practically all the Norman helmets, which are invariably conical and not very high ; they were secured to the head by straps under the chin, and at times by laces to the body armour. The nasal continued in use until about 1140, when it was generally discarded, but isolated examples may be found in every succeeding century down to the seventeenth. It was fixed or movable, and that worn by the Conqueror at Hastings was of the latter description, as he removed it to reassure his force by a sight of his features when a report spread that he had been slain.

A neck defence was at times fitted to the helmet, which reached to the ears on either side and depended to the shoulders: it is shown in Fig. 85, No. 7. Cheek-guards also were in use.

It must not be supposed that the Phrygian-shaped helmet affected by the Saxons became obsolete in the Norman period; on the contrary it is frequently represented in MSS. (*cf.* Harl. MS. 603, eleventh century; Harl. MS. 2800, twelfth century, &c.).

During the period under discussion (1066–1180) various additional weapons were introduced which the exigencies of warfare appeared to necessitate. Foremost among these was the military pick called variously the Bisacuta, Oucin, and Besague, designed to perforate the joints between the metal plates of the hauberk. It is shown in Fig. 109, furnished with one point only, though it commonly had two, as might be inferred from the name Bisacuta. It was a modification of the martel-de-fer. A dagger for the use of foot soldiers was also in use, adapted for rushing upon and disabling knights who had been unhorsed in a cavalry charge; it was termed the Cultellus, and appears to have attained occasionally the dimensions of a short sword. One of the most ancient of weapons is the Guisarme, which, in its earliest forms, is conjectured to have been a combination of the scythe and the prong. The advantage of having a weapon with a cutting edge and also adapted for thrusting, while at the same time serving to ward off a blow by entangling another weapon in the angle formed by the junction of the two, would appeal very strongly to the foot soldier, by whom it was chiefly used. The term "bisarme," by which it was occasionally known, would indicate the dual nature of the weapon, which consisted essentially, in all its multitudinous variations, of a cutting glaive with a rising spike at the back. It was always fixed to a staff six or more feet in length, and at times the knife edge partook more of the nature of an ornamental axe than of the glaive. Frequent mention of "grinding of the guisarmes" occurs in ancient writers, from which we infer that the cutting edge was one of its valuable characteristics, while references to the "deadly" or "destructive" guisarme are very common. Some appear to have had small bells attached to their extremities to frighten the horses of the cavalry. So common was the weapon that in Scotland it became one of the recognised means of offence with which the foot soldier was required to be provided.

The bipennis, or double axe, was still in use, but only by the Saxon element; the complete fusion of the conquerors and the conquered led to its gradual extinction as a national weapon.

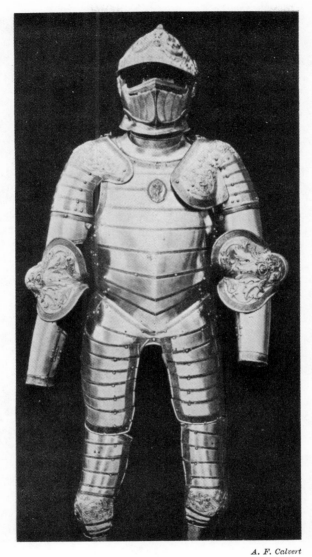

PLATE X *

Armour of Charles V. (Work of Negroli)

CHAPTER VI

THE CHAIN MAIL PERIOD, 1180–1250

THE essential differences between this period and the last are : (1) the substitution of chain mail for the jazeraint, mascled, and scale armour which had formerly been used; (2) the adoption of the pot-helm or heaume as a secondary defence for the head in place of the conical helmet, the coif-de-mailles, or the pot-de-fer under the mail; (3) the introduction of the sleeveless surcoat and the crest.

The Heaume.—The term "heaume" may perhaps by some be deemed to be hardly applicable to the head-defence when first introduced, inasmuch as it was small in size, fitted closely to the head, and was in most respects a helmet. But inasmuch as a second defence was worn underneath it from its very inception, the word "heaume" is an appropriate designation, as it infers a reinforcement to an existing protection in the next few centuries during which it is constantly in evidence. It may readily be divided into two distinct classes, namely, those in which the plates composing it are riveted together so as to form one piece, and secondly, those in which a movable ventail can be affixed. Further subdivisions may be made if desired, such as flat-topped, round-topped, and sugar-loaf. The word "heaume" or helm among the northern nations simply meant a covering of any kind for the head, and we have an example in the Anglo-Saxon wærhelm, of which examples have been given in this work. Of the first heaumes the flat-topped, or those with slightly curved crowns, were probably the earliest, of which the woodcut No. 96 furnishes an example.

A helm which is preserved in the Musée d'Artillerie in Paris probably exemplifies the transition between the

FIG. 96.

Norman helmet and the barrel heaume. The conical Norman crown is preserved, but instead of the pendent neck and cheek guards and nasal, the head and face are entirely covered by a cylinder of iron, which is complete but for a vertical slit covered by a projecting nasal and two transverse occularia, one on either side.

In England very early examples may be seen upon the monumental effigy of Hugh Fitz Eudo, in Kirkstead Chapel, Lincolnshire, and in a slightly modified form in the carvings of the Presbytery arcade of Worcester Cathedral, also in the groups of the Painted Chamber, Westminster. Holes for breathing purposes are entirely absent, the sole openings being a pair of horizontal occularia separated by a perpendicular band. In this class may be included the painted pot-heaume on a parchment MS. dating approximately from

FIG. 97.—Painted "Pot Helmet," c. 1241.

the year 1241, which is shown coloured in green and white diagonal stripes, and is now in the town library of Leipzic (Fig. 97). This flat-topped variety appears to have been viewed with much favour, for we have many examples of it in this period and in that immediately following. For instance, the seal of Roger de Bigod, Earl of Norfolk (1231 to

1240) (Fig. 98), exhibits a heaume which is flat-topped, furnished with two occularia, and nine small square breathing holes on either side, strengthened with cross pieces of iron. The seal of Richard de Clare, Earl of Gloucester and Hertford, who died in 1262 (Fig. 99), shows a flat topped helmet of cylindrical fashion, in which the occularium is formed by one ornamental wavy slit of which the lower edge is slightly cusped. The helmet of Hamelin,

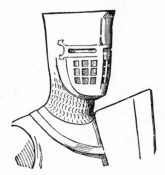

FIG. 98.—From the seal (1231–1240) of Roger le Bigod, Earl of Norfolk.

FIG. 99.—From the seal of Richard de Clare, Earl of Gloucester and Hertford (d. 1262).

Earl of Surrey and Warenne, 1202 (Fig. 100), is of the round-topped variety, and is remarkable for the narrow occularium and the complete absence of any breathing holes. It is taken from the Cott. MS., Julius, C. VII.

It is difficult to see the protection against a lance or sword-thrust afforded by the heaume of Hugh de Vere, Earl of Oxford, d. 1263 (Fig. 101), unless an interior plate was in use to reinforce the numerous openings in the fore part. The peculiarity of the surcoat covering the neck should be noticed, as it is uncommon at this period. From the examples given it will be apparent that from the year 1180 to

1250, the era under discussion, no heaume is represented with a movable visor, and this may be taken as a distinguishing feature, inasmuch as they appear shortly afterwards.

Whatever doubts may exist respecting the presence of true chain mail in the early Norman period in conjunction with mascled, scale, leather, horn, and jazeraint work

FIG. 100.—Helmet of Hamelin, Earl of Surrey and Warenne (*d.* 1202). (From MS. Cott., Julius, C. vii.)

FIG. 101.—From the seal of Hugh de Vere, Earl of Oxford (*d.* 1263).

generally, no misconception can arise with respect to the epoch under consideration, where, together with the heaume and the plastron-de-fer, it formed the sole defence of the knight. Chain mail has existed from very remote antiquity, but owing to its nature is of such a perishable quality, exposing the maximum of surface to atmospheric oxidation, that practically no examples have come down to us of all the vast quantity fabricated in remote ages. There are in the British Museum some aggregations of iron rust brought from the excavations at Nineveh, which experts assert have once been hauberks of chain mail of the true pattern (so far as interlocking is concerned), and hence are credited with being the earliest examples in existence. That the Romans used rings, together with discs and plates, as defensive covering, backed by a sub-stratum of a tough textile fabric, is well known; but whether these rings were so interlinked as to form a true chain mail has been much questioned. Discoveries have, however, been made from time to time which tend to prove that they were not unacquainted with it, and taking into consideration the extent of territory they possessed, and the number of nations owning their sway, it would be a matter for wonder if they were ignorant of its existence. Sculptures may be referred to which appear to indicate true chain mail, but so many conventional styles and methods were used by artists to indicate defensive equipment, that it is difficult to arrive at a definite settlement of the question. That this means of protection originated in the East is undoubted, where its coolness would be a great advantage; that it spread in some mysterious way to the Teutonic nations of the West is also certain, and we must look for its intro-duction there to an age long prior to the time of the Crusades. It was imitated, however, by the unskilful western artificers in such a manner that immense weight occurred and became an inseparable condition, and in this manner during the early Crusades it came into contact with the light chain mail, characteristic of Oriental workmanship, covering the nomadic cavalry of the East. These horsemen were enabled in consequence to move with a swiftness and freedom quite impossible to the crusading knights, thus being forcibly reminiscent of the ponderous Spanish galleons of the Armada, and the small but handy English vessels. In the twelfth and thirteenth centuries the cost of true chain mail was prohibitory to all but the very wealthy, in spite of great quantities which fell to the lot of the victors in Palestine. The manufacture varies under the conditions of time, place,

 and requirements. Wire, or what answered for wire, was made in the earlier periods of a very rough character, in the manufacture of which the hammer evidently played an important part; but later on, when the art of wire-drawing became known, the cross section of a link exhibits as perfect a circle as it would if of modern construction. This wire was wound tightly round an iron core of convenient size, cut off in rings,

FIG. 102.—Interlinked chain mail showing method of construction.

and each ring separately treated by flattening the overlapping ends, piercing them with a steel punch, and inserting a small rivet. This rivet was either hammered to flatten it, or it was finished off in a vice. The general method in almost every coat of mail was for one ring to interlink with four others; a few variations occur, however, such as rows of rings occasionally interlinking with other rows above and below, the use of alternate double rings, &c. From the foregoing it will readily be seen that the cost of production of chain mail in labour alone must have been excessive. The strengthening of the mail by insertion of leather straps was occasionally done, the straps being carried through the links in horizontal rows, while vertical rows of strapping in addition to the foregoing are not unknown. In the metalwork, also, the resistance of mail could be considerably augmented by enlarging the rivet joinings. Considering the intricate nature of mail, it is no matter for wonderment that neither in the centuries under consideration nor in those immediately following do we find the common soldier clad in true chain mail, as every portion, large or small, would be carefully retained by the knightly wearer. The incised slab of Sir John de Bitton, in Bitton Church, Somersetshire, 1227 (Fig. 103), may be taken as an excellent example of this early period preserved in a

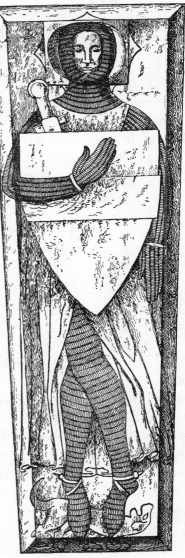

FIG. 103.—Sir John de Bitton, Bitton Church, Somersetshire, 1227.

monumental effigy: the large shield covering the greater
part of the body has no guige, and is necessarily quite
flat, though doubtless convex in reality. The coif-de-
mailles is separate from the hauberk, and has a lappet
overlying the upper part of the gorget to protect the
junction there. The length of the hauberk can only be
surmised, inasmuch as the lower border is not shown,
but from other examples we glean that it reached nearly

to the knees. The mail gloves are
also distinct from the hauberk, and
bands, laces, or straps are used to
protect the junctions with the
sleeves: separate fingers are not
shown, but the gloves are precisely
similar to the mitten gauntlets of
the end of the century. The
chausses are of chain mail, and
continuous with the covering for
the feet. The heaume is not
shown; it is probable that the

FIG. 104—Rich. Wellesburn de
Montfort, c. 1270. Hitchen-
den Church, Bucks.

flattish configuration of the upper part of the head indicates that a pot-de-fer of some kind was worn under the
coif, as in Fig. 104. The sword is long and broad, the
hilt having short, straight quillons and a cylindrical grip,
terminating in a circular pommel. The spurs are of the
short pryck form. It should be noticed that the artist has
drawn the figure too large for the slab, and has consequently
been compelled to encroach upon the bevelled edges.

The Surcoat is of the sleeveless variety, one of
the distinguishing features of this period, and reaches
nearly .to the heels, being, as usual, split up in front and

probably also behind, for convenience in riding. It was introduced in order to guard the mail from rain, and indirectly as some protection against the heat of the sun's rays; but the chief reason for its adoption was that it afforded a means for recognising the wearer, whose features were now completely hidden by the heaume, thus rendering it impossible in the hurly-burly of battle to know friend from foe. Previous to this the nasal helmet, although covering but part of the features, had at times led to confusion, even as early as the battle of Hastings as previously stated. Thus heraldry, which up to this time had only been in an incipient condition, suddenly found itself of the highest importance, and developed in the course of succeeding centuries into a science, the study of which was deemed absolutely necessary for all pretending to the possession of gentle blood. The surcoat had its inception in the long, flowing tunic which during the last period dealt with had been worn underneath the hauberk, as shown upon the two great seals of King Richard I., and the suggestion would be natural to transfer the latter to the outermost position, leaving to the padded gambeson alone the duty of supporting the weight of the hauberk. The first English monarch to appear in this military attire as an outer garment was King John, and he is shown thus habited upon his great seal: while his rival, the Dauphin Louis, who proved such an unwelcome visitor in the latter part of his reign, is similarly represented upon the French seal, as may be seen in the Harl. MS. 43, B. VII., date 1216, to which it is appended. To the Cott. MS., XIX. 2, the seal of Alexander II. of Scotland, 1214-1249, is attached, and this also shows the

surcoat. It was of white material or self-coloured, sometimes diapered, and generally bore heraldic charges. The

length varied, and both long
and short surcoats are seen of
approximately the same date;
the former reaching at times
to the heels and the latter
to the hem of the hauberk.
The material varied with the
means and taste of the wearer;
the better descriptions were of
silk, richly embroidered with
gold and sometimes decorated
with precious stones, cloth of
gold of the richest quality being
also used.

The Crest.—Although much
uncertainty exists among ex-
ponents of the art of heraldry
upon the origin of the crest,
yet a little investigation leads
to the conclusion that it need
not be a matter of speculation
or conjecture. The first example of the nature of a
crest appears upon the cap of
Geoffrey, Count of Anjou, died
1150; his monumental slab in
the museum at Le Mans, which
stood formerly in the cathedral there, exhibits the figure of
a lion (Fig. 105). The helmet of Philip d'Alsace, Count of

FIG. 105.—Taken from the tomb of
Geoffrey Plantagenet, Count of
Anjou.

Flanders (*c.* 1181), shows a lion painted upon the side of the
same character as another appearing upon his shield; but
what is generally acknowledged to be the earliest authenti-
cated example of a crest fulfilling all the desired conditions
is that of Richard the Lion Heart, who upon his great seal
shows a fan-shaped ornament surmounting the heaume,
and upon the base is painted a lion passant (Fig. 106).

FIG. 106.—Heaume, Cœur de Lion.   FIG. 107.—" Pot Helmet," from the
Eneit of Heinrich von Veldeke.

One of the earliest instances of the use of a crest on
the Continent is that afforded by a MS. in the Royal
Library at Berlin, and belonging to the end of the
twelfth century (Fig. 107). In this case an actual figure,
that of a red lion, appears, and not paintings, as in the
two examples previously cited. It is possible that the
adoption of a crest upon the helmet may have been partly
of a defensive character, for the effect of a sword-cut
would be very materially modified after passing through
a stiff erection of steel plate or of tough cuir-bouilli, while

against the mace and the pole-axe it would also afford some slight protection. In support of this conjecture it may be noticed that crests at first were ridged and serrated, somewhat after the style which distinguished the pike-guards of the fifteenth century in their embryonic stage, as if purposely designed to arrest the edge of a weapon. The many examples which occur in an undecorated form preclude the thought that they were invented in order to bear heraldic cognisances, although they were quickly seized upon to fulfil the duty hitherto borne by the shield and surcoat, namely, to afford means of identifying the wearer. Of course the fan-shaped ornament under consideration may have simply been the outcome of that instinct for personal adornment and decoration which appears to be inherent in the human race, and which manifested itself in the mediæval period much more than now; but when it is considered that many of these fans are carried forward well over the face and at the same time far backwards, the conclusion is almost compelled that they originated in an endeavour to secure more protection for the top of the head than the crown of the heaume afforded. The great crests of a subsequent period were never used in actual combat, but were reserved exclusively for tournament purposes.

The Shield during this period was cut off as a rule in a straight line at the top, and was convex, so as to partially enclose the figure (see Fig. 108). It gradually decreased in size, until towards the close it became the small, well-known "heater-shaped" shield which remained in vogue for such a lengthy period. It was invariably decorated with the armorial bearings of the wearer, which in the early part of the chain mail period were mostly fanciful or devotional and of a transitory character, but became hereditary as it progressed. The only weapon of importance introduced was the arbalest, which will be dealt with in the next period.

The equipment of the ordinary rank and file of the chain mail period did not vary in any essential features from that which preceded it. In Fig. 88 we have two foot soldiers from Harl. MS. Y6, one of whom wears the Norman helmet, now truncated, with a nasal, which apparently is very long and wide. A similar helmet, but minus the nasal, defends his companion. The usual hauberk of chain mail or a cheaper substitute covers the body, and the legs are undefended. The mode of wearing the stockings and the cross bar below the leaf-shaped head of one spear tends to the belief that the illuminator was of Saxon blood or depicting others of that descent. The shields are suspended by guiges in both cases, and the fanciful decorations illustrate the assertions previously made in this chapter. In woodcut No. 109 a very characteristic group of soldiery of about the year 1220 is shown, taken from Harl. MS. 4751. The heavily-armed arbalestier in pot-helm and mail is one of a force defending a castle, and has discharged a quarrel which transfixes an archer of the attacking party. Before him, and apparently without any defensive equipment other than a chapelle-de-fer, is a foot soldier with a military pick in his right hand and a sword of short dimensions

FIG. 108.—From the seal (1315) of John de Bretagne, Earl of Richmond.

in the left. An arbalestier is probably shown in the third
position from the front, and an archer fourth, while the
fifth is unmistakably a slinger. As was generally the rule,
no protective covering was allowed the slingers—the one
in question has not even a hat—who from the nature of
their weapon were perforce compelled to be always in open

Fig. 109.—Soldiers, c. 1220. (Harl. MS., 4751.)

order when in action and at a distance from the enemy, and
presumably suffered less than the closely-packed bodies of
men-at-arms, billmen, and even archers. His sling appears
to be in no way different to the Saxon weapon shown in
Fig. 70. The last man is clad in a coif and hauberk of mail,
and is armed with an axe. At this period a weapon appears
in the illuminated MSS. which is apparently of recent introduction, namely the Staff Sling or Fustibal. It is
generally shown in besieging operations pitted against the

defenders on the walls, or in naval warfare as in Fig. 110.
The action of the sling is readily seen, the loop at the end
allowing the bag to disengage itself automatically at the
psychological moment, and to discharge the stone.   In
this case it seems to be
charged with some com-
bustible material to be
hurled on board an oppos-
ing ship.   The slinger is
as usual bareheaded and
devoid of bodily defences.
With him is an archer also
discharging combustibles
affixed to the end of an
arrow.   He is habited
in a sleeveless leather
hauberk strengthened

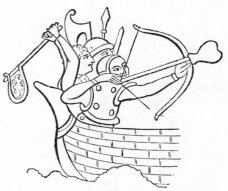

FIG. 110.—Staff-sling, &c.   (MS. by Matthew
Paris.)

with round plates, presumably of metal; a coif of mail or
leather covers his head.   The third figure carries a sword,
spear, and pole-axe, possibly his own, and also the close-
quarter weapons of the projectile throwers.

The equipment of a man-at-arms at the close of this
period is well shown in Fig. 111, from Auct. D. 4, 17,
in the Bodleian Library.   It dates from about 1250, and
illustrates the defensive properties of leather in combination
with iron.   The steel chapelle-de-fer covers a chain mail
coif which may be part of a continuous hauberk, as the arms
and hands are covered with mail of the same description.
Bands of leather round the throat afford the protection of
a gorget: they are affixed to a hauberk composed of leather
scales of large size and leaf-like shape showing the midrib,

while a belt round the waist and pendent leaves on the skirt complete a most effective means of bodily defence. The legs are enclosed in soft leather chausses protected by

FIG. 111.—Armour of cuir-bouilli, *c.* 1250.

FIG. 112.—Chapelle-de-fer, *c.* 1280. Figure of Goliath from Add. MS., 11639.

metal studs, upon which is a cross-gartering of leather thongs. The only weapon shown is an axe of formidable proportions. A spearman of *c.* 1280 is shown in Add. MS., 11639, representing Goliath of Gath, in which a chapelle-de-fer is a feature (Fig. 112).

CHAPTER VII

CHAIN MAIL REINFORCED, 1250–1325

THE special points which distinguish this period are :—

1. The introduction of Banded Mail.
2. The use of Ailettes.
3. The invention of the Conical Heaume borne by the shoulders.
4. The reinforcement of the Chain Mail by Plate.
5. The development of the Crest.

One of the most remarkable brasses in existence is that of Sir John d'Aubernoun, in Stoke D'Aubernoun Church, near Guildford, Surrey (Fig. 113). It is the earliest known example of this form of monumental effigy either in the British Isles or on the Continent, and dates from about the year 1277, the fifth of Edward I. It is to be noted that it is unique among the brasses of this reign by reason of the knight being represented with straight lower limbs, the remainder all having the cross-legged position. Although the figure is somewhat disproportionate, and the partial covering up of the lower parts of the legs by the surcoat is unfortunate, yet as a work of art, and especially as an example of technique and patience on the part of the engraver, it is unrivalled. Every separate link of the mail is faithfully represented. The reinforcement of the chain mail by secondary defences is here exemplified in its primitive

FIG. 113.—Sir John D'Abernoun, 1277. Stoke D'Aubernoun Church, Guildford, Surrey.

stage, a pair of genouillières only appearing, which from their ornamental appearance are presumably of cuir-bouilli, or of plate covered with cuir-bouilli. The reason for the introduction of this defence was not alone the protection afforded : the intolerable drag of chain mail upon the knee or elbow when flexed prevented freedom of action in either joint; but by the termination of the mail at the upper part of the genouillière to which it was affixed, and the continuation of it below, an advantage was gained which was fully appreciated. The coif-de-mailles upon the head descends to the shoulders on either side and covers part of the surcoat, while the hauberk has sleeves which are prolonged to cover the hand with mail gauntlets, not divided for the fingers. The mail chausses are continued like the sleeves of the hauberk, in order to protect the feet as well as the legs. Over the mail appears a loose surcoat reaching to below the knees and confined at the waist by a cord, from below which it opens in front and falls on either side in many folds, being also divided at the back to facilitate riding. It does not bear any ornament or design, but apparently is of rich material, and has a fringed border. The sword is long and straight, with short quillons drooping towards the blade; the grip is slightly swelling, and the circular pommel is enriched with a design. The method of suspending the sword is peculiar to the period : it grips the scabbard in two places, between which a small strap runs as a guide; the weapon thus hangs diagonally across the left front of the figure. The guige bearing the shield is enriched with roses alternating with the mystical cross (signifying good fortune and long life) termed the Fylfot, Gammadion, or Svastika, in which each arm of a Greek cross is continued at right angles; it passes over the right shoulder, and supports a small, flat, heater-shaped shield, upon which the arms appear (*azure*, a chevron, *or*). The spurs are the usual short ones of the pryck variety affixed by ornamental straps. The lance passes under the right arm, and displays a small fringed pennon charged with the same armorial insignia as the shield; it is shortened to permit of its introduction, and shows no grip for the hand. This is the only example of a brass in which the lance is introduced.

Another celebrated brass exemplifying in a remarkable degree the military equipment of the period is that of Sir Roger de Trumpington, 1289, in Trumpington Church, near Cambridge (Fig. 114). This well-known monumental effigy is one of five brasses which portray knights in the cross-legged attitude, concerning which so much has been said and so much written. The popular idea is, that the cross-legged position denotes a pilgrimage, or else a participation

FIG. 114.—Sir Roger de Trumpington, 1289. Trumpington
Church, Cambridge.

in a Crusade, on the part of the deceased, but this supposition is entirely negatived by the existence of monuments to *bonâ-fide* Crusaders, and to persons known to have visited the Holy Land, who are represented with the lower limbs not crossed. It is to be noted that this position is entirely confined to England with the exception of one at Dublin, and the generally accepted ideas are that these persons so represented were benefactors to the Church and died in the odour of sanctity. But it is perfectly admissible to suppose that, after all, this position was entirely an idea of the artist or the engraver, preventing as it did the ungainly stiffness in the d'Aubernoun brass. There are two examples of carved stone effigies both cross-armed and cross-legged—Sir Roger de Kerdeston, 1337, at Reepham, and Sir Oliver d'Ingham, 1343, at Ingham, Norfolk; but neither of these were Crusaders, while both were benefactors to their respective churches.

The armour shown in the Trumpington brass is similar in

general outline to the d'Aubernoun example, but is peculiar in manifesting nothing of an ornamental character. Two or three additions to the equipment, however, are shown which are important. The head rests upon the great heaume, which is of large proportions and conical, adapted for resting upon and being supported by the shoulders. At the apex is shown a staple for affixing either the contoise or the heraldic crest (to be alluded to later), and this feature is also shown upon the heaume of Sir William de Staunton, 1312, at Staunton, Notts (Fig. 115).

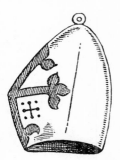

From the lower part of the back of the heaume a chain depends which fastens to a narrow cord tied tightly round the waist; by this arrangement the knight was enabled to regain this most important part of his equipment in the event of his being unhelmed. Later on this chain was affixed to a staple riveted or welded to the plastron-de-fer, openings being made in the hauberk and surcoat to permit of this.

FIG. 115.—Heaume of Sir William de Staunton, 1312.

Ailettes.—This period might almost be termed the "ailette period," but for the fact that this extraordinary adjunct only prevailed during a portion of the time. They were small shields or defences fastened at right angles across the shoulders, designed to lessen the effect of a sweeping cut from a sword or battle-axe, and were prototypes of the passe-gardes of the late fifteenth century, and of the epaulettes of the present day. The fact that a brass has necessarily a plane surface prevents these being seen in their proper place; a perspective representation would afford a vertical line only upon each shoulder, and in order to display the surfaces and avoid any fore-shortening, the artist has turned them at right angles to their real positions. The usual mode of their adjustment may be plainly perceived from a representation of the seal of Henry de Beaumont, Earl of Buchan, 1322 (Fig. 116), where the stiff lower portion is bent upwards and down-

 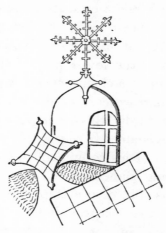

Fig. 116.—From the seal of Henry de Beaumont, Earl of Buchan, 1322.

Fig. 117.—Crest of John de Warenne, Earl of Surrey (d. 1344). (From his seal, 1329.)

wards to prevent a lateral fall; at the same time it is shaped to the shoulder, and probably fixed tightly to the hauberk, or the coif-de-mailles, by rings or rivets. Another example from a seal is that of John de Warenne, Earl of Surrey, 1329 (Fig. 117). Here the ailettes are apparently fastened only by one of the points and the half of one of the sides, but undoubtedly the whole of it was con-cave to the helmet; if so delineated by the artist the remote point would have been invisible, and not proper for heraldic representation as required upon a seal. Ailettes are rarely shown upon brasses and effigies; possibly the Buslingthorpe, Chartham, Gorleston, and Clehongre examples are the only ones in addition to the Trumpington. Upon seals they occur fairly often, but not with any frequency until the commencement of the fourteenth century. An early notice of ailettes occurs in the Roll of Purchases for the great tournament held at Windsor in 1278, where they are stated to have been made of leather covered with a kind of cloth. Silk laces were supplied to fasten them, and it is remarkable, to say the least, that the brass of Sir Roger de Trumpington, who was one of the thirty-eight knights taking part in the tournament, should furnish one of the earliest and best examples which has come down to modern times. In the curious painted window at Tewkesbury representing Gilbert de Clare, Earl of Gloucester, who perished upon the field of Bannockburn in 1314, we have the best illustration of ailettes contributed by stained glass. Probably the windows were made not long after the event, judging from the armour, which would be designed of contemporary pattern. Hewitt engraves a figure of a knight in Ash-by-Sandwich Church in which the ailettes appear as square projections behind the shoulders. In illuminated MSS. of this period the ailettes are very frequently shown, and are figured with combatants in all positions, so that the nature of the defence can be very clearly seen. They are also shown of all shapes and sizes. A lozenge-shaped ailette is seen on the accompanying figure (No. 118) from Roy. MS. 14, E. III., in which the same device appears as upon the shield, thus proving that it is not a square one

worn awry. At times one ailette only seems to have
been used, and that upon the left side; it appears as a
reinforcement to the shield in an illuminated MS. of Sir
Launcelot (Add. MS. 10,293), date 1316 (Fig. 119).
Sometimes the ailettes are so high and wide that they
almost enclose the great heaume by forming a circle round
it, being fixed behind where they meet, and only allowing a

FIG. 118.—Lozenge-shaped ailette
(Roy, MS. 14, E. III.), c. 1280.

FIG. 119.—Soldier
with one ailette
(Roy. MS. 16, G.
6), 14th century.

FIG. 120.—Soldier
with   circular
ailettes.

small opening in front for vision. The proper position is,
as has been stated, upon the shoulders and at right angles
to them, but when enlarged or of an inconvenient shape
they were fixed upon the upper part of the arm or behind
the shoulder. For example, in Fig. 120, which is taken
from a MS. in the Bodleian Library, the ailettes are shown
of a circular form, which obviously would be awkward to
fix upon the shoulder, hence we see them upon the upper
part of the arm.

The use of ailettes is somewhat perplexing, and anti-quarians have held various theories respecting them. That they were not merely armorial is proved by many showing no designs upon them whatever; that they were not for the purpose of distinguishing leaders in a fray is negatived by the fact that a knight's cognisance was much better recognised from his shield, surcoat, and crest; also, the ailettes appear in tournaments where there would be no necessity for recognition. The only supposition which appears to be defensible is that they were shields for the neck and shoulders, but more especially for the latter, as the great heaume protected the neck. In Germany they were called "tartschen," or shields. The defence afforded by a thick piece of leather, quilted material, or steel in that position will be at once appreciated; so low did they reach at times that they covered the junction of the arm with the body at the back, and this is well exemplified in the Clehongre effigy, dating from 1320, in which they are attached to the shoulders by arming points, and are concave to the body. Occasionally for tournaments and pageant purposes ailettes appear to have been made most elabo-rately; thus we find in the inventory of Piers Gaveston in 1313 a mention of a pair garnished and fretted with pearls.

There is a singular figure of a knight in an attitude of devotion illustrated in Roy. MS. 2, A. XXII., dating from about 1290, which has been ably reproduced in Shaw's "Dresses and Decorations of the Middle Ages" (Fig. 121). Many little details of thirteenth-century armour are delineated, affording a valuable acquisition to our knowledge. The mode in which the coif-de-mailles is fastened up to the side of the head by an arming point is well shown; the same method has been illustrated in Fig. 122 on p. 107, where two continuous hauberks

Fig. 121.—Knight (Roy. M.S. 2, A. 22), c. 1290.

are seen looped up in the same way. The palms of the hands are free from rings, in order to afford a better grasp of a weapon; this was the usual mode for constructing the mail gauntlet, and is also shown in Fig. 123. It also permitted the gauntlet being slipped off the hand when required. The gauntlets are continuous with the sleeves of the hauberk. Upon the shoulders are singularly

FIG. 122.—Figures from martyrdom of Thomas à Beckett (Harl. MS. 5102, Fo. 32), c. 1220.

small ailettes, consisting merely of a cross similar in design to those emblazoned upon the surcoat. The thighs are defended by chaussons or haut-de-chausses of mail, apparently with rings only upon the parts exposed. The chausses are of Bezanté armour, formed of small discs, each with a stud in the centre; these are sewn or riveted on to a pliable material, probably leather, which is fastened

FIG. 123.—From "Lives of the Two Offas," by M. Paris (Cott. MS., Nero, D. 1).

together by a series of points down the back of the leg. The chausses are prolonged to cover the feet, upon which are strapped the usual short pryck spur. The heaume is very much ornamented, and its general contour points to an earlier date than *c.* 1290, as does also the absence of genouillières. The lance and its pennon are shown. A leg protection of leather and highly ornamented was in use upon the Continent at

FIG. 124.—Circular ailettes.
(MS. 211, Bod. Lib.)

FIG. 125.—Leg defence (Italian), *c.* 1289.
Relief in Annunziata Convent.

this period ; its form and dimensions may be gleaned from Fig. 125.

In a MS. in the Bodleian Library (No. 211) a knight or man - at - arms is represented carrying a shield and wearing ailettes of a circular pattern, which are fastened to his banded mail at the upper part of the arm (Fig. 124). He wears a hemispherical steel cap and is clothed in a voluminous surcoat. A similar example, but of later date, is shown in Roy. MS. 20, D. 2, British Museum, where a

---

figure habited in banded mail and a conical pot-helm, with sword and shield, wears circular ailettes in precisely the same manner as the previous example (Fig. 126).

FIG. 126. — Knight (Roy. MS. 2, D. 11), 13th century.

THE BANNER, PENNON, AND PENNONÇEL

The knightly Banner of the period was either square or oblong; in the latter case the height was invariably twice the width (see Fig. 127). It was the distinctive mark of the Knight Banneret, and always indicated superiority of command and importance, inasmuch as it required a retinue of at least fifty men-at-arms with their followers to adequately support the dignity. Thus it was a position of distinction which could only be enjoyed

FIG. 127.—Banner of Knight Banneret.

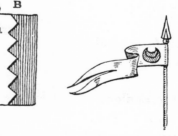

FIG. 128.—Pennon of Henri de Perci, Earl of Northumberland.

FIG. 129. Pavon, Painted Chamber.

by the rich, and the chronicles of the mediæval period record instances of knights who, having specially distinguished themselves on the field of battle, declined the proffered honour of Knight Banneret on the score of insufficient means. If, on the other hand, it were accepted, it was usual to convert the pennon of the knight into a banner on the spot by simply cutting off the tail or tails. The simple knight, or Knight Bachelor as he was termed, carried a Pennon or Pavon, which was furnished with one or more tails, as in Fig. 121, where it is represented with three; that of Henri de Perci, first Earl of Northumberland, with two (see Fig. 128); and in the d'Aubernoun brass, where one is depicted. He became eligible for knighthood at twenty-one, presuming that he had sufficient private property to support the dignity, but had to distinguish himself in the field or otherwise before the honour was conferred. It was not absolutely necessary to be of gentle birth, as many examples may be cited of knighthood being conferred upon those who could not claim such descent. The contingent he led into battle under his pennon varied in number according to his means. The Pennonçel or Pensil was a small, narrow streamer to which the Esquire, or aspirant to knighthood, was entitled. It was necessary for him to serve an apprenticeship in arms, and he generally attended the castle of a neighbouring baron, or the court of the king. Such was, briefly, the etiquette respecting the three different flags of knighthood, quite apart from those of the chief commanders and the great standards. There were, of course, variations introduced. Pennons shown in Figs. 129 and 130 from the Painted Chamber are triangular, and the banner in Fig. 130 is nearly three times as high as it is wide. Before quitting this subject it may be mentioned that knighthood was quite distinct from birth and social position,

and was simply a scheme of military rank, the aspirants having absolutely equal opportunities for acquiring the dignity.

The Heaume. — During the first
thirty years of this period, that is until
about 1280, the heaumes continued to
be generally of the flat-topped variety
not reaching to the shoulders, but
having the addition of a movable visor.
One, however, shown in Fig. 131 and
dating from *c.* 1250, differs considerably, and shows a heaume approaching
the dimensions and shape of a bascinet,
while the visor is adapted for raising
or for removal. An earlier example
without a visor is one seen in a group
from the Painted Chamber in conjunction with helmets having a nasal
(Fig. 130). In Fig. 132 we have an

FIG. 130.—Early heaume and
helmets with nasals.
Painted Chamber.

example of one of
the earliest and plainest of this variety,
in which the ventaille could be removed
at pleasure from the two projecting studs
on the heaume which kept it in place.
Fig. 133 is of the same type, but furnished with a more elaborate visor, and
with a crown surmounting it. Fig. 134
is from the seal of Richard Plantagenet,
King of the Romans and Earl of Cornwall, who died in 1272, and Fig. 135 from
that of Robert de Ferrars, Earl of Derby,

FIG. 131.—Helmet,
c. 1250.

died *c.* 1279 ; in both we trace the tendency to alter the
shape of the lower rim. The movable ventaille was not

in all cases directly detachable from the heaume, but swung outwards upon a hinge on one side, similar to a wicket gate ; as this hinge had a pin running through it which could be

withdrawn, the visor was wholly removed if not required.

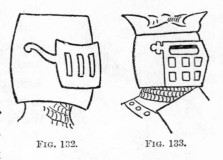

Fig. 132.   Fig. 133.

About 1270 the round-topped variety came into fashion, of which examples are found until the end of the century and even after it. The seal of Patrick Dunbar, 10th Earl of March, affords a good illustration of the heaume with a circular crown; it is furnished with a movable visor. Other examples are shown in groups in

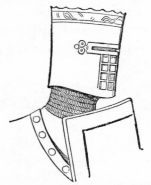

Fig. 134.—From the seal of Richard Plantagenet, Earl of Cornwall, King of the Romans (*d.* 1272).

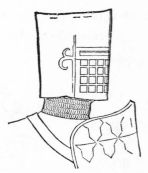

Fig. 135.—From the seal of Robert de Ferrars, Earl of Derby (*d.* before 1279).

the Painted Chamber at Westminster, and two very late specimens are represented in Figs. 116 and 117 on p. 102.

About the year 1280 the conical-topped heaume came into use, whose general form is delineated in Fig. 137, and has already been noticed in the Trumpington brass. It was of great weight, and either hung at the saddle bow, or was

carried by the squire, when not in use ; it rested upon the shoulders, and thus relieved the head of the greater part of its weight. Two heaumes are here shown (Figs. 138, 139) from Add. MS. 10,294 in the British Museum. One is of the plain and ordinary pattern, but the second shows a movable visor which can either be raised or removed entirely. It also illustrates a reinforcing plate protecting the sides of the head. Inside it was thickly padded, and representa-

FIG. 136.—Knight, showing mail over pot-de-fer, 1290.

tions of this feature may often be discerned upon monumental effigies, where the heaume is used to support the head

FIG. 137.

FIG. 138.—Heaume.
(Add. MS. 10,294.)

FIG. 139. — Heaume.
(Add. MS. 10,294.)

of the recumbent knightly figure. To keep it in position laces were attached to the lower edge at the back ; these are clearly seen in Fig. 121, p. 106.

The development of the crest during this period did not make much headway, but a few examples from seals and MSS. will show that there was a certain amount of progress. The heaume of Baron Henri de Perci, *c.* 1300 (Fig. 140), exhibits a highly ornamented crest with the distinctive feature of two streamers affixed to its base, the contoise or mantling in its incipient form. The comb is deeply serrated, and ornamented with gadroons springing from the centre. Upon

FIG. 140.—Heaume of Henri de Perci, *c.* 1300.

the seal of Henry de Lacy, Earl of Lincoln, 1301 (Fig. 141),

FIG. 141.—From the seal of Henry de Lacy, Earl of Lincoln, 1301.

FIG. 142.—From the seal of Richard Fitzalan, Earl of Arundel, 1301.

the conical heaume is shown, not reaching, however, to the shoulders, with a small, plain comb upon its summit, differing in that respect from the crests of Richard Fitzalan, Earl of Arundel (Fig. 142), and Humphrey Bohun, Earl of Hereford (Fig. 143), which both date from the same year. A singularly plain heaume, considering the distinction of the wearer, is that of Edward, Prince of Wales, 1305, as delineated upon his seal (Fig. 144). The crest of John de Warenne, Earl of Surrey, 1329, shown in Fig.

FIG. 143.—From the seal of Humphrey de Bohun, Earl of Hereford, 1301.

FIG. 144.—From the seal of Edward of Carnarvon, Prince of Wales, 1305.

117 on p. 102, displays a startling development upon the preceding examples, and exhibits a high order of decorative design in crests at this early period.

At Acton in Suffolk is a monumental brass to Sir Robert de Bures, dating from the year 1302, which holds the proud position of being the finest early brass in existence, and which may also fairly claim to be the finest military brass extant. The details of equipment differ but little from the d'Aubernoun and Trumpington brasses, but the

PLATE XI

Sir Robert de Bures, 1302.   Acton
Church, Suffolk

guige of the shield, by being partially hidden under the tippet of the coif-de-mailles, indicates that the coif was entirely separate from the hauberk, and was not continuous, as might be imagined from the early brasses. The genouillières are very elaborate, and probably of cuir-bouilli; above them and beneath the skirt of the hauberk are seen the padded and quilted trews covering the chausses from the knee upwards. This garment, whose surface was usually of silk, baudekyn, or other costly material, is shown in the brass to be richly embroidered with fleur-de-lys and an ornament resembling in shape the Greek lyre, disposed alternately in lozenges formed by the reticulations of the silken cords, and a similar decoration appears upon the grip of the sword (Plate XI.).

Sir Robert de Septvans, 1306, is another knight whose brass effigy has the cross-legged position; it is in Chartham Church, Kent, and affords an excellent illustration of the military accoutrement at the termination of the reign of Edward I. (Fig. 146). The singular name of Septvans (or Seven Fans) is derived from the heraldic cognisance of the family, and is shown upon the figure as seven fans of the shape used for winnowing wheat at that period. The coif-de-mailles is thrown back in this effigy, and rests upon the shoulders in folds; the ailettes are square or oblong, and the sleeves of the hauberk are thrown back off the hands and are shown depending from the wrist. Beneath the hauberk the quilted undergarment called the haqueton appears; the trews are of similar material, and apparently are continued under the genouillières, probably to avoid chafing. The latter are of plate, and a stud is shown which fastens them to a strap behind the knee. The sword-hilt and scabbard are enriched with a highly effective diaper design.

Between the years 1306 and 1320 there are no brasses in existence exhibiting the full military equipment of the time, the example at Croft, 1310, being only a half-brass and

singularly devoid of detail (Fig. 145). Two brasses, however, dating from 1320, afford us an opportunity of seeing the marked development in defences which had been adopted in the interval. The Bacon brass in Gorleston Church, Suffolk, has been much mutilated, but sufficient is retained to make it of interest. The coif-de-mailles, hauberk, surcoat, sword-belt, shield, and guige show no differences, but in the

FIG. 145.—Knight in banded mail, 1310. Croft, Lincs.

plate defences a great advance has been made. The back of the upper arms from shoulder to elbow, and the front of the lower arms from the bend of the elbow to the wrist, are protected by plates of steel, fastened by steel straps round the limbs; these are respectively the Demi-Brassarts and Demi-Vambraces. Upon the elbows are the Coudières, and upon the knees Genouillières of plate, while the shins are defended by Demi-Jambarts, all being fixed over the chain mail to fulfil the office of reinforcements. At the shoulder and elbow bends, roundels of plate appear, and over the shoulder are ailettes marked with the Cross of St. George. The shield is small and heater-shaped, and is furnished with a narrow guige. In the Fitzralph brass, 1320, Pebmarsh Church, Essex (Fig. 147), the general arrangement is similar to the Gorleston brass, but no ailettes are shown, and the shield is large and concave to the body. Upon

FIG. 146.—Sir Robert de Septvans, 1306. Chartham Church, Kent.

FIG. 147.—Sir —— de Fitzralph, *c.* 1320. Pebmarsh Church, Essex.

the feet are Sollerets consisting of five lames of plate riveted together and kept in place by two straps passing

FIG. 148.—Figures from " Massacre of the Innocents " (Add. MS. 17,687), c. 1290.

under each foot. The swords of both figures show straight quillons not drooping to the blade as formerly. The pryck

spur is still in vogue, and from the roundels the small
projecting spikes should be noticed. The five cross-legged
brasses thus described and illustrated are all that now
remain to us, and of these five only one, that of Trumping-

FIG. 149.—Soldier (Sloan MS. 346), c. 1280.

FIG. 150.—Swordsman of the chain mail reinforced period.

ton, so far as is known, represents a knight who followed
the banner of the Holy Cross to Palestine.

   The defensive equipment of the ordinary foot soldier of
this period is well delineated in Fig. 148, which is taken
from Add. MS. 17,687 in the British Museum, a German
illumination dating from c. 1290. The subject is the

Massacre of the Innocents, a favourite theme for illustrations in those times: the central figure is holding in the air a child (not shown except the foot) preparatory to dashing it upon the ground, while the soldier to the right has the decapitated head of a child, also not reproduced, in his left hand. The coif-de-mailles are in all three examples peculiar in being continued as a pectoral; in two cases they are constructed of banded mail, and in the third of studded jazeraint. Two hauberks are shown, one of banded mail and the other of jazeraint. The central figure has genouillières of leather which, like those of his companions upon his left, are apparently continuous round the joint: the strips of pendent leather from them have been sewn over the shins and calves, while studded strips over chausses of the same material cover the lower limbs of his comrade. The third figure has simple chausses of banded mail with no reinforcement: long swords with characteristic pommels are worn, and the whole group is a most striking example of the lack of uniformity at the period. Also see Figs. 149 and 150.

Archers.—From the time of the Norman Conquest the practice of archery assumed an importance which did not fall to its lot before in England. The Saxons had not paid particular attention to this arm from a military standpoint, only using it in sport, and the success of the Normans at Hastings was due in a great measure to the skill and superior numbers of their archers. The latter are shown on the tapestry both in hauberks and without, and one is seen on horseback. The bow appears to be of the simplest form of construction, and the arrow decidedly not the cloth-yard shaft of a later age. It became a custom from a very early date for the archer to bear a stake sharpened at both ends which the

front ranks drove firmly into the ground with the second
and uppermost point sloping from them, while the rear
ranks filled up the intermediate spaces with theirs.   When
protected thus in front and on both flanks it was found
that the archers of England could defy the charge of
the heaviest cavalry.   Already in the twelfth century
the English began to develop that prowess in archery

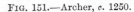

FIG. 151.—Archer, c. 1250.   FIG. 152.—Archer, 1330. (Roy. MS. 16, C. 6.)

which subsequently made them renowned throughout the
Continent of Europe.   At the siege of Messina by Cœur
de Lion we are told by Richard of Devizes that the
Sicilians were obliged to leave their walls unmanned "because no one could look abroad but he would have an arrow
in his eye before he could shut ·it," while Richard himself
did not disdain the use of the weapon, but used it person-
ally with deadly effect when besieging Nottingham Castle,
defended by the adherents of his brother John.   Among

the enactments of Henry I. of England it was provided that if any one practising with arrows or with darts should by accident slay another it was not to be visited against him as a crime.

It was during the period now under consideration, 1250 to 1325, that the archer first stepped into prominent notice, and that the efficacy of his weapon, the most deadly that the art of man devised until the introduction of gunpowder, came to be fully recognised. During the Norman period the infantry as a rule were armed with the bow, but the other weapons they bore were considered of equal if not greater usefulness and importance in battle, owing probably to the undeveloped condition of the weapon. With the advent, however, of the long-bow proper, and the invention of the arbalest, the deadly effect of the arrow

FIG. 153.—Archers.   (Roy. MS. 20, D. 1.)

and the quarrel began to be fully recognised and accepted, and changes consequently occurred in the art of warfare occasioned by the adoption of these weapons. The bow was not at first considered to be of exceptional efficiency in the open field, but to be especially valuable in sieges, and the defence of mountain passes and strongholds. When this idea was proved to be erroneous we find from various Statutes of Arms that a number of the military tenants were ordered to be provided with the long-bow and arrows. The Statute of Westminster, for instance, especially mentions the bow.   Their equipment was considerably augmented also with respect to body armour, for in Fig. 109 on p. 94 we see the bowman of *c*. 1220 defended only by his chapelle-de-fer, whereas in Figs. 153, 155, taken from Roy. MS. 20, D 1, dating from the end of the century, when the conical heaume had been generally adopted, the archers are depicted with the same headgear and the body defended by a hauberk of banded mail. Whether arrows were ever furnished with the small crosspieces as shown is conjectural; they are, however, often shown in MSS. having a foreign origin. In Fig. 154 the archer

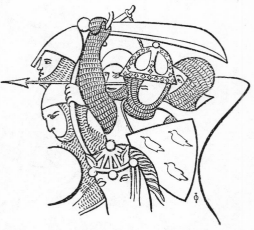

Fig. 154.—Archer, &c., from Painted Chamber.

is seen clad in a coif-de-mailles and hauberk.   The arrowhead is usually barbed as shown, but whether the three-barbed arrow of Spain, shown in the Spanish Codex, Add. MS. 11,695, written in 1109, was ever adopted in England is very doubtful.   The fourteenth century showed the fullest development of the bow, as we shall find, and during that period the archer attained the height of his importance, but by his equipment at this early period we may conclude that he was taking an important place in the military force of the nation.

Arbalestiers.—The arbalest or cross-bow was known apparently as early as the fourth century, and is mentioned in manuscripts of the tenth ; it appears, however, to have been chiefly used for sport at that time. It was not before the close of the twelfth century that it was recognised as a military weapon, or is illustrated in manuscripts.

FIG. 155.—Mounted archer (Roy. MS. 20, D. 1), *c.* 1290.

In the beginning of the twelfth century there appears to have been an effort made for its introduction, but at a council held under Pope Innocent II. in 1139, it was placed under an interdict as a barbarous weapon and unfit for Christian warfare, and this condemnation was subsequently confirmed by Innocent III. In the meantime, however, Richard I. of England and Philip Augustus of France had sanctioned its use during the Crusade

FIG. 156.—Military equipment, c. 1280.

in which they had taken part, Richard being the first to advocate its use, and Philip acquiescing and subsequently adopting his example. The cross-bow thus introduced into England at the end of the twelfth century practically became obsolete at the termination of the thirteenth, when the long-bow almost succeeded in extirpating its rival. This, however, was by no means the case upon the Continent, where it was the leading arm until the introduction of the arquebus, and throughout the thirteenth century cross-bowmen became integral units of every English army, sometimes being mounted. The King's Bodyguard, founded by Richard I., was formed partly of arbalestiers. In the copious records left by Matthew Paris, who died in 1259, the cross-bowman is continually mentioned. His particular post was in the forefront of the battle and upon the wings, where the heavy quarrels discharged from his weapon were supposed to check the advance of the enemy's cavalry; and scarcely a battle is recorded in that part of the thirteenth century where the arbalestier is not credited with performing most conspicuous service. In the battle near Damietta in 1237 a hundred Templars and three hundred cross-bowmen are said to have fallen, and the Emperor Frederick in 1239, writing to Henry III. of England, mentions the very prominent part played in a campaign by the arbalestiers. In the contest with Louis IX., Henry III. had seven hundred cross-bowmen in his force, while the French had a vastly greater number. In King John's time the pay for a cross-bowman on foot was threepence per day, while if mounted he was paid sevenpence halfpenny or fifteenpence, according as to whether he possessed one or two horses. Notwith-

A. F. Calvert

PLATE XII *

Foot Armour of Philip II., made by Desiderius Colman

standing the conspicuous successes of these troops they occupied an invidious position in other countries than our own; for the knights and men-at-arms, if they perceived the day being won by the prowess of the cross-bowmen, did not hesitate to charge through their ranks in order to share in the glory. This occurred many times upon the Continent, though happily no record exists of its happening in England. Like the bowman of his time the arbalestier was clad occa-

FIG. 158.—Archer and arba-lestier, 13th century.

FIG. 157.—Arbalestier, c. 1250.

sionally in heavy armour. In the annexed Fig. 158 of an archer and a cross-bowman, from Add. MS. 15,268 and dating from the close of the thirteenth century, the armour of the latter appears to be of the tegulated or the scale variety, though it is quite possible that it may be intended for banded mail. Upon his head he wears a leather skull-cap strengthened apparently by iron bands, under which appears a linen or soft leather coif. A representation of a similar skull-cap of leather (Fig. 159), ornamented with a strengthening device in iron which is prolonged into a nasal, is shown upon one of the figures in the Painted Chamber, Westminster.

FIG. 159.—Nasal.
Painted Chamber,
Westminster.

The pile of the cross-bow bolt is shown to be quite distinct from the barbed head of the arrow. In Fig. 109, p. 94, the cross-bowman is represented as heavily armed in a pot-helm and hauberk of mail. The supersession of the cross-bow in England by the long-bow was due to natural causes. It was found that as the long-bow underwent improvements it outclassed the cross-bow in more ways than one. A powerful and skilful bowman could discharge half-a-dozen or more arrows during the time necessitated for winding up the cross-bow for a second shot ; also the distance covered by the arrow, together with its penetrative force, were quite equal to that of the quarrel, and is generally considered to have been superior. In consequence of this rapidity of fire the English archer invariably beat down the attack of Continental cross-bowmen, if equal in numbers, and, very often, when they were in excess. Compactness of troops was a great point in mediæval warfare, and the bowmen could stand closer together with their bows vertical than their brethren of the cross-bow with their weapons in the horizontal position. There is little doubt that the cross bow was the ideal weapon for the ordinary soldier of an ordinary race, inasmuch as little intellect was required to direct the aim and little strength was necessary if the usual mechanical means were used to bend the bow. For the efficient use of the long-bow, on the contrary, a keen judgment was an absolute necessity, and it was only a race of considerable physical power that could put forth the strength and maintain the exertion which the long-bow demanded. It is undoubtedly a matter for national self-complacency to reflect upon the fact that while the British gradually discarded the cross-bow and adopted the long-bow almost entirely, the Continental nations proceeded in exactly the opposite direction.

The Hand Cross-bow.—The cross-bow as at first introduced was of a simple construction, and permitted of the bow being drawn by the hands alone, without the aid of mechanical means. Such a bow is that shown in Figs. 109, 157, 160, &c., which when required to be strung was simply placed upon the ground, the left foot inserted in the iron loop at the end of the stock, and the string drawn up with the right hand, until it engaged in the notch. This is termed the hand cross-bow. The oldest arbalest in the Wallace Collection dates from 1450, and is pro-

FIG. 160.—Arbalestier, 1330. (Roy. MS. 16, G 6.)

bably of German construction. The stock is of wood inlaid with plaques of polished stag-horn, which are beautifully carved in relief. The bow is of great strength, partly enveloped in parchment and leather painted, and the original cord remains.

The Goat's Foot, or Hind's Foot, Cross-bow.—The apparatus to bend this bow is essentially a double lever consisting of two pieces articulated together. The smaller piece is divided into two distinct parts, each of which terminates in a catch; one of these engages with the bow-string and the other upon points on either side of the stock. The longer arm of the lever was drawn back, and the catch with the bow-string followed it until, being brought up sufficiently into position, the string was caught by the notch and remained secure until discharged. An arbalest is preserved in the Wallace Collection, dating from 1520, the bow of which is built up of layers of cane, whalebone, hide, and parchment, ornamented and painted; this bow was bent by the goat's-foot lever, a few examples of which are to be seen in the Museum.

The Wheel and Ratchet Cross-bow.—This apparatus is affixed to the bow stock behind the trigger by a stout cord which passes round the stock and holds the mechanism firmly. It consists of a flat, circular, iron case which contains in its outer periphery a small toothed wheel which can be turned by a long handle. Passing through the circular case and engaging with the small wheel is a straight ratchet with one side cogged: this ratchet has a catch at the end remote from the case which engages with the bow-string. By merely turning the handle and so revolving the wheel the ratchet is wound through the case, thus drawing back the string to its resting-place. The apparatus is then detached and hung at the belt until wanted again.

In Plate XL., p. 366, taken at the Rotunda, Woolwich, an arbalestier of *c.* 1450 may be discerned in the act of winding his cross-bow by a one-handled moulinet, the head of the stock, which is very short, resting on his knee and not on the ground. It takes a weight of 400 lbs. to bend this bow.

Moulinet and Pulleys Cross-bow.—A piece of iron bent into the form of a stirrup is affixed to the stock (adjacent to the bow in this case), similar to that of the hand cross-bow,

PLATE XIII *

Philip II., Armour by Wolf of Landshut, 1550

for the insertion of the left foot, so as to gain the largest amount of steadiness and purchase. At the butt end of the stock, against the archer's body, a system of fixed pulleys, having cords running over another system of free pulleys, is firmly affixed by the insertion of the butt into a socket. The free-pulley system has a catch attached to it which engages with the cord of the bow : by winding up the fixed system with a small windlass having a handle on either side, the free system approaches the butt, bringing with it the string of the bow, which after a time is duly caught in the notch provided for it. The tackle is then released and hung at the belt until wanted. An excellent example of Moulinet and Pulleys may be seen in the Wallace Collection, dating from 1490 to 1500 ; it is constructed of steel, and is in good preservation.

The Cross-bow à Galet.—In this type the bow is bent by means of a lever fixed to the stock, and was much used in the sixteenth century for the discharge of stones, spherical balls of lead, &c. In order to afford a good purchase for the lever, the stock between the bow and the string-catch was very often curved downwards into a segment of a circle and made of metal.

The Barrelled Cross-bow was as a rule bent by hand, although a short stick was occasionally used. A half-tube covered the groove through which the quarrel travelled, thus leaving a passage for the string. It did not carry to any remarkable distance, but in spite of this was in much request during the seventeenth century.

The missiles for cross-bows are termed quarrels, or bolts, and generally terminated in a four-sided pyramidal head or pile, being occasionally feathered with wood or brass. One kind was so feathered as to cause the bolt to rotate upon its axis. The cross-bow did not altogether disappear from the army. We find mention in 1572, in the time of Queen Elizabeth, of cross-bowmen being part of a force of six thousand men furnished by the queen to King Charles IX. The slinger of this period is well delineated in Fig. 161. It will be perceived that he carries no protection whatever in the shape of armour; his weapon is the staff sling or fustibal.

FIG. 161.—Slinger with staff sling or fustibal, 13th century.

Banded Mail.—Toward the close of the thirteenth century a new species of armour made its appearance, which is generally known by the name of Banded Mail. It was in extensive use for about a century or more, and appears upon the knight as well as upon the ordinary soldier. Chain mail was apparently superseded by the banded mail, though not entirely, as the former appears upon regal effigies and persons of the aristocratic families, from which we may infer that the chain variety was retained by those who could afford it and banded mail was used by those whose means were limited.

As the structure of banded mail always presents difficulty to the student, and many conjectures made at various times have as a rule rendered the question more difficult still without solving it, it is obviously not out of place in this work to deal comprehensively with the subject and, it is hoped, to definitely decide the question.   The premises from which we may argue are as follows :—

1. From the time of the first Crusade, or approximately about that time, chain mail proper was the flexible defensive covering for the English knight, and various kinds of jazeraint armour, in which leather, metal plates, padded material, &c., were indiscriminately used, for the

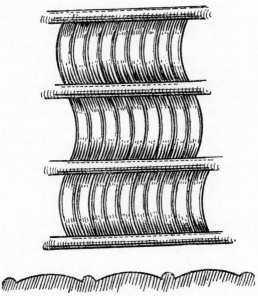

FIG. 162 —Banded mail : knight of the De Sulney family at Newton Solney, Derbyshire.

ordinary soldier.   The chain mail was obviously too dear for the average purse.

2. During the period mentioned above archery was in an incipient condition, and bodily defences were adapted to withstand the weapons in ordinary use, which, if we exclude the javelin, and, under extraordinary circumstances, the lance, were hand and not missile weapons.

3. The simultaneous adoption of banded mail, not only by the common soldier, but also by a large proportion of the knightly forces, points conclusively to the fact that chain mail was no longer considered an adequate defence; in other words that the adoption of a new arm

had rendered it inefficient, and that another description of armour was imperatively demanded to withstand its effects.

4. The use of leather as a means for bodily defence had been known from the most ancient times, and in England had been freely used by the Saxons, as we have seen. From the Conquest onwards it had steadily advanced in favour, and culminated in importance in the first half of the fourteenth century during the Studded and Splinted Armour Period, not finally disappearing until the adoption of total plate defences rendered its use obsolete. Its second rise into favour during the seventeenth century is obviously not connected with this question, except to emphasise the fact that leather has always been considered an efficacious defence against sword-cuts, and also against missiles which are not gifted with too great powers of penetration.

5. The fact that banded mail, whether seen upon the inside or the outside, presents exactly the same appearance (see the Creke, Northwode, and d'Aubernoun brasses) and is delineated in such manner in illuminated manuscripts, and carved the same in monumental effigies, precludes the supposition that rings of metal were sewn down or otherwise affixed to a garment of leather, as had been the fashion with Saxons and Normans. Unless, however, we suppose a total abandonment of leather as a defence which had been growing in favour previously and which culminated afterwards, we must conclude that leather in some form was used in the construction of the mail.

6. The abandonment generally of chain mail and the adoption of banded mail occurred synchronously with the extraordinary development of the long-bow in the latter part of the thirteenth century.

7. Banded mail was of so flexible a character that folds are depicted in garments constructed of this material; it was used for hauberks, camails, chausses, sleeves, and, in short, for every purpose in which its predecessor had been used.

8. It is represented in MSS. with a metallic surface. The colour is always silver, white or grey of various shades, and gold. We have therefore to devise a protection which shall be of greater service than chain against arrows; which shall be comparatively cheap; in which leather plays a more or less conspicuous part; which shall present the same appearance when viewed upon both sides; shall be flexible; and finally shall have a metallic surface or general appearance.

The accompanying diagram (Plate XIV.) is taken from a photograph of a piece of banded mail constructed according to our idea of the structure of the mediæval defence. The rings are iron washers, 1 in. in diameter and $\frac{1}{16}$ in. thick. Through the centre of the washers a piece of leather

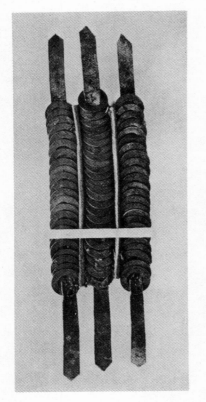

PLATE XIV

Suggested Construction of Banded Mail

exactly as wide as the apertures passes from end to end. The washers are arranged like rouleaux of coin, each one just covering the aperture through the centre of the one below. Between each row of washers a thick piece of leather is placed, the raw edges being visible on either side of the mail where they have been rounded off with the knife. The section of this leather band would be similar to that of a dumb-bell, the centres on each side of the leather being hollowed so as to permit the edges of the rouleaux to approach each other and almost touch, the thin centre only preventing them. To the middle of this leather band the individual rings of the mail are sewn of both the upper and lower rows. The best portion of this example is that immediately to the right of the white band. The appearance of both sides of this example of mail is precisely similar ; it is very flexible, and easily bends in any required direction. The weight, however, would probably be prohibitory, even to a mediæval knight, and in order to lighten it we may suggest that every alternate washer be made of leather, or even that two washers of leather alternate with one of metal. Against this it may be argued that banded mail is represented with a metallic tint, but so also is chain mail, which must have presented ordinarily a rusty-hued mass with simply an outer surface of polished iron. The liability to rust of chain mail must have been excessive, and the two outer and accessible surfaces were undoubtedly the only portions usually polished. So well known is this fact that in the pageants now prevalent brown string is knitted to represent chain armour, the outer surface being subsequently covered with a metallic medium. As a consequence the limners of banded mail would represent it with a metallic surface even though it presented as brown or rusty an aspect as chain mail. The washers used in the modern example would in the mediæval period be flattened rings of metal, and the excessively coarse and large banded mail would be oval rings and not circular. The bands are at times represented by single lines, and the suggestion is obvious that the lines simply represent the junction of the rouleaux which have not the extra defence of the bands of leather, or else the band is so narrow that one line is sufficient for its representation.

We will now deal with its efficiency for defence against arrows, which appears to have been the chief reason for its being called into existence. These missiles would strike either upon the rouleaux or upon the bands, and would impinge either at a right angle to the plane of the surface, or at any angle less than a right angle. An arrow striking the rouleaux at right angles would endeavour to pass through (1) the thickness of a metal or leather disc; (2) the leather running through the discs;

(3) the thickness of a metal or leather disc at the rear. If it struck a metal disc, however, there would be a deflective tendency either to right or left, according to the slant of the disc.

An arrow striking at an acute angle upon the rouleaux would glance off if the discs slanted in its direction ; if the discs sloped from it the arrow might insert itself between two of them, penetrate the band of leather running through the centres, and then endeavour to pass between two discs at the back. So tightly, however, would these discs be pressed together, by the leverage of the arrow-head itself in enlarging the opening between them in the front, that it is questionable if the inertia remaining in the arrow would enable it to overcome such resistance, remembering that the discs are firmly fixed both at the top and bottom to the leather bands. If an arrow struck upon one of the bands it would have to penetrate at least half-an-inch of leather and force apart the rouleaux firmly sewn, or affixed in other ways, to the band on either side.

The specimen of banded mail constructed in accordance with the foregoing method possesses in actual practice the resisting power claimed for it ; the apparent weak point is the penetrability between the discs. If, however, the rings are firmly sewn to the lateral bands the resistance to an arrow is almost if not quite equal to that of any other part of the mail ; the arrow becomes firmly fixed in the discs without penetrating to the body. It is an unsettled question as to whether or not complete armour of leather discs was ever introduced into England : certain it is that the armour of William Longuespée, first Earl of Salisbury, in Salisbury Cathedral was originally painted brown, but that might signify, as we have said before, rusty chain mail and not leather ; whereas upon the few sculptured effigies in banded mail preserved to us the colouring has altogether disappeared.

CHAPTER VIII

THE CYCLAS PERIOD, 1325-1335

PROBABLY at no time in the history of defensive armour has it presented a more picturesque appearance than during the brief ten years of the Cyclas Period. Fitting closely to the figure, the various garments followed the outlines of the human form, and in no parts showed any marked peculiarities or eccentricities. The evolution of the style was undoubtedly derived from the experience gained during the Chain Mail Period, when that defence was proved to be ineffectual against the terrible effects of lance and sword. Both of these weapons, even if they did not actually pierce the mail, either bruised the body, or broke bones, and thereby incapacitated the wearer; while the protection afforded by the loosely hanging folds of the surcoat of previous periods, especially against sword-cuts, has been duly noted. Hence during the Cyclas Period we meet with the introduction of multitudinous coverings, whereby the lance, the sword, and the arrow were opposed by plate and mail, and by various padded garments of a textile nature. The superposition and nature of the defensive equipment will now be described.

1. *The Haqueton.*—This consisted of a stuffed and padded garment covering the whole body from the neck to the knees, and the upper part of the arms; it rested immediately upon the under-shirt of wool. The padded char-

acter of the garment may be seen from the Creke and
d'Aubernoun brasses, where the lower edge reaches the
genouillières.   In the Clehongre effigy the haqueton, though
doubtless worn, is not apparent.   The padding, besides
being defensive, served to protect the body
from the pressure of the mail and plate defences.

  2. *The Hauberk.* — During the Cyclas
Period this garment appears to have been
generally made of banded mail, which consisted of rings or discs firmly attached on
two sides to bands or strips of leather,
and overlapping each other right and left
in alternate rows.   The protection afforded
by this defence was so good, and the flexibility so great, that banded mail was in very
common use during the greater part of the
fourteenth century for hauberks, camails, and
chausses.   The hauberk either terminated in
a point in front at the knees, in similar
fashion to the camail, or was rounded, or
cut squarely off, according to the individual
taste of the wearer.   The sleeves in nearly
all cases terminate a little below the elbow.   It probably
extended well up the neck and reinforced the camail.

FIG. 163. — Sir
Robert Shurland,
1300;   showing
the gambeson.

  3. *The Breastplate, or Plastron-de-fer.*—So far as we
are aware no exact description of this defence is extant; we
only know that it was of steel, that it covered the upper part
of the front of the body, that it was invariably of a globular
shape, and that it was securely attached to the hauberk, but
whether it had a companion backplate so as to form an

entire cuirass is entirely conjectural. Staples were affixed to it for chains, which at that period were so often attached to the hilts of the swords and daggers, and sometimes also to the great heaume, the chain seen in the Northwode brass being for the latter purpose. The globular form it imparted to the cyclas is well seen in monumental effigies, but not so readily discernible in brasses.

4. *The Gambeson* was a body-covering stuffed with wool, padded as a rule in vertical parallel lines of needlework, and worn over the plastron-de-fer and hauberk. In the monumental effigy of Sir Robert Shurland (who in the year 1300 was made a Knight Banneret), engraved in Stothard, we have probably a unique representation of a knight habited only in the gambeson, which in this particular case is furnished with sleeves covering those of the hauberk, although as a rule it was sleeveless. It fitted closely round the neck, and reached to within a few inches of the knee. In Fig. 163 this garment alone is shown, all other details of the effigy being omitted.

5. *The Cyclas.*—This extraordinary garment differed from its pre-

FIG. 164.—Sir John de Creke, 1325. Westley Waterless Church, Cambs.

decessor, the flowing surcoat, in being laced up at the sides, reaching to the knees behind and being cut short in front, so as to expose the lower portions of the gambeson, hauberk, and haqueton. It was of a thin material easily falling into folds, silk being the ideal substance, and was usually girded round the waist by a narrow cincture.

A great diversity of bascinets were in use at this period, but all of them fitted more or less closely to the head, the chief modifications being in the extensions at the side of the face and at the back of the head. In the typical brass of Sir John de Creke (Fig. 164) the bascinet is fluted, while an ornamental

FIG. 165.—Vervelles, showing method of affixing camail to the bascinet.

apex furnishes the attachment for a crest or the flowing contoise. To this headpiece is affixed the camail (or capmail), a means of protection for the neck which was first introduced at this period and remained in fashion for nearly one hundred years, when it was superseded by the gorget of plate in the time of King Henry V. The upper portion of this camail was securely fixed to the bascinet by means of staples or vervelles (Fig. 165), a cord or lace being threaded through which may be perceived in the Creke brass. A narrow strip of mail with a very ornamental border is carried round below the rim. In all cases the camail covers a part of the cyclas. The upper portions of the arm are

defended by demi-brassarts with coudières, while roundels
fashioned to represent the heads of lions protect the joints
of the limbs.   The forearms are en-
tirely cased in vambraces of plate.
The chausses are of banded ring mail
protected in front by jambarts and
genouillières, while the sollerets are
of mixed mail and plate.   Upon the
effigy of Aymer de Valence, however,
who died in 1323 and is buried in
Westminster Abbey, only roundels
are shown protecting the upper parts
of the arm, and incipient coudières;
upon one of the small figures surrounding the effigy a gorget of plate

FIG. 166.—Small figure from
tomb of Aymer de Val-
ence, 1323.

of a very crude form appears to be indicated, superposed
upon the camail and lying also upon the cyclas (see
Fig. 166).   Upon the
Creke brass there are no
indications that a visor
could be affixed if re-
quired, but in the Add.
MS. 12,228 in the British
Museum a bascinet is
shown of an ornamental
character which is pro-
vided with a small defence

FIG. 167. — Bascinet
and visor, c. 1320.
(Add. MS. 12,228.)

FIG. 168. — Bascinet
and visor. (Add.
MS. 10,294.)

of this nature which could probably be removed entirely if
required.   The neck-guard is seen to be well developed and
to be provided with a projecting rim.   Two small feathers
surmount the helmet, and were worn in place of the flowing

contoise (see Fig. 167). The man-at-arms of the period
was provided with a bascinet which was more of the character of a simple pot-de-fer; in Fig. No. 168 an example
is shown to which a visor is attached and capable of being
thrown up when not in use. The sword is suspended in
front of the knight by a device which is very simple when
compared with that which formerly obtained; a belt passes
round the figure and the two ends are
affixed by swivels to the scabbard. The
weapon has apparently a 36-inch blade,
the quillons are straight, swelling slightly
at the ends and drooping in the centre;
the grip is swelling and wire bound and
has a wheel pommel. In Roy. MS. 16,
G. 6, many swords of this period are shown,
and are all characterised by their plainness
and simplicity of form (Fig. 169). The
brass of Sir John d'Aubernoun who died
in 1327 and lies in Stoke d'Aubernoun
Church, Surrey, shows a figure similar in

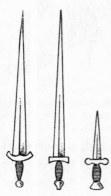

FIG. 169.—Swords and
dagger, c. 1330.

most respects to the Creke brass. The roundels at the elbows
are fixed by arming-points, the helmet is less elaborately
decorated, the method of fastening the sword is old-fashioned,
and he wears pryck spurs and not roundels as shown in
the Creke brass. A very noteworthy and curious brass
of this period is that at Minster in the Isle of Sheppey, in
memory of Sir John de Northwode, who died c. 1330. The
bascinet is of a peculiar swelling form so suggestive of the
globular head-pieces fashionable on the Continent at that
period, and the camail is finished over the chest in engrailed
escallops. A chain is joined to an ornamental staple attached

to the breastplate, and passes over the left shoulder to its attachment with the tilting helm.   Only escalloped coudières and roundels protect the upper arms and scale-like plates of steel the lower; these vambraces may possibly be of cuir-bouilli, so prevalent at the period. The grip of the sword swells considerably and the quillons are short.   Only the upper part of this brass is shown in Fig. 170, but it has been restored and now shows the complete figure. The shield at this period was of the heater shape and small; it was concave, so as to enclose the figure, and a narrow guige passing round the neck secured it.   The effigies of Prince John of Eltham, d. 1334, in Westminster Abbey; that of Sir John d'Ifield at Ifield in Sussex;

FIG. 170.—Sir John de North-wode, c. 1330. Minster, Isle of Sheppey.

FIG. 171.—Knight of the Cyclas Period.

and also that of Humphrey de Bohun, Earl of Hereford and Constable of England, d. 1321, in Hereford Cathedral, and the Pembridge knight at Clehongre Church, Herefordshire, may be studied with advantage as exhibiting varieties in detail of this style of armour.   A knight of the Cyclas Period is figured in Cotman having the same peculiar swelling helmet, and also the addition apparently of a plate gorget in place of the camail; this may, however, be simply a leather covering for the throat (Fig. 171).

CHAPTER IX

THE STUDDED AND SPLINTED ARMOUR PERIOD, 1335-1360

THE Studded and Splinted Armour Period was essentially an era of transition, intermediate between a mode of defence which had proved inadequate by reason of its sheer cumbersomeness and multiplicity of details, and the light and easy effectiveness of the succeeding style, the Camail and Jupon, which was ushered in about 1360. During the studded mail period the prolonged struggle of King Edward III. for supremacy in France occurred, and the fierce old English blood found many channels for venting its superfluous ardour. The defensive and also offensive equipment of knight and soldier underwent many and sudden changes as exigencies suggested, and keen was the contest between the three styles then prevailing, viz. chain mail, cuir-bouilli, and plate. From accredited sources of information we glean that the partisans of chain mail passed through this stirring period relying almost entirely if not wholly upon its efficacy ; the believers in cuir-bouilli clothed themselves in fanciful garments of that material reinforced by a substratum of banded or other mail ; while the advocates of plate essayed various departures of a more or less cumbrous character, which must have proved abortive by reason of their weight and crudity, although containing, as many did, the germs of improvements which, when elaborated, made the armour of

PLATE XV *

Tilting Armour, Prince Philip II., by Wolf of Landshut, 1554

later periods so effective. There were other experimenters
who believed in a judicious mixture of all three kinds of
defence, and as they far outnumbered the remainder the
period has gained the name which heads this chapter.

In an age which saw so many varieties, and when each
man did that which was pleasant in his own eyes, it is
difficult to distinguish essential characteristics by which the
amateur may readily recognise armour of this period, but a
few salient features may be mentioned which were fairly
persistent throughout.

1. *The Surcoat* or skirted jupon was sleeveless and fitted
the upper part of the body tightly, but below the waist was
made full so as to hang in folds to the knees·; as a rule it
opened up the side, but sometimes was slit only a short
distance up the front and then laced at the neck. It dis-
played the armorial bearings of the wearer above the
sword-belt, then worn round the waist or a little below it,
and in some few cases the skirt was dispensed with and
terminated at the belt. The lower part of the skirt was
either plain or escalloped, the latter feature sometimes
partaking of the nature of gadroons and extending upwards
to the belt. The skirt also at times was of a different
colour to the upper part, a feature which is well shown in
one of the windows at Ely Cathedral, dating from 1335,
where six figures are shown in contemporary armour, and
the skirts of three surcoats are darker in colour than the
upper part, one being ornamented with a band of a still
darker colour. All the skirts shown reach below the
knees and have no sleeves.

2. *The Hauberk* beneath the surcoat was of chain-
mail of various patterns, or banded mail, and reached to

the knees, being about an inch longer than the upper garment. It was furnished with a high collar and with sleeves reaching to the wrists, plate gauntlets being almost universal at this period. The hauberk exemplified all the various kinds of chain mail known in the mediæval period. The banded mail, already spoken of in the preceding period, had varieties; instead of the rings being merely superposed as in Fig. 162, they were at times interlinked and given a slight twist, so as to lie flat similarly to an ordinary curb chain, each of these continuous chains being sewn to the usual raised leather band on either side. In some examples, chains of large and thick links an inch or more in diameter are shown merely fastened down to the under leather or material without any separating bands. But probably the most effectual defence, though of enormous weight, was the usual system of putting rings or discs of metal face to face, like rouleaux of coins, and known as the pure banded mail, which afforded effectual protection against the deadly arrow of the period, which could neither penetrate nor force apart the tightly wedged discs. We read of knights emerging from the fray bristling with arrows, which were pulled out of their harness by the squires.

3. *The Breastplate* was undoubtedly worn at this period, as the globular conformation of the upper part of the body and the chains sometimes affixed to that part through the surcoat prove. It can hardly be imagined that these chains could be fastened to a hauberk. It is probable that the breastplate was always worn immediately below the surcoat; and there are indications that the haqueton or gambeson was sometimes worn at this period under the hauberk.

4. *Chausses* of mail were universally worn protecting nearly the whole length of the legs and covering the feet.

So far as uniformity is concerned, the four articles enumerated above are all that can be cited with any degree of accuracy. The bascinet of the period was of many and varying shapes, and at times approached the grotesque. Two are given here from Roy. MS. 16 G. 6 (Figs. 172, 173), which are adorned with acanthus - shaped crests: the camail depending from both is of banded mail, and the vervelles by which it is affixed are shown. It is probable that this style prevailed more upon the Continent than in England. The form of helmet shown in the Ely window before

FIG. 172—Bascinet, c. 1330.
(Roy. MS. 16, G. 6.)

FIG. 173.—Bascinet, c. 1330.
(Roy. MS. 16, G. 6.)

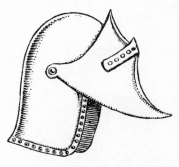

FIG. 174.—Bascinet and visor, c. 1330.
(Roy. MS. 16, G. 6.)

mentioned is globular, the lower part covering the ears and cheeks; a comb much flattened and of no great height traverses it from the forehead to the back of the head. A common form of bascinet is shown in

Fig. 174, which covers the head and neck, and is provided with one of the cumbrous visors of the age. This

revolves upon pivots fastened well back, and not only protects the face, but partly fulfils the duty of a gorget. The occularium is formed by a row of circular apertures in a reinforcing plate. This massive form of visor is well shown on the head of Thomas de Beauchamp (Fig. 175) on the celebrated Hastings brass, one of the few brasses of this period of armour which have been handed down to us, and which in consequence is simply invaluable. The visor is provided with a reinforcing plate and slits for the occularium, with breathing holes below, while the

FIG. 175.—Helmet, Thos. Beauchamp, 1347. (Hastings brass.)

FIG. 176.—Bascinet and gorget, c. 1350. (British Museum.)

FIG. 177.—Bascinet, &c., Almeric, Lord St. Amand, 1347. (Hastings brass.)

great projection at the lower part (when allowed to fall) not only protects the neck, but also a portion of the chest. A bascinet is preserved in the British Museum which dates from *c.* 1350, and illustrates the manner in which the gorget plate was affixed (Fig. 176). The bascinet of Almeric, Lord St. Amand (Fig. No. 177) is provided with a singular adornment, the chapelle-de-fer or steel bonnet: the brim, being movable upon pivots at the sides,

FIG. 178.—Bascinet with laminated gorget. (Add. MS. 12,228.)

FIG. 179.—Bascinet and gorget of plate. (Add. MS. 12,228.)

could be brought down so as to protect the face. But such an arrangement left the chin and throat open to injury, and to obviate this a mentonnière of massive proportions is shown, thus anticipating the protection of the same nature as required by the salade a century later. This illustration of the chapelle-de-fer is the only one engraved upon a brass, but another example of it on a monumental effigy

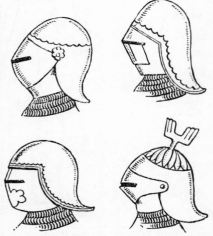

FIGS. 180 and 181.—Bascinets, Meliadus MS. (Add. 12,228.)

may be seen in Westminster Abbey upon an equestrian figure on the tomb of Aymer de Valence, *c.* 1296. A late example of the war hat dating from 1515 and of German make is No. 135 in the Wallace Collection, while a

FIGS. 182–184.—Figures from the monument of Lady Percy in Beverley Minster, *d*. 1330.

pictorial representation of it may be seen in Julius, E. IV., the life of Richard Beauchamp, Earl of Warwick, written at the close of the fifteenth century. Bascinets not very unlike those in vogue in the reigns of Henry V. and Henry VI., and later on in the Tudor period, were in use, as may be seen from the illustrations taken from

FIGS. 185–187.—Figures from the monument of Lady Percy in Beverley Minster, d. 1330.

Add. MS. 12,228, Figs. 178, 179, and the romance of King Meliadus, Figs. 180, 181.

In the spandrels of the canopy of a monument to Lady Eleanor Fitzalan, wife of the first Lord Percy of Alnwick, in Beverley Minster, who died in 1330, are seven military figures exemplifying this period of armour, and in one or two cases the helmets are reinforced by a larger plate

which descends to the back of the neck and to each shoulder, over which it curves outwards so as to nearly cover the camail. These pieces are riveted on to the bascinet proper, which is generally furnished with a huge visor.

A complete set of the figures in the canopy are here delineated, not in the cramped original postures, but in erect positions. They all possess points of difference, and a comparison of the various defences exemplified by each will give an excellent idea of the feeling which characterised the armour of this difficult period (Figs. 182–188).

The heaumes of the period were generally round-topped and furnished with movable visors, while the crest and its adjuncts at times assumed large, if not formidable, proportions. That of Sir Geoffrey Luterell, 1345,

FIG. 188.—Figure from the monument of Lady Percy in Beverley Minster, d. 1330.

from the famous Luterell Psalter, is shown in Fig. 189, and that of Sir Hugh Hastings, 1347, in Fig. 190.

The shoulders were generally left unprotected, except

by the mail of the hauberk, but occasionally roundels are used similar to those of the Cyclas era. Demi-brassarts covered the upper arms, shown in many illustrations of the period as overlapping lames of plate, occasionally complete and protecting the front as well as the back of the limb. Coudières, if worn, were invariably of cuir-bouilli, and of a pattern which is almost stereotyped, and shown in Fig. 191, the genouillières being of similar design.

In Add. MS. 12,228 at the British Museum many combats of the period are depicted, and almost without exception coudières and genouillières of this pattern are shown.

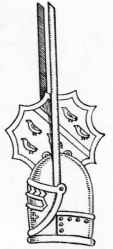

FIG. 189. — Helm and crest, Sir Geoffrey Luterell, 1345.

FIG. 190.—Crested helm, Sir Hugh Hastings, 1347.

Vambraces were generally dispensed with, the hauberk sleeve being deemed sufficient together with the large cuff of the gauntlet. Where used the vambrace or demi-vambrace may be of plate, as in the Cyclas Period, or of cuir-bouilli as on the brass of Sir John de Northwode on p. 145. They were also of pourpoint as on the arm here illustrated (Fig. 192). As this curious variety of defensive equipment is now mentioned for the first time, it may be stated that not only in this period but in the succeeding, it was most exten-

sively used. Pourpoint in its simplest form is merely a
padded garment; studded pourpoint, or studded mail, as
 it was occasionally called, consisted of metal
discs or roundels, generally of steel, secured
by rivets to the padded garment, or to leather
or cuir-bouilli. These roundels were made
very similar to the modern stud, but with a
short neck; where large roundels are seen,
as in the vambrace shown, the smaller head
is buried in the pourpoint, or boiled leather,
and the larger back, as we should term it,
is visible. This is generally reversed in the
case of other defences which we shall have
to consider, where only the small heads
appear upon the surface for ornament, and
the real defensive disc is buried in the pour-

FIG. 191.—Bascinet
and coudières, Me-
liadus MS. (Add.
12,228.)

point. It is probable from
the illustration that the
pourpointerie shown were
stiff, moulded pieces of cuir-bouilli slipped
on over the underlying hauberk sleeve.

Genouillières were invariably of cuir-
bouilli, and where illustrated in MSS. or
shown in stained-glass windows are of a
yellow colour. There was not much
variety in form, and they generally followed
the design of the coudière. A simple
and very common form, dating from *c.*

FIG. 192.

1330, is shown in Fig. 193, from Roy. MS. 16, G. 6.

Cuissarts.—There was seldom any special defence for
the upper leg, but occasionally haut-de-chausses of studded

mail are met with, especially as we approach 1350. An
effigy at Tewkesbury exhibits studded cuissarts, and may
be ascribed to *c.* 1350 (Fig. 194). Whether
this pourpoint supplemented the chausses of
banded mail or was worn in their place is a
moot point.

Grevières or Jambarts.—These, if of plate,
are rare, but demi-grevières are common (Fig.
195). Perhaps the defence most in vogue
was of the splinted kind, which consisted of
parallel bands of steel arranged in vertical
lines and embedded in pourpoint with studs
showing, or affixed to cuir-bouilli. The latter
was often used for vambraces and cuissarts

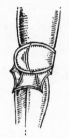

FIG. 193.—Genou-
illière and re-
inforcement, *c.*
1330. (Roy.
MS. 16, G. 6.)

(Fig. 196). Perhaps the
best example of splinted
armour and banded mail
combined is that shown
in the brass of Sir Miles
de Stapleton on p. 188,
and many references to

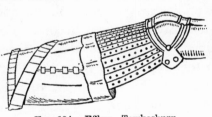

FIG. 194.—Effigy. Tewkesbury.

this style of defence will appear in the
chapter on the Camail and Jupon Period.
Sollerets, if worn at all, were invariably of the
pattern shown in the Creke brass, and seldom
covered all the upper part of the foot. Occasionally we find the ubiquitous cuir-bouilli
being used, and a brass as late as 1375 shows
an example ; it is that of Sir William Cheyne
at Drayton Beauchamp, Bucks. (Fig. 197).

The Shield.—Very few representations of
the shield of the period occur, but that in use was of the

FIG. 195.—Leg of
man - at - arms.
(Add. MS. 12,228.)

small heater-shape variety.   An early shield occurs at Whitworth, Durham (Fig. 198).

This work would be incomplete without a reference to

the famous Hastings brass in Elsing Church, Norfolk, dating from 1347, which gives details of armour of that most interesting period of English military history for which we generally look in vain to other brasses, to monumental effigies, and to MSS.   A full

FIG. 197.—Sollerets of cuir-bouilli, Sir William Cheyne, 1375.

description of this invaluable record has been written by Mr. Albert Hartshorne, F.S.A., which appeared in *Archæologia*, Vol. 60, and is more comprehensive than any account previously published.   He relates the recovery of one of the missing figures from the Fitzwilliam Museum and its subsequent restoration to the original position

FIG. 196.—Demi-jambart, &c., of studded cuir-bouilli.

it occupied.   The figure of Sir Hugh Hastings occupies the centre, surrounded by a much mutilated canopy, in compartments of which are represented four contemporary warriors, &c.   The work is of foreign origin, possibly Flemish or French. The bascinet is of the globular form so well shown in French MSS. of the period; it is furnished with a visor which would come down well over the gorget.   The latter is of plate,

FIG. 198.—Early shield at Whitworth, Durham.

and the first shown upon a brass; it is acutely pointed

in front and of massive proportions, and guards the neck and chin, thus anticipating the protective character of the mentonnières a century later. It lies directly upon the camail, and was doubtless articulated, fastening at the back by buckles. The rings of the camail and hauberk are very small, and show distinct signs of interlocking. The usual skirted jupon of the period covers the body to the knees, upon which is emblazoned the Hastings Arms, a maunche differenced with a label of three points, which also appears upon the shield. Roundels of unequal size protect the arm-pits, that upon the left being the larger; demi-brassarts cover the upper arm, and demi-vambraces the forearm, being arranged as in the Bacon brass in Gorleston Church, and the Fitzralph brass in Pebmarsh Church (Fig. 147), whilst a roundel

FIG. 199.—Figure from Hastings brass, 1347.

protects the elbow-joint. The sleeves of the hauberk are slipped off the hands, as in the case of Sir Robert de Septvans (Fig. 146), and depend from the wrist, thus showing the quilted haqueton or gambeson under the mail; the latter is also apparent beneath the lower hems of the hauberk and jupon, quilted in vertical lines. The cuissarts are of studded mail, from which depend broad bands of cuirbouilli passing round the knees; upon the latter the genouillières appear as a reinforcement provided with fluted bosses curiously spiked. The legs from this point downwards are missing, but a rubbing in the British Museum, taken in 1782, shows that the figure wore mail chausses, and that the feet were provided with rowelled spurs. Sir Hugh Hastings served in Flanders 1340 to 1343, and also in Brittany : he took part in the operations at Bergerac and Auberoche in 1345, and was present at the siege of Aiguillon in 1346.

In two of the niches of the canopy are the figures representing King Edward III. and Henry, Earl of Lancaster. The king holds a drawn sword but has no scabbard; laminated epaulières and reinforced coudières appear on each figure but no roundels; gorgets are absent and the shins are protected by demi-grevières of plate. Both the king and his cousin have cuissarts of studded mail. Another figure represents Thomas Beauchamp, Earl of Warwick; he carries a pennoned lance in his right hand, and is chiefly remarkable for the visored bascinet (Fig. 175), which, with its dependent guards for the neck and its huge visor protecting the neck and part of the chest as well as the face, may be compared with the armed figures from the tomb of Lady Eleanor Fitzalan at Beverley, 1330. It is similar to that worn by a companion figure, Ralph, Lord Stafford, on the same brass, and also by that representing Lawrence Hastings, which is now missing. The latter is known to have shown a figure with a gorget of plate similar to Sir Hugh Hastings, with roundels at the shoulders and elbows. Another lost figure is that of Hugh le Despencer, whose stone effigy may be seen at Tewkesbury.

The newly found figure is that of Roger, Lord Grey of Ruthin; it shows defences similar to the others, but has complete brassarts of plate, with demi-grevières, and the gambeson appears above the mail collar. The figure is bareheaded and leans upon a pole-axe, which would apparently be about four feet long: the inclusion of this weapon is remarkable so far as brasses are concerned.

The last figure represents Almeric, Lord St. Amand, whose headpiece is extremely peculiar (Fig. 177). The globular bascinet appears to be protected by a steel bonnet, or chapelle-de-fer, having a wide projecting rim which worked upon pivots at either side and could be brought down when required level with the eyes, while the back would afford some protection for the neck. A comb or ridge is also shown, probably hollow, and enclosing a similar small ridge on the bascinet, upon which it would run as a guide. This is the only example of a headpiece of this fashion engraved upon a brass, but on the monumental effigy of Aymer de Valence at Westminster, c. 1296, one of the equestrian figures is shown similarly habited. The gorget is different from that of Hastings in being hollowed out at the sides; it rests directly upon the camail, which is shown with very large and coarse markings.

In all the figures the sword is suspended at a single point and not at two as in the Cyclas and previous periods, while the cord round the waist is also dispensed with. The woodcut heading our Preface indicates crudely the armour prevailing in this period. The subject of the illustration is unknown, but it probably represents an episode at a mediæval garden-party, where a section of the guests indulge in a little "gentle and joyous sport" for the edification of the others.

In connection with the armour of the Studded and Splinted Periods the representation of the sovereigns of England upon the coinage is of considerable interest, inasmuch as it illustrates in a remarkable degree the extraordinary conservatism of the moneyers and die-sinkers of the mediæval period. The first representation of regal defensive equipment occurs in the reign of King Edward III., and in the Studded and Splinted Period. The gold noble of the second coinage of this monarch represents him standing in a ship bearing a shield upon his left arm and a sword in his right. The shield is large and heater-shaped, and the sword has a short grip, a globular pommel, and short quillons drooping towards the blade, which is long, and narrows gradually towards the point. Camail of very capacious extent covers the body nearly to the waist and extends down the arms to the elbow; from below this the sleeve of a mail hauberk appears, covering a small portion of the forearm and pendent about a foot. The forearm is apparently unprotected, but a gauntlet covers the right hand, which alone is visible. Upon the jupon appearing below the camail are four studs, indicating pourpoint defence. In 1346, the half-noble exhibits a much more contracted camail, a tightly fitting jupon with short sleeves, and the sleeve of a chain mail hauberk apparently reaching to the hand. The noble of 1351 shows camail, a short-sleeved jupon revealing a hauberk reaching to the elbow, from beneath which issues a loose sleeve to the wrist, of soft folding material, probably part of the gambeson. The jupon is loose and plain to the waist, below which appears studded work. The half-noble is the same, except that the chain mail hauberk reaches to the wrist. In 1360, the noble presents the same characteristics with regard to the camail and jupon, but a loose sleeve, fringed at the wrist, is apparently attached

to the jupon.   The half-noble of the same date has a rough
indication of a coudière, with mail brassarts or hauberk
sleeve, and a gauntlet.

Richard II. nobles have the camail with a tippet of
material reaching nearly to the waist, below which appear

FIG. 200.—Man-at-arms, c. 1350.   FIG. 201.—Knight, c. 1350.

the studs; the arm is encased in the short sleeve of the
jupon, and a long sleeve of material beneath it; but on
the half-noble a hauberk sleeve of mail is depicted to the
elbow.   Henry IV. is represented in his first coinage habited
almost the same as his predecessor, but in 1412 a gold
noble was issued showing the arm in a brassart, coudière,

and vambrace, but with the same unaccountable studs below
the waist. The gold coins of Henry V. continued to be
of the same pattern as those of Henry IV. In Henry VI.'s
first coinage the arm is encased in laminated brassarts,
coudière, and a scoop-shaped piece of chain mail emerging
from the coudière and reaching nearly to the wrist, where
a gauntlet or glove with a flexible cuff is shown. Otherwise the coin is the same as in Henry IV.'s time. The
rose-noble of Edward IV. exhibits the same characteristics,
as does also the angelet. With this reign the type of the
king standing in a ship ceases, but is revived again in the
time of Henry VIII., whose first coinage comprehended
a regal on which the peculiar scoop-shaped piece of mail
upon the arm is shown, an indefinite kind of cape serves
for the upper part of the person, and the inevitable studs
appear below the belt. On the George noble, issued
between 1526 and 1533, we get, for the first time in more
than a hundred years, an approximation to contemporary
armour in the figure of the Saint, who is clothed in Maximilian plate from head to heel, with large pike-guards
appropriate to the time. On subsequent coins of Edward
VI., James I., and Charles I. the armour is correct.
Summarising the above respecting the persevering studs
we find them represented on coins a century and a
half after they ceased to be worn ; camail is shown sixty
years after it was disused ; plate does not appear until a
hundred years after it came in vogue, and the drooping
sleeve of mail, though used on the Continent, was not seen
in England after the Cyclas Period. Speaking generally,
Richard II. and the monarchs immediately succeeding had
the pleasure of seeing themselves represented upon the

coinage in the same equipment as the ordinary soldier of the time, with the sole exception of the crown.   Upon the

FIG. 202.—Military equipment, *c.* 1360.
(Add. MS. 12,228.)

silver coinage the head only of the monarch is represented until we come to the reign of Edward VI., when the Maximilian type is shown, and subsequent coins exhibit contemporary armour.

CHAPTER X

THE CAMAIL AND JUPON PERIOD, 1360–1410

WITH the advent of the camail and jupon we enter upon a period which presents a certain amount of uniformity, and is in marked contrast to the tentative styles which preceded it. Throughout the Surcoat, Cyclas, and Loose-skirted Jupon Periods, defensive armour was in a state of transition; warriors sought to render themselves immune by every conceivable expedient, discarding those which failed upon trial, and augmenting those which proved efficacious. The cumbrous mentonnières and gorgets of plate; the enormous visors; the great globular bascinets; the multiplicity of garments in the Cyclas Period, and the indiscriminate use of cuir-bouilli, horn, pourpointerie, chain, and plate, in that which followed, were all in this period relegated to the limbo of forgetfulness, and a uniformity of attire was adopted which was the more striking when compared with those which immediately preceded it. This similarity or prevalence in fashion in military dress has lasted to the present time, for in all the different periods we shall deal with after this uniformity commenced, we shall notice that certain features are prominent, and that only minute deviations call for our attention. As human knowledge is but the consolidated result of experience, so we may attribute the Camail and Jupon Period to the French wars of Edward III. and Philip of Valois, which for nearly twenty years devastated France, and in

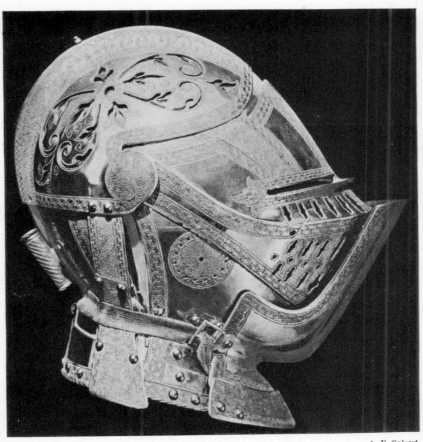

PLATE XVI *

Helmet of Philip II., by Wolf of Landshut, 1554

which the two decisive battles of Cressy, 1346, and Poictiers, 1356, are included. During that long period the various defences underwent the fiery ordeal of actual use, and only those which emerged triumphantly from the struggle were retained.

To the student of armour and arms, this period is of exceptional interest by reason of the unwonted facility with which it may be studied, inasmuch as there is hardly a cathedral, or church of any importance in the kingdom, which does not possess, in some manner, details of military equipment relating to it. Brasses and monumental effigies simply abound, stained glass is by no means uncommon, while carvings in wood and stone exhibit details which are at times of great importance. The wealth of technical matter thus preserved enables the student to reconstruct the period with a fidelity which is wanting in those earlier. It must not be supposed that the great and salient features of the style were at once adopted; there was a transition period of nearly twenty years, during which the old defences were in part retained, and only discarded by degrees. Before pointing out these exceptions, however, it may be as well to take the several features of the equip-ment in order, as has been done in preceding styles.

The Jupon.—The jupon was a sleeveless outer garment reaching from the neck to midway between the hips and the knees. It was tight-fitting, as may readily be gleaned by inspection of brasses and effigies, and no folds or creases can be observed in it. In construction it consisted of several thicknesses of material sewn through, thus becoming almost homogeneous, and upon this firm sub-structure a layer of silk, velvet, or other rich material was firmly fastened down, and bore in the great majority of cases the

armorial insignia of the wearer. There are exceptional
cases in which the jupon was stuffed and quilted. The arm-
holes became decorated in the later years of this style, but
owing to the covering camail we have no knowledge of
any decorations upon the neck. The skirt was finished
with an enriched border of either escallops, or acanthus
leaves, or dags—dagging being a mode of ornamenting the
hems of civilian garments prevailing in the reigns of
Edward III., Richard II., and the fourth and fifth Henrys;
it consisted in cutting out borders of sleeves, skirts, &c.,
into open work of various devices. This rich and splendid
covering to the real body defences was always laced up at
the sides, occasionally only on one side, under the left arm.

    The Breastplate.—This was worn underneath the jupon
and over the hauberk to which it was affixed, and gave

FIG.203.—Breastplate,
Camail and Jupon
Period. (Roy. MS.
15, D. 3.)

the swelling, globular appearance to the
knights so characteristic of the period; its
termination at the waist imparted a contour
of body almost wasp-like at times. We
are unaware of the form of this defence,
and also as to whether or not it possessed
a companion backplate, so as to form a
complete cuirass; however, the appearance
of the back of many effigies of this period
leads to the supposition that a similar plate was used to
protect that part of the body. In the MS. Roy. 15, D. 3,
a foreign knight is shown wearing his breastplate upon his
jupon, and it is of the form depicted in Fig. 203; it may
perhaps be taken as the general shape of this defence.
Upon a sculptured effigy of the year 1370 in Bamberg
Cathedral, a copy of which is reproduced in Boutell's
" Monumental Brasses," a heart-shaped breastplate is shown,

but there are no British examples of the exposed defence. In the Bamberg effigy chains are shown depending from staples in the breastplate for attachment to the sword-hilt and misericorde, and the brass of Sir Ralph de Knevynton at Aveley, Essex, 1370, also has this feature (Fig. 204.)

The Hauberk.—During the earlier portion of the Camail and Jupon Period the hauberk was invariably constructed of banded mail, but towards the end of the century it was superseded by linked chain mail, although late examples of the banded may be found, such as that of Lord Berkeley, 1392, at Wotton-under-Edge, Gloucestershire, and Sir Nicholas Hawberk, 1407, Cobham Church, Kent. The defence reached to about the middle of the thigh, and

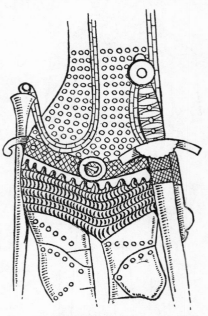

FIG. 204.—Sir Ralph de Knevynton, 1370. Aveley, Essex.

subsequently to 1380 became sleeveless. The lower edge appears as a rule about two inches below that of the jupon, and is, in some cases, made ornamental by pendent rings, as in the case of Sir Robert Swynborne. Under the hauberk the quilted gambeson, or haqueton, was worn as usual, but no portion of it appears in brasses or effigies.

The Bascinet.—The bascinet was very tall at the commencement of the period and acutely pointed at the apex; it gradually lessened in height as time advanced. It

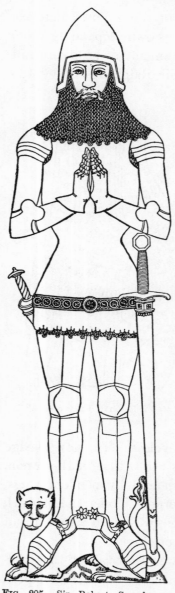

FIG. 205.—Sir Robert Swynborne, 1391. Little Horkesley Church, Essex.

descended on both sides well over the ears, and was carried round to the back of the neck, as a rule, in a straight line. The apex was not over the centre of the head, but more towards the rear; when the knight couched his lance and bent forward in the saddle the point was thus brought forward to a perpendicular position. This detail cannot be perceived in brasses, but is very apparent in monumental effigies, and is shown on the opposite page (Fig. 206), taken from a stained-glass window in St. Peter's Church, St. Albans, and approximately of the date 1380. The visor is represented in gold-coloured glass, and this feature of gold gilding is by no means uncommon in MSS. of the early part of this period, from which it is possible to infer that the visors were either of cuir-bouilli, latten, or were enriched by gilding. At first the visors were removable at will, being merely hung on projecting knobs at the sides; but afterwards, when the snout-faced variety came into

vogue, they were invariably fixed, and could only be raised
or lowered.   An earlier form of bascinet is shown in the
windows of the same church which has a close-fitting visor,
very similar to those which
marked the advent of the
pot-helm in the thirteenth
century (Fig. 207).   To-
wards the close of the fourteenth century the adop-
tion of the " snout-faced,"
or " pig-faced " visor (Fig.
208) became universal,

FIG. 206.—Bascinet.   FIG. 207.—Bascinet. St.
St. Peter's Church,   Peter's Church, St.
St. Albans.   Albans.

eliciting much uncomplimentary criticisms from contemporary writers and being the subject of many caricatures
in carvings of the period.   In the Tower of London
a bascinet weighing 5¼ lbs. is
preserved (Fig. 209); the visor
or ventaille, which weighs
1 lb., originally hinged up to

FIG. 208.—Snout-faced bascinet.   FIG. 209.—Bascinet. (Tower of London.)

a pivot in the centre of the skull.   In the Wallace Collection, Fig. 210 shows a beautiful example which was
formerly in the Meyrick Collection; it is French, and
dates from c. 1400.   An early example of this form of
visor bascinet is preserved in the collection at Parham

dating from 1365, which shows the ventaille partly
covering the neck, and this form is common in the

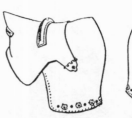

FIG. 210.—Snout-faced bascinet, c. 1400.
(Wallace Collection.)

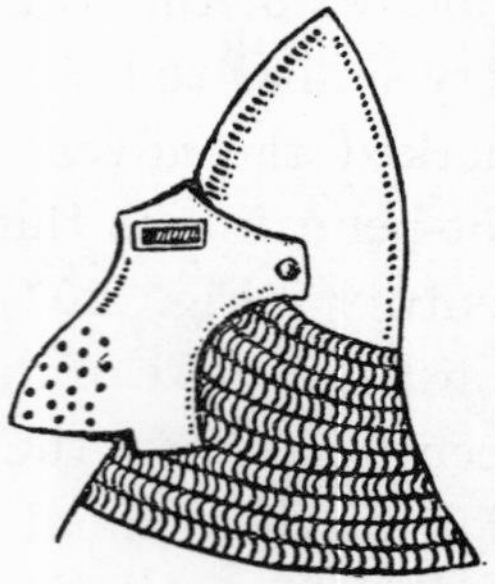

FIG. 211.—Visored bascinet
from Roy. MS. 20, C. 7.

Roy. MS. 20, C. 7, in the British Museum, dating from
1400 to 1415 (Fig. 211). Here, however,
the feature is made of such huge dimensions, reaching doubtless as far as the
collar-bones, that a feeling is engendered
of disproportion, or of caricature; but as
the examples are very numerous, and all
appear the same, the thought is perforce
dispelled. Huge visors are also depicted
in a History of Richard II. of England
preserved in the Bibliothèque du Roi (a
figure from which is here shown, Fig. 212),
which must have provided a large amount
of breathing space and also acted to some
extent as a gorget. The bascinet termed
the Barbute is essentially Italian, and
does not occur upon any English brass
or effigy; it appears to have been prevalent on the Continent, and some of the head-pieces shown upon the common

FIG. 212.—Knight.
(Richard II. MS., in
Bibliothèque du Roi.)

soldiery in English MSS. partake of the character of this defence. It was worn without any visor, but a portion of the camail, adapted for the purpose, was lifted in order to cover almost entirely the small opening left in front, being fastened to the staples with which these helmets are almost always provided. The Barbute in the Wallace Collection (Fig. 214) shows this feature very distinctly, as it is provided with two staples for the purpose, while the nasal thus formed by the camail is well shown in the effigy of Ulrich Land-

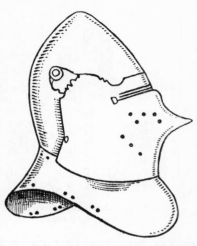

FIG. 213.—Snout-faced helmet, c. 1400.

schaden, 1369, in Neckarsteinach (Fig. 215), which, however, is defended by the ordinary bascinet, though strange to note, the figure is entirely without any visible plate armour for the limbs. A bascinet with an iron nasal of rigid form is shown in the MS. Roy. 14, E. 4, and

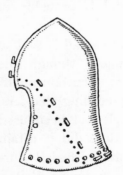 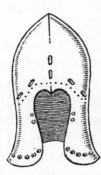

FIG. 214.—Barbute, c. 1400. (Wallace Collection.)

depicted in Fig. 216. It will be seen by the various figures illustrating the Camail and Jupon Period that the height of the bascinet became less towards the end of the time when it prevailed, and showed a distinct tendency to

FIG. 215.—Effigy at Neckarsteinach, 1369, showing nasal.

FIG. 216.—Nasal from Roy. MS. 14, E. 4

merge into the globular form of the succeeding period. The bascinet of Sir William Burgate, 1409, in Burgate Church, Suffolk (Fig. 217), is remarkable for its high comb or apex, and is probably of foreign origin.

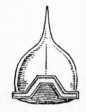

FIG. 217.—Bascinet. Sir William Burgate, 1409.

The Camail.—The term camail is said to be a derivative of " cap-mail," though one authority deduces it from " curtain-mail." As we have seen in the preceding chapters, this protection for the neck had been used for centuries, but at no time did it attain the dimensions and efficiency which distinguished it during the period under discussion. It is probable that a gorget of plate of some description was worn underneath it, to which we shall refer when speaking of the epaulières. The well-known representation from Nero, D. 7, in the

FIG. 218.—Sir John de Argentine, 1360. Horsheath Church, Cambridge.

FIG. 219.—Sir John Wingfield, c. 1400. Letheringham Church, Suffolk.

FIG. 220.—Sir George Felbrigge, 1400. Playford Church, Suffolk.

British Museum, representing the Black Prince receiving a
grant of Aquitaine from his father, shows the prince with
his helmet and its depending camail doffed, but no gorget,
however, is disclosed. At first the lower portion of the
camail fell almost perpendicularly to the shoulders, and
covered but a small portion of them, as may be seen in the
brasses of Sir John de Argentine, 1360, Horsheath Church,
Cambridge (Fig. 218); Sir John de Paletoot, 1361, Watton
Church, Herts (Fig. 224); and Sir John de Cobham, 1375,
Cobham, Kent; but as the period progressed, the mail expanded so as to cover not only the shoulders, but the upper
part of the arm. At first banded mail was universally employed, and examples may be found of its use even as late as
1405, on the brass of Sir Thomas Massyngberde, but by the
year 1380, chain mail of varying patterns had become popular.
The links were arranged either in horizontal lines or vertically, and examples may be found where they vary in size
from that of a coarse dog chain down to extremely fine
links. For examples, see brasses of Sir John Wingfield,
1400, Letheringham Church, Suffolk (Fig. 219); Sir John
Hanley; Sir John Bettesthorne, Mere Church, Wiltshire;
Sir George Felbrigge (Fig. 220); the painting of the Black
Prince in St. Stephen's Chapel, Westminster, &c.

The method of attaching the camail to the bascinet was
by a lace running through staples termed vervelles, which
were visible until about the year 1387, when the fashion
was introduced of covering them with a more or less enriched
border. To the student this forms a valuable clue to the
date when inspecting a brass or monument, but must of
course be used in conjunction with other characteristics.
The brass of Sir William de Echingham, 1387, is one of

the latest showing this feature (see Fig. 221). Towards the latter part of the period mixed mail and plate made their appearance (see Fig. 222, knight of the d'Eresby family).

Plate Defences.— One of the features of this period was the enclosure of the limbs in plate defences which conformed generally to the natural curves, and present a striking contrast to the distortions which appeared during the greater part of the fifteenth century. Upon the shoulders laminated epaulières occur, the upper plates of which are habitually hidden by the camail and jupon, but were probably affixed to or depended from the gorget of plate before

FIG. 221.—Sir William de Echingham, 1387.
Etchingham Church, Sussex.

FIG. 222.—Knight of the D'Eresby family,
1410. Spilsby Church, Lincs.

mentioned. Brassarts of plate enclosed the upper arms, while coudières of a close-fitting pattern protected the bend of the arm. There was no distinct fashion during this period for the outer projecting plate of the coudière; at first a roundel appeared as in the case of Sir John de Argentine (Fig. 218), and Sir John de Paletoot (Fig. 224), but the general form was that exhibited in the brasses of Sir John Wingfield (Fig. 219) and Sir George Felbrigge (Fig. 220). Cylindrical vambraces of one plate guarded the forearms to the wrist, where they were covered partly by the cuffs of the gauntlets. The latter during this period attained to a higher degree of perfection than had previously been the case, and great attention was paid to detail and careful fitting. The fingers and thumbs were distinct and articulated; a plate covered the back of the hand and another was

formed into a cuff.   The introduction of gadlings, or
spikes of steel upon the knuckles and joints, occurred at
this time, not solely for ornament but for actual weapons
of offence when other means had failed.   In a trial by
combat fought before Edward III., one of the combatants gained the advantage by striking the gadlings of
his gauntlet into the face of his adversary.   At times
they are shown of great size, projecting a considerable
distance from the knuckles.   Towards the close of the
fourteenth century the terminal parts of the finger-guards
are shown with imitation finger-nails,
and many of the gauntlets seen upon
the effigies are richly decorated.   A
most interesting specimen, unique in
England and of great rarity, is Fig. 223,
in the Wallace Collection, dating from
the latter half of the fourteenth century
and of French make.   The plates for
the fingers are missing; the covering

FIG. 223.—Gauntlet, late
fourteenth   century.
(Wallace Collection.)

for the back of the hand and the cuff is formed of one piece,
with the exception of a small plate, which, however, is not
movable.   The decorations are bands of latten.   The
gauntlets of the Black Prince hanging over the tomb in
Canterbury Cathedral are often referred to; they are of
the same period as those in the Wallace Collection, but
made of latten, gilded, and cannot vie with them in workmanship.   The gadlings are well seen upon the various
brasses of this period, those of Sir George Felbrigge being
perhaps one of the most prominent (Fig. 220).

The mail defences for the lower limbs have the same
characteristic of following the outline closely, and of being
what may be termed skin-tight.   The thighs were enclosed

in cuissarts of steel, back and front plates hinging upon the outside of the legs and buckled between the thighs, thus differing from the Splinted Armour Period, when front plates only were invariably used. The knees were guarded by genouillières of plate, which at first were of simple construction, and consisted of a single plate (*vide* Sir John de Argentine, Fig. 218), but eventually these were reinforced by lames of steel above and below. Steel grevières protected the shins and calves, and a small plate depending from the genouillière, or from one of its lower reinforcements, gave an additional protection to the front plate. The sollerets were invariably of plate jointed, like the epaulières, after the manner of a lobster's tail; they were long and pointed, and gave rise to the fashion which prevailed until sabbatons were introduced, of pointing the toe downwards through the stirrup when riding. At the back of the knee-joints, and also at the joints of the shoulders, elbows, and ankles, small pieces of mail were introduced called goussets or gussets, being fixed generally upon the garment worn underneath the plate, but at times to the inside parts of the plate itself. They served as reinforcements to the hauberk.

One of the peculiarities of the Camail and Jupon Period is the magnificent hip-belt, of far more elaborate workmanship and finish than in any preceding or following age. It generally consisted of raised square or oblong brooches, veritable triumphs of the goldsmith's art, and occasionally studded with jewels, linked to each other to form a continuous band, and fastened in front by an enriched morse or clasp. At times roundels were used, and occasionally a running pattern in gold or embroidery.

In the early figures it is shown with a buckle and a loop, a piece of pendent belt passing through and fastened like the Order of the Garter. A brass exemplifying very plainly the loop and buckle lies in St. Michael's Church, St. Albans, and dates from *c.* 1370 (Fig. 223A). (It is remarkable for showing two tabs of leather or plate upon each shoulder, issuing from beneath the camail; we may have here a replica of the French fashion of epaulière at the period, which generally was encircled by tabs of cuir-bouilli.) See also Fig. 218, Argentine, and Paletoot, Fig. 224. This seldom occurs upon late examples. The general method of wearing it was horizontally round the hips,

FIG. 223A.—Brass in St. Michael's Church, St. Albans.

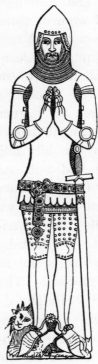

FIG. 224.—Sir John de Paletoot, 1361. Watton Church, Herts.

but a few exceptions will be found upon searching the engraved figures. This fashion was copied by the ladies of the period, who wore hip-belts, showing beneath the super côte-hardi, of equal richness to their lords.

The Sword was attached to the belt at the uppermost part of the scabbard, and hung perpendicularly at the left side. It generally had a wheel pommel and a swelling grip, with quillons either straight or drooping slightly towards the blade. The latter was about an inch and a half broad at the hilt, thirty inches in length, and tapered to the point, while the section was either of a flattened or a lozenge shape. It was double-edged, and had a grip of varying dimensions, ranging from four inches in length to an extent which, in some examples, almost suggest a two-handed weapon, or the hand-and-a-half or bastard sword of a later period (compare the d'Eresby and Felbrigge brasses). The pommel, grip, and scabbard were at times elaborately enriched with a profusion of ornament. A new weapon was introduced at this period, the misericorde or dagger of mercy, used for despatching a fallen foe whose wounds were beyond all surgical aid, in the combat *à outrance*, or in the field; or as a last resource for defence when other weapons had failed. It was a straight dagger with no guard as a rule, and having both the hilt and scabbard curiously ornamented; the blade had but one edge, the section being triangular. From its occurrence upon many monumental effigies, we gather that as a rule the misericorde was attached to the belt by a chain, but this feature is not as a rule shown upon brasses. The curious brass to Sir Ralph de Knevynton, however, exemplifies it, though the chains for attachment of both sword and misericorde are affixed to the

FIG. 225.—Misericorde, John Cray, 1380.

breastplate (see Fig. 204). The misericorde of John Cray, 1380 (Fig. 225), shows it depending at an angle from the belt, while towards the close of the reign of

King Richard II. the knights have the weapon slung hilt downwards to the front, though this curious fashion was soon discarded.

The Shield in use at this period is but rarely shown, and never upon brasses. Upon the tomb of Robert Wyvill, Bishop of Salisbury, 1375 (Fig. 226), a shield occurs which has a central boss riveted on and is concave to the person ; a projection is shown at the upper part, upon the back of which the guige is apparently fixed. In the "Pilgrimage of Human Life" in the French National Library we have represented the discarded habiliments of a knight who is departing upon a pilgrimage : the shield is

FIG. 226.—Shield, 1375.

small, notched in the right-hand corner for the lance rest, and presents a concave surface to the front. The snout-

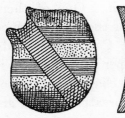

FIG. 227.—Shield, Hereford Cathedral, 1375.

faced visor upon the bascinet shows it to be of the period now dealt with. A sculptured effigy in Bamberg Cathedral, dating from 1370, has a shield which is notched in the corner and also concave to the front ; while another shield from Hereford Cathedral affords us an example of an English pattern dating from 1375, which also is concave to the front (Fig. 227). It occurs upon the tomb of Sir Richard Pembridge. For the emblazoning of arms the heater-shaped shield is invariably used.

The Heaume.—During the period under consideration the great heaume was in use for tilting purposes, the visored bascinet being reserved for warfare. The heaume retained its conical crown in order to fit over the bascinet, but the lower rim was still too high above the shoulders for the latter to afford any support to it, and the curve as shown is not adapted (Fig. 228); we must therefore infer that the whole weight was borne by the bascinet, and that the inside

of the heaume was padded in order to make it fit securely. In the lower part of the front a hole or staple is generally found, by which it could be fixed securely by a thong or chain to the cuirass. It is doubtful whether any great heaumes are in existence which date back to the thirteenth century, and there are only a few authentic examples of the fourteenth. One of them is the heaume of the Black Prince in Canterbury Cathedral (Plate XVII.), the upper part of which is covered by the chapeau or cap of

FIG. 228.—Heaume of Thomas de Mowbray, Earl of Nottingham, and Earl Marshal. (From a drawing of his seal, 1389: MS. Cott., Julius, C. vii.)

dignity bearing the heraldic lion. No breathing-holes are shown, and the occularium is extremely narrow. As weight was apparently of no object at this period, a secondary defence was often introduced in the form of a large plate of iron covering the whole of the left part of the face, hinged at the termination of the occularium upon that side, and falling lower than the rim of the heaume, to which it was further affixed by bolts and nuts. This *pièce de renfort* may be viewed as the prototype of the "grande garde" of the succeeding century: an excellent example is preserved in the

PLATE XVII

Heaume, Crest, and Shield of the Black Prince in Canterbury Cathedral

collection of Lord Zouche at Parham.   It will be observed that the lower or cylindrical portion of the Black Prince heaume consists of two pieces riveted together, and this was the usual method at the time.   In the heaume of Sir Richard Pembridge, Hereford Cathedral (Figs. 229, 230), however, the three pieces (cylinder, truncated cone, and crown) are welded together, and the rivets are more for ornament than for increased strength ; the metal is thickened round the

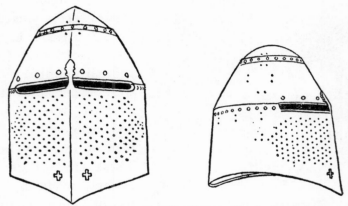

FIG. 229 and 230.—The Pembridge heaume, Hereford Cathedral.

occularium, and the lower edge is roped so as not to present a cutting edge.   There are a number of holes in the upper portions to permit the aglets of the laces to be passed through, by which the crest and lambrequins could be attached to the heaume.   In the lower front portion are the two holes in cruciform shape to allow passage for a T-bolt appended to the chain for securing to the breastplate. A very rare example of the great heaume, which may date from the early part of the fourteenth century, is one preserved in the Rotunda at Woolwich.   The crown is conical; the visor hinges on the left side, and closes with a spring on the right, and numerous small holes are pierced in it for air. The occularium is a narrow slit above the visor and below the crown. It is much corroded, and probably when new weighed more than at the present time (9½ lbs.) (Plate XXXIX., p. 364). During the studded and splinted style of English armour, heraldic crests had been intro-

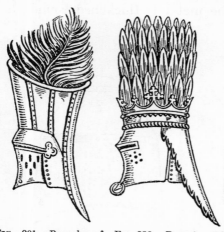

duced as we have seen, following upon the fan-shaped decorations of an earlier period: in the latter part of the four-teenth century all warriors of distinction adopted the fashion, and subsequently all men of knightly rank. These crests were in-variably made of cuir-bouilli, which material allowed itself to be

FIG. 231.—Panache of Wm. de Latimer, 1372.   FIG. 232.—Panache, Ed-ward Courtenay, 1400.

moulded into any desired shape, and had the advantage of being unaffected by the weather, besides affording some protection from a sword-cut. Crests of all shapes, sizes, and degrees of grotesqueness sprang into being, some tending to enormous proportions and thus fore-stalling the mantling of extravagant size so character-istic of the fifteenth century. The contoise or flowing scarf invariably accompanied the crest. A panache of feathers was a favourite form of crest, by reason pre-sumably of its lightness and gracefulness; that of Sir

Wm. de Latimer, 1372, and of Edward Courtenay, 1400, are reproduced as examples (Figs. 231, 232). As a foreign specimen of the great heaume of the Camail Period we may refer to the example preserved in the Historical Court Museum at Vienna, dating from about *c.* 1360, and known locally as the "Pranker heaume" (Fig. 233). It is made of four strong hammered-iron plates with

smaller reinforcements, and weighs about twelve pounds, being probably used only for tournaments. The crest, two golden horns with silver combs, is of the usual cuir-bouilli, and weighs about three pounds. A late heaume of this period, dating from *c.* 1410, is that of Sir Edward de Thorpe, which is of sufficient height to rest

FIG. 233.—Pranker heaume.

upon the shoulders (Fig. 234). A panache surmounts the elaborate coronet; the occularium is very high, and could hardly allow of a bascinet being worn underneath. The usual ring for affixing it to the breastplate is shown at the base.

The orle or wreath is of the greatest rarity upon monumental brasses of the Camail and Jupon Period; Sir Reginald de Cobham, 1403, has a small jewelled orle, however, and one of the same character is shown on the brass of a knight of the d'Eresby family, 1410 (see Fig. 222). This piece of ornament originated in the band of cloth, silk, or velvet placed round the bascinet to support, and act as pad to, the heaume, and subsequently, when the latter was discarded, remained to be a foundation for the crest.

The earlier effigies and brasses of this period are in many of their details exemplifications of the studded and splinted style of defence, and are in fact of greater use in that respect than the few contemporary brasses and effigies which remain and are generally used as examples. The lost brass of Sir Miles de Stapleton, 1364 (Fig. 235), once in Ingham Church, Norfolk, is, for instance, an excellent example, probably the best; he has a studded jupon fitting tightly to the figure and escalloped at the hem, with haut-de-chausses or cuissarts of the same

FIG. 234.—Heaume, Sir Edward de Thorpe, c. 1410.

material. His genouillières are of single plates with two rows of reinforcing cuir-bouilli tabs depending below, while the jambarts are of metal splints affixed by rivets to the cuir-bouilli beneath. The long pendent tab of the belt should be noticed. The remarkable brass of Sir Ralph de Knevynton, 1370 (see Fig. 204), at Aveley, Essex, may also be quoted as showing the same features respecting the jupon and cuissarts; but the shape and position of the belt, the great length of the misericorde,

FIG. 235.—Sir Miles de Stapleton, 1364. Formerly in Ingham Church, Norfolk.

its quillons, the crude genouillières, the long hauberk
pointed in front, the pose and shape of the figure, and
the chains depending from the breastplate,
make this brass, which is of Flemish workmanship, one of the most singular of its kind.
Sir John de Argentine, 1360 (Fig. 218) and
Sir John de Paletoot, 1361, have cuissarts
of studded material and pendent belts; Sir
Thomas Cheyne, 1368, also has studded
cuissarts, and jambarts of studded splints
similar to those of Sir Miles de Stapleton,

FIG. 236.—Genouil-
lière, Sir Thomas
Cheyne, 1368.

but his genouillières are most remarkable and quite unique.
They appear to be constructed entirely of cuir-bouilli with

FIG. 237.—Sir Humphrey Littlebury, Holbeach, Lincs.

pendent tabs of singular form reinforcing the jambarts (Fig. 236).
The Cheynes appear to have been
a family addicted to peculiarities,
as Sir William Cheyne, 1375, has
laminated sollerets of remarkable
construction and also quite unique
(see Fig. 197). Sir Humphrey
Littlebury, Holbeach Church, Lincolnshire (Fig. 237), has cuissarts
of cuir-bouilli with studs of an
ornamental form; his genouillières
are crude and of single plates, but
the hem of his jupon is remarkable
for graceful beauty, being deeply
dagged into acanthus-leaf form. A rich hip-belt has a
pendent tab at the side, but, strange to note, the sword
is not suspended by it, but has a separate belt passing

diagonally round the waist. This second belt is not
unfrequently found in sculptured effigies but seldom upon
brasses. The brass of Robert Albyn, *c.* 1400 (Fig. 238),
Hemel Hempstead, Herts, where two belts are shown,
has the sword suspended from both belts. Sir John de
Cobham, 1375, the founder of Cobham College, has
studded cuissarts and genouillières reminiscent of those of Sir Thomas Cheyne. The
brass of Sir John de St. Quintin, 1397
(Fig. 239), in Brandsburton Church, Yorkshire, is remarkable for the very wide and
elaborate hip-belt, which is fixed higher
than is usual upon a shortened jupon,
necessitating a small subsidiary belt from
which to suspend the sword, and also an
extra length of hauberk, which is curiously bent round the
limbs. The coudières are larger than usual, and together
with the genouillières are ornamented. After 1380, many
jupons are shown with fur round the arm openings, as in
the brass of Sir Nicholas Dagworth, 1401, where the great
length of the sword-grip, ornamentation of the armour,
great height of the bascinet, and elaborate hem to the
jupon are special features.

Fig. 238. — Robert
Albyn, 1400. Hemel
Hempstead Church,
Herts.

The years between 1400 and 1410 must be looked
upon as a transition period, inasmuch as features distinctive of the Camail and Jupon and of the Surcoatless
overlap each other. For example, the brass of Sir Thomas
Braunstone, Constable of Wisbeach Castle, in Wisbeach
Church, Cambridgeshire, dating from 1401 (Fig. 240), has
taces, apparently five in number, although his neck is
camailed, the jupon being dispensed with; whilst Sir John

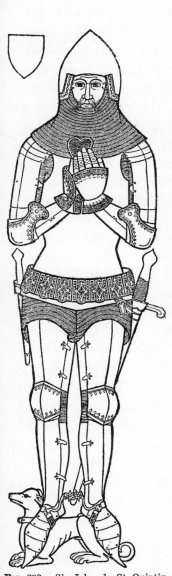

FIG. 239.—Sir John de St. Quintin, 1397. Brandsburton Church, Yorkshire.

FIG. 240.—Sir Thomas Braunstone, 1401, Constable of Wisbeach Castle. Wisbeach Church, Cambridgeshire.

FIG. 241.—A knight, c. 1405. Laughton Church, Lincolnshire.

Hanley, who, together with his two wives, is shown upon a brass in Dartmouth Church, dated 1403, has five or six taces and a shortened jupon, edged with fur round the arm-holes, but with a camailed neck.

Sir John Wylcotes in Great Tew Church, Oxfordshire, although wearing camail, has a reinforcing gorget of plate super-posed upon it. The latter ex-ample is a strange mixture of old and new styles; high pointed bascinet and camail being blended with palettes and taces. Lady Wylcotes, who is shown upon the same brass, wears the nebule head - dress which went out of fashion thirty years previously. A knight of the d'Eresby family, 1410 (see Fig. 222), exemplifies a strange mixture of transition styles. The orle has been pre-viously noted, but the bascinet is provided with a bavière which is placed upon the camail. The laminated epaulières are curiously brought forward in order to cover the goussets, over which they

form protecting arches.   Round the waist is seen the

ornamental belt worn by all knights of that period round the hips; it carries no sword or misericorde and is therefore purely ornamental, and, if we may say so, entirely superfluous. The sword-belt across the body from the right hip is the fashion of the Surcoatless Period. (A knight in Laughton Church, c. 1405 (Fig. 241), also exhibits this feature of the sword-belt, though otherwise he conforms to the period.) A waved fringe of mail appears below the five taces; the genouillières have prominent projections over the knee-caps and are very ornamental, while the sollerets have a decorative gousset of chain mail. Altogether the armour is eccentric, and probably both the wearer and his wife were of the same character, inasmuch as the lady is shown in a reticulated head-dress without the veil and the high-waisted gown then only prevailing on the Continent. The knight's suit is beautifully enriched with a design which imparts a very characteristic aspect to the entire figure.

CHAPTER XI

THE SURCOATLESS PERIOD, 1410-1430

WITH the advent of this period we find the knightly defence consisting essentially, for the first time in English history, of a complete suit of plate with no textile covering whatever worn over it. Hence the term "Surcoatless Period," which distinguishes it from any preceding or succeeding era. The camail was now finally abolished after being in vogue in one fashion or another for over one hundred years. Its great recommendation was mobility, as it enabled the wearer to move his head easily in almost any direction, but the great detraction was undoubtedly the weight. The bascinet itself was heavy, but when the thick curtain of chain mail was added it must have been almost insupportable, as practically the whole weight was borne by the head. Now, however, a gorget of plate was substituted for the camail (Fig. 243), and in order to relieve the pressure upon the head still further, the bascinet was so formed as to rest upon the gorget, to the upper part of

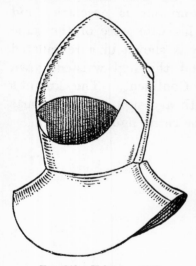

FIG. 242.—Helmet, c. 1415.

194

which it was affixed in such a manner that it allowed
the head to be turned right and
left. Thus the defences for the
head and neck, instead of being
supported by those parts, were
transferred to the shoulders. The
bascinet, as it gradually developed
into the barbute type, became more
globular in form, although still re-
taining the pointed apex (Fig. 242) ;
the lower portion which protected
the chin, and known as the *bavière*,
was riveted to the upper, generally
near the temples. The breastplate,
now visible for the first time, is of
globular form and provided with a
backplate ; from it one can easily
perceive how the knights of the
Camail and Jupon Period obtained
the peculiar globose formation of
the upper portion of the body.
From the waist, and connected
with the breastplate, depended a
row of plates or lames of steel
overlapping each other and made
in various designs ; these were denominated the *taces*. To support
them a lining of leather or other
strong material was used underneath, to which they were firmly
affixed. At first the skirt of the hauberk is generally

FIG. 243.—Robert, Lord Ferrers
of Chartley, 1407. Merevale
Abbey Church, Warwickshire.

shown, similar to its former appearance under the jupon, but after a time, probably about 1420, the hauberk was discarded, and the knight relied for protection upon his plate armour and padded gambeson alone. Round the taces the hip-belt was worn horizontally during the earlier part of this period, with the sword and misericorde depending as in the time of the camail and jupon; but subsequently the style was modified, and innovations crept in which will be dealt with later. Laminated epaulières were still in use to protect the shoulders, but instead of the lames being prolonged in front to protect the goussets (as shown in the Braunstone and d'Eresby brasses), a plate of varying form, called a *palette*, was affixed to the cuirass by a strap, which admitted of greater freedom for the arms. The brassarts were often formed of lames of plate riveted together, though the older form of front and back plates was in use. The coudières are remarkable for the beautiful fan-like shape of the outer plate, which was enlarged in order to afford extra protection to the elbow-joint, and in some cases was of very large proportions. The vambraces show no change. The gauntlets were larger in the cuffs than those of the preceding period: they retained the gadlings and were often of most elaborate workmanship; the fingers remained separate and conformed to the natural shape, finger-nails being often engraved upon them to complete the resemblance. The cuissarts, genouillières, grevières, and sollerets, did not differ essentially from those of the Camail Period, except in the richness of ornamentation which was at times shown. One point, however, and an entirely new one, is exemplified upon a few brasses—the protection of the back part of the knee-joint by small lames

PLATE XVIII *

Armour made for the Infante, afterwards Philip III.

of steel. The skilful and costly nature of this defence prevented its general adoption; it was revived, however, at a later period, during the early part of the sixteenth century, and became fairly prevalent.

The sword was but slightly altered from its former shape, the chief difference being the quillons, which were straight and of considerable length, and the general elongation of the grip, whereby it developed into more of a hand-and-a-half, or bastard sword, than formerly (Fig. 244). It should be explained that in wielding this weapon the right hand only would be generally used, but upon occasion, in order to give extra effect to a stroke, the left hand could be brought up to the pommel, which was invariably pear-shaped in order to insure a firm grip. The misericorde was suspended as usual upon the right side, but the point of the blade is now directed towards the rear, and is generally hidden in brasses by the body of the knight (Fig. 245). One of the characteristics of this period should be specially noted, viz. the mode of suspension of the sword by a narrow band passing diagonally over the front of the body from the right hip to the left side, and occasionally, but rarely, furnished with a buckle. The inception of this style is shown upon the brass of a knight in Laughton Church which exhibits both hip-belt and sword-belt worn over the jupon; it prevailed in England for approximately sixty years (Fig. 241).

One of the earliest examples in brasses of this period is that at Great Tew Church, Oxfordshire, referred to on p. 192 as being of a transition character, in consequence of the camail appearing beneath the gorget. The bascinet and bavière are in one piece, and the whole revolves upon

FIG. 244.—Knight, 1410. South Kelsey Church, Lincs.

FIG. 245.—Sir Thomas Swynborne, 1412. Little Horkesley Church, Essex.

the gorget, which is probably prolonged upwards inside the headpiece. The placcates are oviform; the upper lame of the taces covers the lower part of the breastplate; the hauberk and hipbelt are in use, and the great heaume is shown under the head, to be worn as usual over the bascinet. Robert, Lord Ferrers of Chartley, 1407 (Fig. 243), presents a very unornamental suit of this earlier portion of the period, showing the globular helmet with the mentonnière riveted to the upper portion and revolving within the gorget; it should be compared with the Wylcotes brass. Sir Simon de Felbrygge, K.G., 1413, is shown with the royal banner of King Richard II., and wears the diagonal sword-belt; he is furnished with many lames in his epaulières and has shield-shaped palettes, while the coudières show the fanshaped plates in their incipient stage. The Yorkshire St. Quintins appear to have been eccentric in the style of their armour. We have referred to peculiarities in respect of Sir John de St. Quintin and his brass, 1397 (*vide* p. 191), and in that

FIG. 246.—Sir Thomas de St. Quintin, *c.* 1420. Harpham Church, Yorkshire.

of Sir Thomas de St. Quintin, in Harpham Church, York-shire (Fig. 246), we have more characteristic originalities. The orle round the bascinet is of very large proportions, and

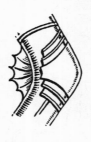

ornamented with a brooch in front; the gorget consists of three plates, the upper one

FIG. 247.—Coudière, Lord Camoys, 1424. Trotton Church, Sussex.

FIG. 248.—Coudière, Peter Halle, 1420. Herne Church, Kent.

of peculiar form, showing ridged projections over the cheekplates of the bascinet, while the epaulières are more of the nature of the pauldron of a subsequent period,

in being composed of a single piece. The arm openings are protected respectively by a roundel and a shield-shaped palette, and roundels are also used at the elbows, these being strongly reminiscent of the early camail days (*vide* Sir John de Argentine, 1360, p. 175).

FIG. 249.—Bascinet, Sir William Cal-thorpe, 1420. Burn-ham Thorpe Ch., Norfolk.

The hip-belt is among the latest examples of that fashion, having been generally dis-carded by this date; it is very elaborate, and suggestive in point of width of that of the brass of Sir John de St. Quintin in 1397 (p. 191). The hem of the hauberk is wavy, and so also is that of the gambeson showing beneath it; this is possibly the only example of the gambeson being visible at this late period.

But perhaps the chief points to be observed are the laminated defences for the back parts of the genouillières. If
they are lames they probably represent the earliest development of this nature ; on the other hand the artist may have
intended to represent banded mail, and omitted the small
vertical lines. The development of the fan-shaped coudière
may be well observed in the brass of Lord Camoys, in
Trotton Church, Sussex (Fig. 247), where the defence, both
inside and out, may be seen, but the strap or other fastening
joining the two sides of the opening is not shown. The
coudière may have been riveted to the brassarts and vambraces, in which case it was not needed. A brass in which
the fastening is apparent is that of Peter Halle, c. 1420,
in Herne Church, Kent (Fig. 248), where the strap may
be noticed crossing the mail. Upon the brass of Sir
William Calthorpe, 1420, in Burnham Thorpe Church,
Norfolk, the bascinet is shown very highly ornamented
with a border; he also wears a collar of Esses round the
neck (Fig. 249).

The brass of Sir John Lysle (Fig. 250) in Thruxton
Church, Hampshire, bears the date 1407, and if the effigy
were executed at that time, or approximately so, we have
the earliest example of complete plate in existence in England. There are, however, certain points about the armour
delineated which lend themselves to the supposition that the
brass was executed some ten or more years later, viz. the
absence of any hauberk ; the development of the fan-shaped
coudières ; the position of the misericorde and the sword-belt,
&c. The distinction probably belongs to the Ferrers brass.

The brass of Sir John de Leventhorpe, 1433, at Sawbridge-
worth Church, Herts (Fig. 251), is interesting as showing the

development of the lowermost tace into the subsequent

FIG. 250.—Sir John Lysle, 1407.   FIG. 251.—Sir John de Leventhorpe, 1433.
    Thruxton Church, Hants.   Sawbridgeworth Church, Herts.

tuilles of the Tabard Period. In this effigy the lame in

question is divided into two tuilles which still have the same width, and partake of the nature of taces ; each tuille is suspended by two buckles. This is one of the earliest representations of this feature in England.

The shields used in the Surcoatless Period were similar to those in the preceding, but manifest infinitely greater varieties. They were invariably small in size and notched for the lance, but as every knight apparently designed his own, it is obviously impossible to enumerate or illustrate them. They all, however, agreed in presenting a concave surface to the opponent's lance, whereby it was prevented from glancing upwards or downwards and thus inflicting injury, while the general tendency was to deflect the lance-point to the left, whereby it touched neither horse nor rider. The examples here given are from one of the Harleian MSS., No. 4379 (Fig. 252), and may be taken as a general type of the knightly shield in this and also in the preceding period.

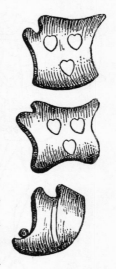

FIG. 252.—Shields.
(Harl. MS., 4379.)

Remembering that there was no arbitrary law regulating the military equipment and dress of the ordinary soldier at this period, it is somewhat difficult to deal decisively with the subject, but a few examples and some broad outlines may probably be sufficient to enable the reader to grasp a general idea of the subject.

The Man-at-arms in the middle of the fourteenth century was generally armed with the lance, sword, and mace, the

martel-de-fer or a military pick at times supplanting the
latter. The shield was heater- or heart-shaped and notched,
but sometimes circular, and of various sizes. A hauberk or
jacque reaching to the knees, and having sleeves to the
elbow, constructed of any
of the numerous kinds
of jazeraint work, or of
banded mail, covered his
body; it was reinforced at
the shoulders, elbows, and
knees with roundels, caps,
or plates, while two mam-
melières were in use to
cover the chest and act
more or less as breast-
plates. Greaves and vam-
braces of leather streng-
thened with splints of iron,
with thick leather gaunt-
lets and shoes, guarded the
limbs, while a skull-cap
with banded camail or a
thick leather gorget de-
pending, protected the
head and neck. Either a

FIG. 253.—Richard de Beauchamp, Earl of
Warwick, early 15th century. (From
the Warwick Roll.)

gambeson or a leather tunic under the jacque completed
the equipment.

Billman, Pikeman, or Foot Soldier.—The pikeman of
the period was equipped with a more elaborate defence
than is generally credited, and consequently his comparative immunity from hurt by the lethal weapons of the time

goes far to explain the determined resistance made by the infantry. The very fact that there was no uniformity in his accoutrement rendered him a formidable foe to the knight, who naturally directed his lance to that portion of an enemy's person possessing the least defensive equipment;

but it required more than human divination in the excitement of a contest to discern the weak points in the equipment of men all armed in a different manner. The broad rule respecting the armour of the infantry in mediæval times was that the knightly defence of one period became the soldier's salvation in the succeeding period. At the same time many a contemporary piece of equipment was obtained from the field of battle and used to augment the personal defence. The figure (Fig. 254) (taken from the British Museum MS. Roy. 20, C. VII.) may be taken as a general type of the billman of the reigns of Edward III., Richard II., and possibly Henry IV. and V. Upon the head he wears a skull cap com-posed of two pieces of iron riveted together

FIG. 254.—Billman, Richard II. (Roy. MS. 20, C. VII.)

with reinforcing strips of metal; from this depends a camail of banded mail which is strengthened by a plate defending the cheeks, chin, and throat, in imitation of the bavière then coming into vogue with the knightly class. Possibly this piece was home-made, and the village black-smith had a hand in its fabrication. The body is protected by a leathern jacque having roundels at the shoulders with crude brassarts, coudières, and vambraces, possibly of leather. A tegulated skirt of pieces of leather, horn, or iron plates reaches to the knees, which are defended by

metal genouillières, from which depend grevières of metal or cuir-bouilli. Indications of cuissarts are apparent, and the legs are covered with chausses of banded mail in addition. It will thus be seen that the billman's equipment for defence was but little inferior to that of the knight. No sword or mace is shown, but these were in common use. The fauchard he wields is nine feet in length, with cutting edges upon both sides, a sharp pike-point at the end, and a hook with which to dismount a horseman. A second example from the same MS. (Fig. 255) shows a head-covering of cuir-bouilli in the form of overlapping leaves or scales, while the camail is of soft pliable leather. In this cut the small badge is delineated upon the left breast that denoted the leader under whom the soldier fought. Another soldier with a circular shield and armed only with a sword, is taken from the MS. above named (Roy. 20, C. VII.); he wears a piece of tegulated defence, probably leather, over a leathern jerkin, while his sleeves appear to be of a stuffed and quilted nature, similar to a gambeson. He has demi-plate upon the legs and is furnished with a bascinet (Fig. 256). A soldier is also shown wearing the high bascinet so characteristic of the knight of the early Camail Period; it had doubt-

FIG. 255.—Cuir-bouilli headpiece. (Roy. MS. 20, C. VII.)

FIG. 256.—Soldier, c. 1400. (Roy. MS. 20, C. VII.)

less formed part of some loot, and the wearer added to
the defence a large bavière which
also partially served the function of
a breastplate, while a tippet of
banded mail covers the shoulders
(Fig. 257). Some of the foot soldiers carried a small circular shield or
buckler about 9 inches to 12 inches
in diameter and furnished with a
boss in the centre; the left hand
would be able to grasp both it and
the pike as well. Towards the end
of the reign of Richard II. the fashion
of wearing a houppelande over the armour came in vogue

FIG. 257.—Soldier with plate
gorget, *temp.* Richard II.
(Roy. MS. 20, C. VII.)

FIG. 258.—Spear-
man, *c.* 1400.
(Roy. MS. 20,
C. VII.)

both for knights and common soldiery, thus
preventing the armour from being seen, except
the lower parts of the legs (see Fig. 258). With
this incongruous habit appeared also the snout-
faced or pig-faced visor of alarming proportions, serving as a visor, gorget, and pectoral
combined. The annexed cut is taken from a
group of combatants in Roy MS. 20, C. VII.,
who are all defended in the same ungainly
manner. With the advent of the reign of
King Henry IV. this visor became of less size
and different shape, while reinforcements to
the bascinet were added to compensate. In
Fig. 259, from Roy. MS. 15, D. III., a
soldier is shown with bascinet and neck-
guard affixed; to protect the throat an
extra plate is used swinging upon pivots on either side

of the helmet—a crude bavière.   Another foot soldier is
shown with a similar defence (Fig. 260), but his bascinet is

FIG. 259.
(Roy. MS. 15, D. III.)

FIG. 260.
(Roy. MS. 15, D. III.)

globular at the top and furnished with a projecting neck-
guard, in which we cannot fail to see the salade in its early
stage.   We may refer this to the reign of Henry V., as well

FIG. 261.—Soldier, Richard II.,
gorget over camail.   (Roy. MS.
20, C. VII.)

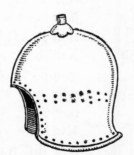

FIG. 262.—Bascinet, *temp.*
Henry V.

as that shown in Fig. 259.   Another bascinet of the same
period is given in Fig. 262, where the small holes for fixing
the lining are shown, and also those round the lower edge

and opening for the face, for the camail. This bascinet still further suggests the salade, as does also the one in the British Museum (Fig. 263).

The Archer.—The equipment of the archer was essentially of a lighter nature than that of the billman. A pot-de-fer upon the head, with coif-de-mailles or camail; a brigandine or jacque of pourpointerie, covering at times a small plastron-de-fer; upon the left arm a bracer, otherwise legs and arms in cloth stockings and sleeves; a girdle with axe, sword, or scimitar depending therefrom; a quiver at the right hip with its burden of goose- or pigeon-feathered arrows, and the long yellow bow slung at the back in company with a small round target—such was

FIG. 263.—Bascinet from Brit. Mus.

FIG. 264. — Quivers and scimitar. (Roy. MS. 14, E. IV.)

the war dress of the mediæval bowman. At times a stake sharpened at both ends was carried to hinder a charge of cavalry, but this was generally improvised upon the spot. In Roy. MS. 14, E. IV., the quivers at this period are shown to be of an elongated bag form, and quite different to the late fifteenth-century style. A very favourite weapon with archers, judging by the number of men represented wearing it in all MSS. of the time, is the scimitar, which is invariably of the shape shown in Fig. 264. The curious guard for the fingers, springing from the pommel, is very characteristic.

The weapons used by the billmen of this period are

well shown in Roy. MS. 20, C. VII., and are reproduced in Fig. 265. No. 1 is shown in use by a soldier whose left hand is guarded by the circular projection, which, together with the long point, was made of steel. The shaft of this formidable pike or partisan was about five feet in length, the point three feet, and it depended for its efficacy upon

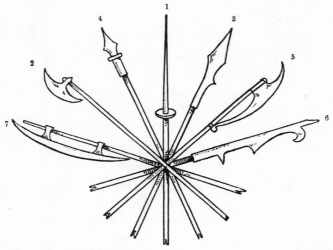

FIG. 265.—Weapons from Roy. MS. 20, C. VII. Nos. (left to right) —7. Pole-axe (the voulge); 2. Pole-axe; 4. Pike; 1. Pike; 3. Pike; 5. Pole-axe (bardiche); 6. Fauchard (guisarme).

its armour-piercing qualities. Nos. 2, 5, 7 are the pole-axe with varying modifications, the total length, including shaft, being about eight feet; it was apparently a favourite weapon, and is many times represented, No. 5, the bardiche, however, being somewhat uncommon. Nos. 3 and 4 are simple forms of pikes, with a cross-guard in one case, and an armour-piercing spike in the other. No. 6 is the deadly fauchard, a variety of the guisarme, evolved originally from the scythe; it was a common weapon in the Middle Ages, but inflicted such ghastly wounds with its razor-like edges back and front, that its use in Christian

FIG. 266.—Combat with pole-axes between Earl of Warwick and Sir P. Malacat.
(Cott. MS., Julius, E. IV.)

warfare was often deplored. Its total length was usually about eight feet.

The antiquary, John Rouse, of Warwick, has left us some excellent drawings of military equipment of the fifteenth century, which are preserved in the Cottonian MS., Julius, E. IV. They illustrate the romantic adventures of Richard de Beauchamp, Earl of Warwick, and one of these spirited sketches is introduced here (Fig. 266).

It represents a combat with pole-axes between the earl and Sir Pandulf Malacat at Verona, when Sir Pandulf was badly wounded upon the left shoulder, and would probably have fared worse had not the combat been stopped. We gain an excellent idea from this sketch of the mode in which the gorget was adjusted, which is difficult to realise from a brass. The misericorde is suspended as in the later days of Richard II., and a central prolongation of the front taces is represented, which occurs upon several English brasses. The shape and character of the formidable weapons are well delineated in the sketch.

PLATE XIX *

Armour of Philip III., made by Lucio
Picinino of Milan

CHAPTER XII

THE TABARD PERIOD, 1430–1500

THE sources of information for this period are considerably enlarged when compared with those preceding it, as, in addition to MSS., missals, brasses, and monumental effigies we may add paintings by the old masters, crude woodcuts following upon the introduction of printing, and, what is of still greater value, actual examples of arms and armour in our public and private museums, churches, &c. The fifteenth century probably saw a greater output of armour than any other in English history: the stirring times in France under the Duke of Bedford and other leaders at the end of the Hundred Years' War was followed almost immediately by the thirty years of intestine strife of the Wars of the Roses. Under the stress of these conditions armour continued to improve in defensive power until, in the reign of Richard III. and the earlier part of that of Henry VII., it attained to its maximum stage of efficiency in England. In the combat during this century between the forgers of weapons of offence and the armour with which to resist them we have the greatest struggle ever witnessed in this country; so invulnerable did the plate become by completeness of covering and dexterity in tempering that all the efforts of the bowyer, fletcher, weapon-forger, and gunsmith had to be enlisted to break down the solidarity of the defence, and it was not until the succeeding century that the victory could be fairly claimed for the attacking faction. The Tabard Period witnessed every device in armour that the wit of man could evolve, and it was produced under those circumstances which would best achieve the desired result, namely the stress of urgent need. The name by which this age is known, that of the Tabard Period, has been selected by reason of the tabard being practically the only distinguishing feature which did not change, and was fairly persistent throughout. It is also used in contra-distinction to the preceding Surcoatless Period. The tabard was a surcoat which was generally long in the body (to mid-thigh), and had sleeves to the elbow in the earlier portion of its existence; but in the later period

FIG. 267. — Tabard, William Fynderne, 1444. Childrey Church, Berks.

the sleeves were much shortened, and the tabard at times only reached to the waist. It was split upon both sides, and the front and back portions fastened together by points, drawn closely together or left wide apart to show the armour beneath; occa-sionally no points whatever were used, and the front and back hung loosely from the shoulders.

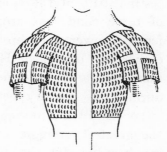

FIG. 268. — Tabard, Sir Ralph Shelton, 1423. Great Snoring Church, Norfolk.

It served as a protection against sun and rain, and also

as a means of personal adornment, being generally emblazoned upon the body and also
on the sleeves with the armorial
bearings of the wearer. It was
of silk or other material, sometimes padded so as to hang stiffly;
in most examples it depends in
folds. An early brass showing
this feature is that of William
Fynderne, 1444, at Childrey in
Berkshire (Fig. 267), where the
armorial bearings are depicted
upon the body and sleeves, both
of which are long. An early
tabard is that shown upon the
brass of Sir Ralph Shelton, 1423,
in Great Snoring Church (Fig.
268), which fits tightly to the
figure, and the tincture of the
body of the tabard has apparently
been attempted by the engraver.
Another early example is that
of John Wantele, 1424, at Am-
berley Church, Sussex, where
the arms are shown upon the
body (which reaches almost
to the knees) but not on the
sleeves. Later examples are
those of Sir John Say, 1473, at
Broxbourne, Herts, and Piers
Gerard, 1492, Winwick, Lancs.

FIG. 269.—Brass in the Scarisbrick
Chapel of Ormskirk Church, co.
Lancs., to a member of the Scaris-
brick family of that name, c. 1500.

In the Roy. MS. 18,

E. V., is a very spirited drawing of Julius Cæsar crossing the Rubicon, in which he is represented as wearing a tabard.

A very elaborate example, *c.* 1500, is on the brass in Ormskirk Church, Lancashire, commemorating a former member of the Scarisbrick family (Fig. 269). The figure in question wears sabbatons.

The Helmet. — During the earlier part of the Tabard Period, until about 1450, the helmet differed but slightly from those shown in the Surcoatless, the modifications being chiefly in the form of the apex and the addition of a close-fitting visor. In the example shown (Fig. 270) the visor

FIG. 270.—Bascinet of one of the Neville family, Brancepeth, Durham.

was probably rapidly adjusted to the lower studs in time of danger, or the heaume could be worn. The shape of the apex should be noted, and this feature is also somewhat similar in the helmet of John, Duke of Somerset, A.D. 1444. In those cases where the knight trusted to the bascinet only, the bavière is raised considerably to guard the face. This is well seen in the brass of Sir Humphrey Stafford, 1450 (Fig. 271), where the orle is a prominent feature. An example is

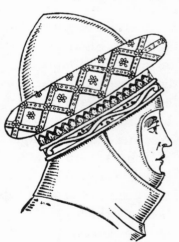

FIG. 271.—Bascinet and orle, Sir Humphrey Stafford, 1450.

given here of a brass of a later period exhibiting armour of an earlier date, an occurrence which at times causes confusion.

Sir John de Harpedon's brass (Fig. 272) is well known in Westminster Abbey, and dates from 1457; the armour is most unusually simple for that period, and could well be attributed to thirty years earlier, except in regard to the gauntlets. There are no less than eleven lames in the taces.

About 1450 the Salade (Germ. *schallern*, from *schale*, a shell, or Italian *celata*) was introduced into England, and for a considerable time formed the headpiece of knights, men-at-arms, and archers. It rested entirely upon the head, and was not affixed in any way to the body armour. Its coolness was a great recommendation, as was also the facility with which the head could be moved in all directions. There appear to be two distinct headpieces from which the salade could owe its development; the chapelle-de-fer is one, and it probably suggested the German shape. This was in use from the thirteenth to the fifteenth centuries, and consisted of a light iron headpiece with a flat broad brim turned

FIG. 272.—The brass of Sir John de Harpedon.

down. In the earlier examples the brim projects equally all round, but later it is much flatter at the front than at the back, where it was drawn out to a point (see Fig. 273). The Italian *celata* was the second model from which the salade could trace its evolution; it was the helmet of barbute form referred to on p. 173, and which was undoubtedly founded upon the Greek model. It gradually developed in the fifteenth century into the shape shown

FIG. 273.—Chapelle-de-fer, *c.* 1485.

in Fig. 274, losing its pointed apex and swelling outwards at the back of the neck. Upon their introduction into France, both German and Italian forms were classed under the name Salade. The salade in its primitive form was a head protection forged at first out of one piece of metal (Fig. 275 and Fig. 276) with a comb upon the crest and an occularium, which was

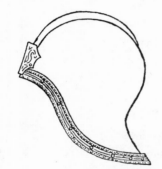

FIG. 274.—Italian celata.

FIG. 275.—German salade, *c.* 1440.

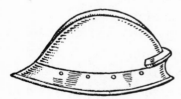

FIG. 276.—Early salade.

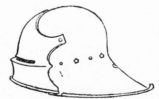

FIG. 277.—Salade from Rhodes, *c.* 1470.

made available by pulling down the front of the helmet until it rested level with the eyes. This was superseded by one having a movable visor which could be raised or lowered at pleasure, and generally when lowered was locked with a spring catch (Fig. 277). A few examples occur in which the long projection at the back is jointed after

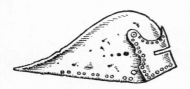

FIG. 278.—Salade, 1450.
(Tower of London.)

FIG. 279.—Salade, c. 1460.
(Wallace Collection.)

the form of the lobster's tail, and at times the salade measured as much as sixteen or eighteen inches from front to back. An example weighing 5 lbs. is in Case 25 at the Tower of London, dating from 1450: it is of German make and still bright, though much pitted all over (Fig. 278). A very interesting example is Fig. 279, in the Wallace Collection, dating from about 1460, which was probably used by a mounted archer. As in the Tower example, it is bright but pitted: the crown is without a ridge, but becomes combed at the tail; the form of the salade enables it

FIG. 280. — Mentonnière, in Whissonsett Church, Norfolk.

to be thrown well back upon the head when not in use. The small holes round the visor were probably intended for the sewing in of a lining, and the pairs of holes at the sides show where the strong lining was affixed which supported the helmet itself. Salades of this shape are shown in contemporary paintings, those of Albert Dürer for example. The mentonnière was habitually used with the salade: it was a plate fastened by one, two, or three screws or almayne (sliding) rivets to the upper part of the breast-plate, and was moulded so as to cover the lower part of the face to the lips or nose and reach to the ears on

FIG. 281.—Schallern, with Crest of Bavaria (Duke Ludwig of Bavaria, 1449).

FIG. 282.—German type of salade and armour, 1450.

both sides (see Fig. 280). In use the visor of the salade when lowered fell outside the mentonnière, thus effectually protecting the face of the wearer. A plate cheek-guard or bavière was worn at times, and this reinforcement is plainly seen in the salade, with crest, of the Duke Ludwig of Bavaria, 1449 (Fig. 281). A salade of German pattern with a very high crown is shown in Fig. 282; the general type of armour prevailing upon the Continent in 1450 is here presented, the laminated brassarts being a special feature. As a rule, however, a collar or standard of mail was deemed to be a sufficient protection under the mentonnière. An example of the mentonnière dating from about 1480 is No. 840 in the Wallace Collection; it has two plates, of which the upper one is held in position by a spring catch;

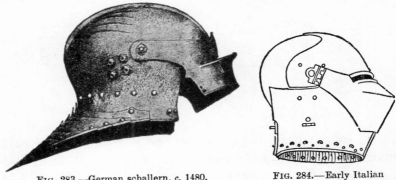

FIG. 283.—German schallern, c. 1480.   FIG. 284.—Early Italian armet, c. 1450.

it suggests the falling bufe of a later period. Fig. 283 represents a salade of the end of the fifteenth century; it will be seen that a comb runs over the crown, and that a sliding neck-guard is used in place of a rigid tail. A magnificent example of Milanese workmanship is shown on Plate VII.*, p. 60.

The Armet.—Towards the end of the Tabard Period the armet was introduced into England, and partially superseded the salade and other forms of head-protection. The origin of this helmet and the derivation of the name are equally involved in obscurity; but it probably first saw the light in Italy, and gradually spread through Germany into England. "Armet" may be derived from "elmetto" or "armetto," little helm, or "heaumet," the diminutive of "heaume." The essential difference between the armet and all those headpieces which antedated it was that, while the older styles had been put on by lowering them over the head and the weight had in nearly all cases been

FIG. 285.—Armet, c. 1470.
(Wallace Collection.)

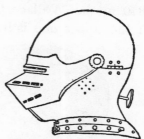

FIG. 286.—Armet, probably
Italian, c. 1480.

borne by the head, the armet opened out in its lower part upon hinges, and could thus be closed round the head and neck, while the weight was transferred to the gorget and

FIG. 287.—Armet, c.
1480. (Wallace Col-
lection.)

thence to the shoulders. It was in all respects neater, lighter, and handier than either the salade or the bascinet, while providing a fine defensive form for both head and neck. The armets, like the bascinets, had in their earlier stages a camail attached by a row of vervelles (Fig. 284) and a reinforcing piece upon the forehead. The same pin and hinge arrangement peculiar to the bascinet is used for affixing the visor, which latter, by falling, secures the opening of the helmet in front, at the same time forming the occularium by leaving a space between its upper edge and the lower edge of the reinforcement covering the

forehead. Under the hinges or pivots of the visor are the
upper parts of the two chin-pieces, hinged to the crown,
which overlap in front and are strapped together at the
chin.   At the back occurs a tailpiece from which projects
a short stem to which is attached a flat disc, probably to
protect the back of the helmet, which was its weakest part.
An example in the Wallace Collection (Fig. 285), dating
from 1470, has the stem remaining but not the roundel,
while the holes for attaching the camail are well seen.
The pivots for the visor are in the reinforcement in this
case.   Another armet from the same collection has the
pointed visor and bavière in one plate, while the roundel
is shown at the back (Fig. 286), and the latter example
shows the camail superseded by the laminated gorget with
which the armet articulated.   Fig. 287 also has the
disc in position; it dates from 1480, is without any reinforcing piece upon the forehead, and the occularium is
contained in the visor. No. 46 suit of armour in the
Wallace Collection has an armet dating probably from
1490, with pointed visor and bavière in one piece; the
neck portion is furnished with a hollow roping running
round it, which fits upon and grips the upper lame of the
gorget, which being perfectly circular, like the neck of the
gorget, allows the head to be turned right and left.   This was
a feature of the close helmets of the succeeding century.

   Body Armour; the Breastplate.—The breastplate from
approximately 1430 to 1450 remained of the same globular
form which had characterised it in the Surcoatless Period,
but after that date we often find it reinforced by another
plate, called a demi-placcate, springing upwards from the
waist, the upper part as a rule being moulded into a

FIG. 288.—*Cap-à-pie* suit of Gothic armour, c. 1470. (Wallace Collection.)

graceful system of cusps. In some cases, a second reinforcing plate is added over the first, but it is doubtful if these plates reached to the waist in any single case. By the system of introducing almayne rivets the breastplate could be given a certain amount of mobility, and adapt itself to the movements of the wearer. The goussets at the armholes were ridged or roped and sometimes turned back upon the breastplate. The backplates, also, about 1450, were made in several pieces, in order to obtain freedom of movement; the well-known *cap-à-pie* suit (Fig. 316) in the Wallace Collection has no less than five pieces in the backplate. Towards the end of the century, the breastplate was reinforced with goussets of plate adapted to the movement of the arms by judiciously-placed rivets. This is shown in Fig. 289; in the Tower Collection, *c.* 1490 or 1500, in Case 48; it shows a roped border in the upper part, holes for affixing the lance-rest, one in the centre for the screw of the gorget or mentonniere, and an articulated lame of the taces at the lower part. The section is shown with it. The suit of armour, No. 10 in the Wallace Collection, has the breastplate fitted with plate goussets; it dates from 1470. A demi-placcate of one plate is

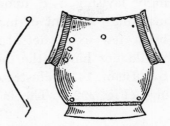

FIG. 289.—Breastplate, *c.* 1490. (Tower of London.)

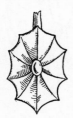

FIG. 290.—Palette suspended from pauldron, *c.* 1470. (Wallace Collection.)

well delineated in Fig. 291 from Roy. MS. 18, E. V., 1473, being a portion of the defence of "Goliath of Gath" in that manuscript.

Arm Defences.—These were of great variety and, as the century progressed, of the most original and complicated description, giving to this period the most characteristic forms by which it can be identified. Soon after 1440, and perhaps before that

time, the defences of the right and left arms in England began to be of different construction, similar to changes which had already become well advanced upon the Continent in the same direction. The right arm was encased in steel which, compared with other portions, was comparatively thin, light, and cap-

FIG. 291.—Demi-placcate, &c. (Roy. MS. 18, E. V.)

able of the greatest flexibility and mobility; this was occasioned by the need of extreme quickness of sword-play in combat after the lance had been shivered in the charge. Laminated epaulières and laminated brassarts were accordingly lavishly used upon the right arm as affording the maximum amount of movement, these being strengthened by a few extra defences of plate adapted so that they would not hinder the flexibility so obtained. A brass at Swaffham, 1470, illustrates the use of lames upon the right arm (Fig. 292). The left or bridle arm, on the contrary,

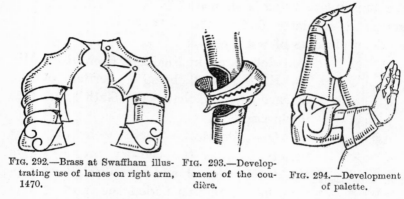

FIG. 292.—Brass at Swaffham illustrating use of lames on right arm, 1470.

FIG. 293.—Development of the coudière.

FIG. 294.—Development of palette.

was guarded by extra strong and thick plate defences and reinforcements of all descriptions, shapes, and sizes; in fact the general idea was to render the whole of the left side of the knight impenetrable to the weapons then in use. Probably this was occasioned by the partial or total disuse of the shield in warfare, as being an encumbrance whose disadvantages more than counterbalanced any possible benefits which might have been derived from it. It can be readily seen that in combat with an ordinary right-handed swordsman the left side of the body would be liable to receive more hurts, both in number and intensity, than the right, hence this extraordinary strengthening of the defences upon that side.

Pauldrons.—The defence known as the Pauldron was introduced in England about 1430, and may be looked upon as a development of the palette, which, becoming larger and larger, finally ended by covering the epaulières. This enlargement may be readily seen from the accompanying Fig. 294, where the palette is seen to have reached the shoulder. The right arm defences of Walter, Lord Hungerford, 1459, from his effigy in Salisbury Cathedral (Fig. 295), afford us an example of the pauldron in its early stage;

FIG. 295.—Pauldron of Walter, Lord Hungerford, 1459. Salisbury Cathedral.

it is plain and of small proportions, just sufficient to fit upon the lames beneath. The peculiar shape of the coudière with its flutings should be noticed. A pauldron consisting of long lames of plate is shown in Cott. MS., Julius, E. IV. (Fig. 296), and also on the Staunton brass; it, however, invari-

FIG. 296.—Laminated pauldron. (Cott. MS., Julius, E. IV.)

ably consisted of a strong and rigid plate, which is well exemplified in the brass of Sir Miles Stapleton in Ingham Church, Norfolk, 1466 (Fig. 297), where the defence, beautifully ornamented by curves and cusps, is not only designed as a protection to the shoulder and upper arm but also to a certain extent for the neck, which is also encircled by a standard of interlinked chain mail. In this ridging for neck defence occurred the first idea of passe-gardes or pike-guards, an innovation which in different forms was in vogue during

FIG. 297.—Pauldron, &c., Sir Miles Stapleton, 1466. Ingham Church, Norfolk.

the latter part of the fifteenth and nearly the whole of the sixteenth centuries. It is still further indicated in the brass to Thomas Colt, Armiger, 1475 (Fig. 298), at Roydon, Essex, where a serrated ridge is shown traversing a large part of the pauldron with the evident object of arresting a sword-cut. The pauldron is of large dimensions, and projects well over the breastplate. William Yelverton, 1481, whose brass is shown at Rougham in Norfolk, has the passe-garde well developed and rising

  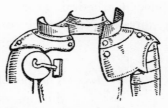

FIG. 298. — Pauldron, Thomas Colt, 1475. Roydon, Essex.

FIG. 299.—Pauldron, William Yelverton, 1481. Rougham, Norfolk.

FIG. 300.—Pauldrons, &c., 1490. (Wallace Collection.)

in a high ridge on the left side of the neck; the pauldron is of fair dimensions, but strange to note does not cover the left gousset (Fig. 299). It is probable that the wearer bore a shield. The pauldron and its passe-garde or pike-guard is well shown upon a suit of Gothic armour in the Wallace Collection, dating from about 1490 (Fig. 300); here the great difference in the sizes of the two pauldrons is shown, the small one upon the right shoulder necessitating a palette in the form of a roundel being introduced to guard the gousset of the right arm.

The Coudières.—Until about 1450 the coudières were of normal sizes and proportions, but when the shield was discarded and the left side of the knight was strengthened, the left coudière became of supreme importance in the warding off of a blow, and hence underwent changes which in some cases can only be termed monstrous and extravagant. Probably the brass of Sir Robert Staunton, 1458, in Castle Donington Church, Leicestershire, furnishes the maximum example of immensity in coudières, though the peculiarity of having both of the same size and pattern should not be overlooked. Another and later brass, that of Thomas Playters, 1479, in Sollerley Church, shows a coudière of a peculiar shape and of great size, reproduced in Fig. 301. A secondary defence was introduced about the middle of the century to protect the inside bend of the left arm, called the

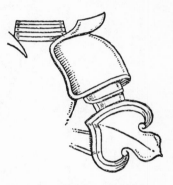

FIG. 301.—Coudière, &c., Thomas Playters, 1479.

garde-de-bras, well seen upon the brass of Sir John Peryent the younger, 1450, at Digswell, Herts (Fig. 302); in the accompanying Fig. 303 is shown an example of a left coudière from the Wallace Collection (No. 46), dating from about 1490.

The Taces, Tuilles, and Tuillettes.—The taces introduced into armour during the Surcoatless Period reached approximately to the mid-thigh of the wearer, and during that period short lames were attached in front at times, making the skirt of plate even longer. As the Tabard Period progressed, however, the taces showed a tendency to decrease in number, thereby shortening the skirt of plate and permitting more of the thigh to be uncovered. In order to remedy this, separate plates, rounded so as to encircle the limb to a certain extent, were affixed to the lowermost tace by straps in front

of each thigh, and as the taces contracted the "tuilles," as they were termed, grew longer and broader. An excellent example is that of Henry Parice in Hildersham Church, Cambridgeshire, 1465 (Fig. 304), who has tuilles, genouillières, and elbow-pieces of extravagant size; the tuilles are here shown suspended by straps to the lowermost of three taces. Incidentally the skirt of the gambeson is disclosed in this figure, and apparently the edge of some defence of mail worn under the taces. A precisely similar example occurs at Roydon, Essex, upon the brass of Robert Colt, 1475. Towards the end of the century the taces had so far contracted that they reached only to the hips, as shown in the brass of Sir Anthony de Grey, 1480, in St. Albans Abbey Church

FIG. 302.—The brass of (Fig. 326), but another mode was some-
Sir John Peryent the times adopted, as seen in the brass of Sir
younger.

Robert Harcourt at Stanton Harcourt, Oxfordshire (Fig. 305), where the tuille was not attached to the lowest tace but to a higher one, the intermediate space being filled up with short lames and mail. Other smaller plates were at times added to protect the outer part of the thighs, called "tuillettes." If the front tuilles are themselves composed of several plates, or jointed, then the term "tuillette" is also applied to them.

Leg Defences.—These did not undergo such decided transformations as the remaining portions of the armour, but a few innovations deserve attention. Until 1450 there was no decided change from the style prevailing in the Sur-coatless Period, with perhaps the exception that the reinforcing plate of the genouillière protecting the grevière had a tendency to lengthen, but was still cut off square. After the above date we find that it is generally

FIG. 303.—Garde-de-bras, *c.* 1490. (Wallace Collection.)

pointed in the lower part and laminated, while reinforcing plates begin to appear above the genouillière protecting the thigh and often overlapping each other. An unusual re-inforcement for the genouillière is shown in Fig. 306; it is of chain mail and occurs

FIG. 304.—Tuilles, &c., Henry Parice, 1465. Hildersham Church, Cambs.

upon a suit in the Wallace Collection dated 1470. The actual cap covering the knee did not undergo much change, except that it was often prominent and ridged, but one innovation, and a marked one, is exhibited upon a few brasses (in the Grey brass, St. Albans, for example), where the usual outer

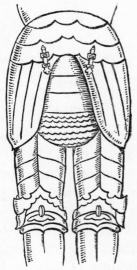

FIG. 305.—Sir Robert Harcourt, *c.* 1472. Stanton Harcourt, Oxon.

guard is prolonged round the back of the knee in order
to protect the gousset generally shown there.   A peculiar
variety of genouillière is delineated in Fig. 307, where a
spike is seen projecting from the guard, and a considerable
number of lames and reinforcements are shown.   It is
difficult to see the possible use of this spike, and one can
only suppose that it was so placed to annoy the horse of

  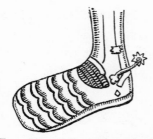

FIG. 306.—Rein-
forcement to
genouillière, c.
1470. (Wallace
Collection.)

FIG. 307.—Spiked
genouillière.
(Roy. MS. 18,
E. IV.)

FIG. 308.— Sabbaton of Piers
Gerard, 1492.   Winwick,
Lancs.

an antagonist when at close quarters.   It is from Roy.
MS. 18, E. IV.   The sollerets remain pointed, and were
often of extravagant length, but with less lames as a rule
than in the early part of the century; towards the end,
about 1490, they disappeared and became extinct, the
broad-toed "sabbatons" taking their place.   Those of
Piers Gerard, 1492, Winwick, Lancashire, are early examples of this fashion (Fig. 308).

Until about the year 1460 the sword was worn at
the left side suspended by a narrow band passing over
the right hip, as in the Surcoatless Period, but after the
above date it appears upon brasses and monumental effigies

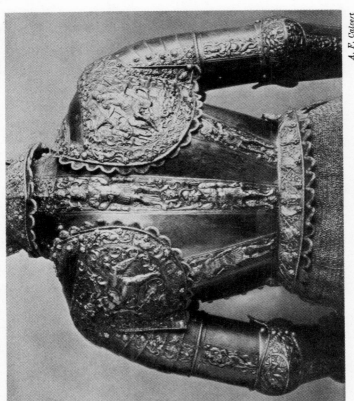

PLATE XX *

Armour of King Sebastian (Backplate)

in front of the body, with the point slightly inclined to
the left as a rule, but sometimes hanging perpendicularly.
It has a singularly short and ill-proportioned hilt, with a
much-swollen grip and a pommel pear-shaped or circular,
while the quillons are straight, with a slight droop at the
ends towards the blade. The lance-rest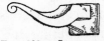
was added in the latter half of the cen-
tury, and is shown projecting from the
breastplate in many brasses. Upon some
existing suits of the period and later the
rest is capable of being folded up when not in use, and
kept in place in both positions by a spring. The lance-
rest shown in Fig. 309 dates from 1480, and has a strut
or support beneath it to aid in bearing the weight of the
lance.

FIG. 309. — Lance-rest, 1480. (Wallace Collection.)

Tilting Armour.—From the very earliest times since
man bore arms he has engaged in friendly contest with
others, not only as a means of recreation and engendering
mutual respect, but it was readily recognised that the
only way to obtain skill in deadly combat was to constantly
practise the art of war in the time of peace. It was also
natural and proper that these friendly combats should be
governed by rules and regulations whereby the minimum of
risk should be run, and so avoid the possibility of turning
a manly pastime from a source of enjoyment into a combat
of deadly earnestness. Although history records that the
latter result really occurred at times, it was the exception
that proved the rule, and tilting was part and parcel of a
knight's everyday life, and the glories of the tournament
the hoped-for goal. During the early part of the Middle
Ages single encounters, and also the mêlée, were fought

in the usual harness which the knight was in the habit
of wearing in battle, and no other precautions were taken
excepting the use of blunted spears and restricting the use
of the sword to the edge only.   As time advanced, however, and armour became heavier and more cumbersome,
the being hurled out of the saddle by a dexterous thrust
of an opponent's lance was a matter of moment, seriously
endangering life and limb, whereas it had formerly been
deemed comparatively trivial when the defences were of
mail or textile fabrics.   Hence as time progressed it became necessary to have special armour for the tilt, or to
add such extra defences to the fighting armour that the
increased weight promised security in the saddle, and the
multiplicity of plates between himself and the weapons
of his opponent practically guaranteed immunity from
harm.   This idea, once established, eventually led to the
result that a knight armed for the joust could not mount
to the saddle, but had prominent portions of this armour
fitted when mounted.   He became an apparently impreg-
nable tower of steel, immovably fixed in a huge saddle.
The student of armour must carefully discriminate between
these tilting suits and actual war harness; the former
were never used upon the field of battle, although at
times we know that certain of the tilt defences were
borrowed in order to reinforce the usual harness.   The
fifteenth century witnessed the inception and almost the
culmination of the idea, and a few of the tilting suits of
the latter part of that era are still extant.   Fig. 310 represents the upper portion of a suit of tilting armour from
the collection in the Museum in Vienna; it dates from
1480, and is eminently typical of the period.   The half-suit,

No. 21 (Fig. 418) in the Wallace Collection, is very similar to the suit illustrated. The great tilting heaume is composed of three plates of varying thickness, ranging from nearly half an inch in the principal portions of the front

FIG. 310.—German tilting armour, 1480, from the Collection in the Museum at Vienna.

to an eighth of an inch in the back. A comb, convex in section, runs down the centre of the crown, and radiating flutings are seen to ornament the back. The neck of the heaume is firmly fixed to the backplate, and three screws serve the same purpose in front for the breastplate. The occularium, formed by the aperture between the crown plate and the front, appears somewhat large when seen in this position, but remembering that the lance is held considerably lower than the heaume it is possible that an opening half an inch or even less would be presented to it.   It was quite possible to have comparative freedom of

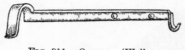

movement for the head inside the heaume, which was invariably furnished with a quilted lining.   The specimen in the Wallace   Collection   weighs

FIG. 311.—Queue.   (Wallace Collection.)

twenty pounds.   The breastplate is globular in form, and flattened upon the right side to allow of the queue (Fig. 311) being affixed; this singular addition consists of a bar of steel rectangular in section and screwed firmly

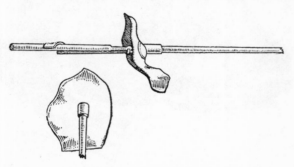

FIG. 312.—Queue, vamplate, and lance.
(Tower of London.)

into the breastplate, bearing at the rear extremity a turned down hook which resisted the upward pressure of the butt of the lance.   The front portion of the queue has another hook turned upwards, in which the lance rested, and behind which it was gripped by the hand. This hook was omitted when the lance-rest was separate and affixed to the right side of the breastplate, as seen

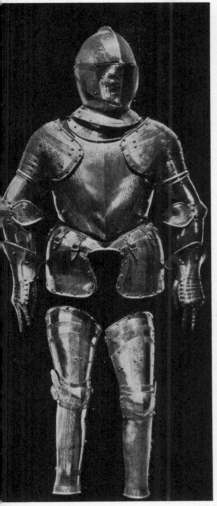

A. F. Calvert

War Armour, early Seventeenth Century,
Milanese make

Armour of Prince Philip II., German
make, 1549

in the figure, where it appears to be forged in one piece and secured by two screws. An excellent example demonstrating in a practical manner the use of the queue is exhibited in the Tower Collection, where the lance is seen in position, and a large vamplate of curious design is affixed for the protection of the hand and arm (see Fig. 312). In order to admit of the free passage of the lance the large palette protecting the right armpit is slightly hollowed at its lowest part ; the Wallace suit has a companion palette protecting the left arm. Upon the shoulders are pauldrons of two plates, decorated with radiating fluting, and upon these in the Wallace suit are two upright iron pins or projections to which were attached the flowing ends of the lambrequin, contoise, or mantling, depending from the crest. In the example from Vienna eyelets occur upon the pauldrons for the same purpose. The brassarts are laminated and overlap each other downwards. Upon the right arm appears the Polder mitten (a corruption of *épaule de mouton*, so named from its shape), an additional reinforcing piece which is screwed to the vambrace and protects a large portion of the arm. It has fine flutings radiating from the bend. No gauntlet is seen, the vamplate generally affording a sufficient protection for the hand. A similar reinforcement for the right arm is upon the Wallace suit, which differs only in a few details, whilst a very fine example of this reinforcement, but dating from a later period, is preserved in the Tower (No. 371, Case 25) (Fig. 313), which exhibits excellent workmanship. The elbow-joint of the left arm is protected by a *garde-de-bras* similar in form to that upon the right arm ; this is riveted to a manifere (or *main-de-fer*) of one plate protecting the bridle hand, and decorated with flutings radiating from the wrist. The protection for the left arm in the Wallace suit is represented in Fig. 314; it is a large and finely fluted piece secured to the vamplate by three screws. A small oak shield covered with leather and painted is secured by a guige passing through two holes in the left upper part of the breastplate; it is not

FIG. 313.—Polder mitten. (Tower of London.)

FIG. 314.—Garde-de-bras. (Wallace Collection.)

connected in any way with the arm, but simply hangs in position. This is the Stechtarsche. In Fig. 310, no armour is shown below the waist, but the Wallace suit is furnished with taces of four plates, to the lowest of which are fixed the tuilles; while the breastplate is reinforced by a placcate. Judging from the deep grooves and indentations upon the heaume and palettes this suit has been donned at times in the combat *à outrance*, when the war spear was employed, as the lance-head or coronal customarily used in the Joustes of Peace would not effect such damage. The Joustes in question were conducted upon the original methods, namely, in the open lists or field and without any obstruction between the combatants; the system of running with a barrier between the horses was termed the Italian course, and was not used generally in Europe until the sixteenth century. This Italian course is known as *Uber die Pallia* (over the barriers), or *Welsches Gestech,* in contradistinction to the open course or *Das Deutsche Stechen.* The Wallace suit, including the heaume, weighs 96 lbs., and bears the Augsburg guild mark. A few extra tilting pieces which came into vogue upon the Continent in this period will be dealt with in a subsequent chapter.

A fine suit of Gothic armour to which reference has been previously made is in the Wallace Collection (Fig. 288) which dates from 1470. The salade is of fine covering form and is fitted with a lifting visor; the mentonnière has one plate which falls if required. The breastplate is reinforced with a large placcate and has laminated goussets protected by fluted roundels. The taces are of three plates, to which the tuillettes (so called because they consist of more than one plate) are suspended. Espalier pauldrons of very fine workmanship protect the shoulders and upper arms; the coudières are peculiar to the period, while mitten gauntlets with long cuffs and demi-vambraces are also used. Demi-cuissarts of three plates have the genouillières fixed to them, while the jambarts are complete. The sollerets and a few other parts of the suit are restorations. The chain-mail reinforcements to the jambarts are of rare occurrence.

A suit of armour in the Tower of London deserves special mention by reason of its being the oldest *cap-à-pie* suit of plate in the collection. It is shown in Fig. 315, and probably dates from the middle of the fifteenth century, having practically no decorations of any importance. It is furnished with a visorless salade having a long tailpiece, and a gorget with a roped border which is probably of a later date. The epaulières consist of five laminated plates; the coudières are small, while demi-brassarts and complete vambraces cover the upper and lower arms respectively. The gauntlets are of overlapping plates with large cuffs.

FIG. 315.—Gothic armour from the Tower of London

The breastplate has two demi-placcates reinforcing it, and the backplate is of three pieces. The taces are three in number, to which tuilles of one plate are affixed. Demi-cuissarts, plain small genouillières with fan-shaped guards, and grevières of complete plate (probably recent) protect the lower limbs. There are no sollerets. The figure is equipped with a pole-axe of an original pattern, the shaft being partially sheathed in iron. Another suit, No. 26, probably dates from the last years of the fifteenth century, as it is furnished with a chain-mail skirt. The breastplate has a demi-placcate strengthening it; the gauntlets are very elaborate with fine gadlyngs and cuffs (probably the cuffs only are original); the cuissarts have four lames upon the upper parts, while the sollerets are of beautiful construction but recent workmanship. The

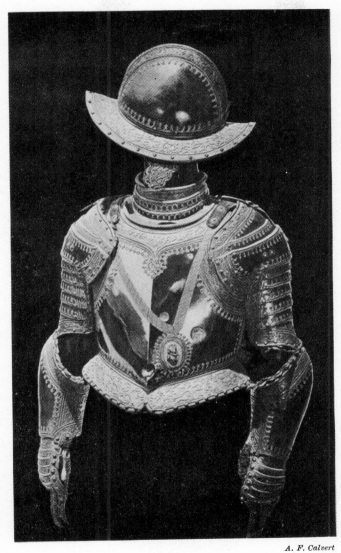

A. F. Calvert

PLATE XXII *
Half-suit, Pamplona Armour, Philip III.

backplate is of two plates, and a garde-de-rein is affixed below. The suit has been much restored.

The finest example of complete war harness for man and horse to be seen in London, and probably in England, of the very early period of 1460 is that which occupies such a prominent position in the Wallace Collection (Fig. 316). It was formerly in the famous collection of the Count de Nieuwerkerke, who purchased it from M. E. Juste, of Paris, for £1200, but probably if it came under the hammer now it would bring in four to six times that sum. As one might expect, it has had to be made up in a few parts to its present complete condition, but nothing whatever has been done to the armour for the lower limbs, which is original and well preserved. This is the more to be wondered at inasmuch as those are the parts more liable to suffer injury and need replacement than any others. The salade is of fine form and furnished with a visor, the occularium being formed between the upper part of the visor and the lower edge of the crown-piece. The mentonnière is attached by a screw to the breastplate, and is in two parts, the upper one falling if required, similar to the buffe of a later period, while a demi-placcate is affixed by an almayne rivet to reinforce the breastplate. The backplate is in five plates, all riveted in such a manner as to afford the maximum of movement for the back. A garde-de-rein of four plates is affixed below. The left coudière is of a graceful form and large proportions; the right differs in pattern, and has a garde-de-bras riveted to the vambrace protecting the inner bend of the arm. The cuissarts, composed of a number of plates, are of a most ingenious design, whereby tuilles are rendered superfluous. But perhaps the chief point of interest is centred in the sollerets, which have extreme lengths of pointed toe-caps; to these are attached the spurs, the necks of which are ten inches in length. At a period when it was necessary to cut the straps of sollerets when fighting on foot, and so remove the projecting point as to enable the knight to walk, it is curious to find in this suit that no provision is made for such a contingency, and that the long, pointed toe is riveted on. The genouillières are of latten, and below them deep pointed plates extend, to which are affixed the grevières, which fasten by spring catches on the inside. The whole of the armour is of a most graceful form, and the eye, accustomed to mediæval representations of contemporary equipment, dwells with delight upon this beautiful example of art from the Middle Ages. The use of latten as a means of adornment for the edges of various plates gives a rich contrast to the dull grey of the steel. Another fine suit of *cap-à-pie* armour dating from the fifteenth century, in the Wallace Collection, is No. 46, which may be of German origin, and dates from about 1490. The head is protected by an armet of very fine proportions, opening down the centre of the chin-piece, and having a bavière and visor in a single plate. The breastplate is very globose, and is an example of the mediæval fashion of engraving mottoes, texts, invocations to the saints, &c., upon armour, as it bears a prominent inscription. It is furnished with sabbatons, and partakes in many characteristics of the nature of armour of the succeeding century.

The second half of the fifteenth century saw armour not only in its highest development, but also of the most beautiful form, for nothing can exceed the graceful lines and excellence of workmanship characterising the Gothic

FIG. 316.—Equestrian figure. (Wallace Collection.)

style, as it is usually called. It was made to fit the human form and to adapt itself to the movements of the wearer. One of the most valuable relics we possess, illustrating its features, is the absolutely unique effigy of Richard Beauchamp, Earl of Warwick, in the Beauchamp Chapel, St. Mary's Church, Warwick, *temp.* 1454 (the earl died in 1439). It is of latten, gilded, and in perfect preservation : every feature, turn, and curve of the original copy is faithfully reproduced not only upon the front part or upper surface, but also upon the back ; it was turned over some time since in order to be copied, and was found to be as carefully and accurately finished there as in the parts usually visible. Every detail is represented except the mentonnière, which is usually absent in effigies, though the catch for its attachment is shown. The points calling for special notice are the passe-guards or pike-guards upon the pauldrons which constitute a very early example of this adjunct, and also the presence of two large tuilles and two smaller tuillettes. The coudières are large and of the beautiful butterfly pattern, covering the inner bend of the arm ; they are both equal in size and of the same pattern. Although the work was executed by an Englishman, William Austin, the armour is undoubtedly of Milanese manufacture, and may be ascribed to the Missaglias. An early example, foreshadowing the changes which occurred in defensive armour in the second half of the fifteenth century, is that of Thomas de St. Quintin, 1445, in Harpham Church, Yorkshire (Fig. 317). The figure is represented in pointed bascinet and mentonnière, beneath which the laminated epaulières are partly visible. These are almost covered by two palettes of

FIG. 317.—Thomas de St. Quintin, 1445. Harpham Church, Yorks.

singularly large size, that upon the left being the greater; the reinforcement to the breastplate appears below. Upon the right coudière is an additional plate termed the garde-de-bras, and another of larger proportions and different form covers the left. The breastplate is of the short form, and necessitates the addition of six taces, to which are appended the tuilles. The figure shows the sword and misericorde being worn as in the Surcoatless Period. The effigy of Sir Richard Vernon, 1452, at Tong Church, Shropshire, is an excellent example of mediæval Gothic armour, and as portrayed in "Shaw's Dresses and Decorations" is simply magnificent. Our frontispiece is adapted from the illustration.

FIG. 318.—Walter Green, 1450. Hayes, Middlesex.

The orle surrounding the bascinet is gorgeous with chased work and pearls; the head rests upon a ponderous heaume, shaped for the shoulders, and bearing crest and mantling. The mentonnière is here in place: the breastplate is reinforced by a demiplaccate, and there are eight lames of taces with short tuilles. The genouillières have only a lower reinforcement, and the sollerets are comparatively short. A very late example of the hip-belt is shown, from which the misericorde is suspended, the sword-

FIG. 319.—John Gaynesford, 1460. Crowhurst Church, Surrey.

belt being quite distinct. The pauldrons are dissimilar, the right being the smaller and hollowed for the lance; while the upper parts of both are fluted. The coudières are distinctly beautiful, with radiating flutings upon the butterfly shape, which is folded inwards over the goussets.

Of the same date as the Beauchamp effigy is the well-known brass of John Daundelyon at Margate, 1455, whose breastplate is of the short character, as shown in the effigy; the bascinet is very pointed at the apex, and the mentonnière appears of singularly graceful form. The palettes are large and dissimilar, the left covering a considerable portion of the breastplate; upon the left arm is a circular garde-de-bras attached to the coudière, while an extremely large coudière is shown upon the left arm which may be regarded as a second garde-de-bras: the gauntlets are characterised by long pointed cuffs. Walter Green, 1450, whose brass occurs at Hayes, Middlesex, is represented without any bascinet, but with the head resting on a visored tilting helm (Fig. 318). The epaulières consist of a number of lames which extend upwards to the neck, where they are confined by a band, and over these are two symmetrical pauldrons of plain pattern. His armour bears a remarkable resemblance to that of John Gaynesford, 1460, in Crowhurst Church, Surrey, even to the plain gauntlets of four plates covering the hands. In both examples the taces are numerous and worked into broad escallops, tuilles being omitted (Fig. 319). An early example of the garde-de-bras is that represented upon the memorial effigy of Sir John Verney, Albury, 1452, where a small garde is attached to the coudière of the right arm and an enlarged one of peculiar shape to the left (Fig. 320).

Upon the same effigy also occurs a complicated genouillière, which, fitting closely to the knee, is provided with

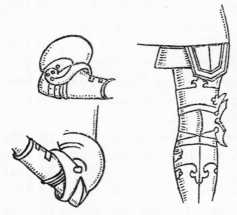

two reinforcements
above and below, the
extreme plates being
worked into highly
ornamental forms (Fig.
321). A coudière of
large size and graceful
form is shown upon the
brass of Henry Parice,
1464, at Hildersham,
Cambridge, where arm-
ing points are seen
attaching it to the bras-
sart and vambrace: it

FIG. 320.—Right and left   FIG. 321.—Genouillière,
coudière, Sir John Ver-   &c., Sir John Verney,
ney, Albury, c. 1452.   Albury Church, c. 1452.

is serrated in the upper extension, and the same decoration is repeated upon the pike-guard of the pauldron. In
this figure the lance-rest is shown affixed
to the breastplate (Fig. 322). Upon the
same brass there is an example of extravagant tuilles attached to the lowest of three
taces by straps, while the rare occurrence
of the skirt of the haqueton with the
edge of a defence of mail (possibly a hauberk) is shown, another instance being that
at Roydon, Essex, upon the brass of Robert
Colt, 1475. Sir Robert Staunton's brass,

FIG. 322.—Coudière,
&c., Henry Parice,
1464. Hildersham,
Cambs.

1458, in Castle Donington Church, Leicestershire (Fig. 323),
affords us the best example of extravagant coudières, and
is also remarkable for showing the salade, which is of ex-

treme rarity upon brasses
and effigies. The latter is
represented very wide in
form, with a falling visor
having the occularium in
it, and guided by a pro-
longation which apparently
runs backwards and for-
wards upon a hidden comb.
The gorget is of plate, over
which the laminated epau-
lières are shown, apparently
meeting over the chest:
other details of the arms
are hidden by the enormous
coudières, which, strange to
say, are of similar size and
form. They are cusped and
fluted in the upper parts.
Upon viewing these arm
defences the reason may
readily be perceived why
the knights deemed the
shield superfluous. A demi-
placcate is added to the
breastplate. The armour
shown upon the brass of Sir
Robert del Bothe, 1460, in
Wilmslow Church, Cheshire
(Fig. 324), is characterised

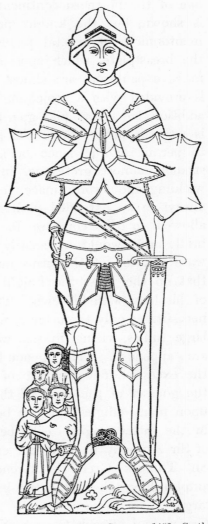

FIG. 323.—Sir Robert Staunton, 1458. Castle
Donington Church, Leicestershire.

by excessive singularity of contour, suggesting an origin in one of the northern continental countries. No headpiece is shown, but the knight probably wore the salade: a mentonnière of several plates covers the upper part of the breastplate, which apparently is not reinforced. The massive pauldrons are almost similar in outline, and each is provided with a projecting ridge upon the shoulder in addition to a low pike-guard. The chain mail gousset is very apparent where the pauldron has been cut away to permit of the lance being held. The coudières are strange, almost grotesque, in form. The right arm in wielding the sword, mace, and lance, would be almost always in an extended position, hence the small latitude allowed in the coudière for bending it: the left, or bridle arm, would necessarily be bent more. The awkward position of the arms may be explained by stating that on the brass the knight is holding the right hand of his lady with his own. The long form of breastplate necessitates only three taces, which are escalloped, and two large tuilles, vieing in size with those of Henry Parice, are appended. The genouillières are remarkable for the excessive development of the guard-plate protecting the gousset at the back of the knees; this guard is seen upon many effigies but few brasses, and where it occurs in the latter might easily be overlooked—see the brass of Sir Anthony de Grey for example. Upon the brass of Sir Thomas Grene in Grene's Norton Church, Northamptonshire (Fig. 325), the knee-guards are, if anything, larger than those upon the Bothe brass, while Henry Green, in Luffwick Church, Northamptonshire, 1467, who wears a tabard, has similar guards. Sir Robert del Bothe is among the first, or is the first, to exemplify the wear-

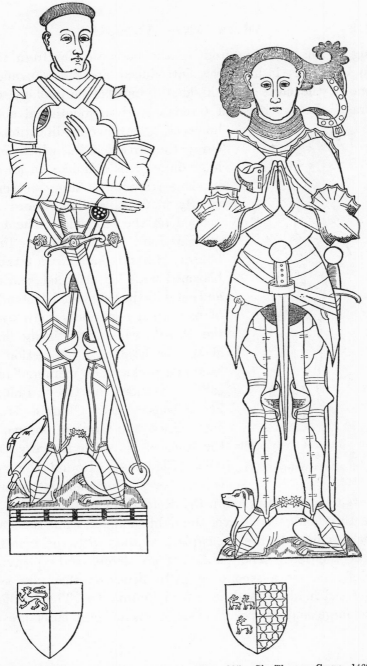

FIG. 324.—Sir Robert del Bothe, 1460.
Wilmslow Church, Cheshire.

FIG. 325.—Sir Thomas Grene, 1462.
Grene's Norton Church, Northants.

ing of the sword in front of the body sloping from right to left: this fashion was introduced about 1460, and is one of the clues used in identifying the chronology of a brass. In the brass at Grene's Norton, mentioned above,

however, a curious modification occurs; the misericorde, which is of huge dimensions and like an anelace in some respects, is slung perpendicularly in front, and the sword suspended on the left side. The brass of Sir John Say, 1473, at Broxbourne, Herts, is habited in a tabard blazoned with his armorial bearings, and exhibits the hausse-col or standard of mail then commonly worn round the throat when the tilting helm alone was used as a protection for head and neck. The memorial brass to Sir Anthony de Grey, 1480, in St. Albans Abbey Church, Herts, exemplifies the armour known as the Richard III. style in every particular (Fig. 326). Round the neck is a hausse-col or standard; the head

FIG. 326.—The brass of Sir Anthony de Grey, 1480, in St. Albans Abbey Church, Herts.

rests upon a tilting helm, the occularium and projection beneath it being visible over the right shoulder, while the staple for affixing it to the breastplate appears with the mantling over the left. The pauldrons are large, and apparently reinforced by a secondary plate beneath; they are symmetrical in shape and have no pike-guards. The coudières are large and of peculiar shape while long cuffs are appended to the shell-gauntlets. This form of pauldron was fairly prevalent at the time, and also during the early part of the next century. Two demi-placcates appear upon the breastplate: the taces are only three in number, and short tuilles appear in front with tuillettes covering the hips: the genouillières appear with reinforcements extending well up the thigh and a guard-plate passes behind the goussets. The sword is slung in the prevailing mode, but the misericorde is in an almost horizontal position at the back. Similar armour in its broad outlines is used upon the figures in the Warwick Roll of John Rouse, written and illustrated in the reign of Richard III., of which we give examples. Richard Neville, Earl of Salisbury, is represented in a salade with an unusual knob upon the summit (Fig. 327); the short taces and dependent tuilles are here exemplified, as are also the shell gauntlets. The shield with its bouche at the corner is concave to the front, and the sword is shown with a disproportionately short grip and much swollen, similar to that in the De Grey brass. The figure of King Richard III. (Fig. 328) habited in a tabard also occurs in the Roll; the coudières are peculiarly spiked, but otherwise the armour has the usual Yorkist characteristics.

Among the most interesting pieces of armour in the British Isles we must include the Rhodes armour preserved in the Rotunda at Woolwich. The Knights of St. John of Jerusalem occupied Rhodes after their expulsion from the Holy Land, and subsequently migrated to Malta. In the early part of Queen Victoria's reign General Sir J. H. Lefroy was sent by the British Government to Turkey, and while there secured the Dardanelles cannon described

elsewhere, and also the Rhodes armour, left behind by the
Knights. This is one of the most valuable of late "finds,"
and the whole of it is in the Rotunda. Much is in bad
condition and would not bear cleaning, but one suit has been

Fig. 327.—Richard Neville, Earl of
Salisbury, from Warwick Roll.

Fig. 328.—Richard III., from
Warwick Roll.

made up and is illustrated in Plate IX., p. 72. The salade
is of a very deep form with a large visor; there is a lobster-
tail neck-guard of two lames. The mentonnière is more
of the nature of a gorget, and is not affixed to the breastplate. The pauldrons are laminated and continuous with
the brassarts, which have turners, while the coudières are
of the sixteenth century. The vambraces are late fifteenth

century, as are also the gauntlets. The breastplate is globose and furnished with a placcate, while the backplate has been provided with a garde-de-rein from the Tower. The cuissarts and genouillières are late fifteenth century, but the jambarts are of a still later date. In order to complete the figure a chain-mail hauberk has been lent from the Tower, and the tuilles and sollerets have been made. The two-handed sword is a fine example, dating from c. 1510. The whole suit may be looked upon as an example of the style prevailing c. 1490.

The period under discussion, from 1430 to 1500, saw the common foot soldier, whether bowman, arbalestier, billman, petardier, or cannonier, much better equipped, and in every way more carefully provided for, than in any preceding age. It had early been perceived in England that the native infantry was as effective in battle as the flower of foreign chivalry, and instead of being jealous of this fact, as were the foreign nobles as a rule of their own foot soldiers, the knights of our own country sought by every possible means to add to the deadly prowess of the soldier, and to defend him by every artifice that wit could devise. It came to be recognised as an article of military knowledge that a charge of cavalry against English archers armed with the long-bow resulted, under ordinary conditions, in disaster, and that no good result was to be obtained by it, but on the contrary it was simply to court destruction. The lessons of Crecy and of Poictiers had been well learnt, and it was remembered that the French chivalry, although encased in steel and the horses defended by bardings, simply melted away before the deadly sleet of arrows emanating from the English position, and in

spite of their most strenuous efforts only managed to reach
the archers in such a disorganised form that an effective charge was out of the question. So long as the bowmen stood firmly in their position and preserved order and
discipline they had nothing to fear
from the most determined charge of
cavalry. The secret of this undoubtedly was that although the
knight himself was impervious to
the arrow so long as it did not
strike a gousset or the junction or
joint between two plates, his horse
was by no means equally well protected, and it is well known that
the arrow was in most cases directed
towards the unfortunate steed in pre-
ference to the invulnerable rider. It
thus became a custom for the knights
and heavily-accoutred men-at-arms
to dismount and advance on foot to
the charge, in imitation doubtless of
the example set by the Black Prince
at Poictiers. But the slow progress
of such a mass of heavily-armed men against a body of
archers gave the latter plenty of time to select their opponents, and with unerring aim to challenge the weak points of
their adversaries' defences with the deadly cloth-yard shaft.
The invariable result was that the archer came off victorious,
and the discomfited mail-clad knight thus found himself
unable to reach the enemy with whom he desired to close
either on horseback or on foot. In this dilemma the

FIG. 329.—Bowman, 1473.

invention of the pavise came to his help, and for a time the archer was to a certain extent nonplussed. This was at first an upright wickerwork defence, square in form and plane of surface, sufficiently large to cover the knight and also the page or squire who bore it. The knight also carried his own shield as an additional defence, and thus effectually protected from arrows could advance to close quarters, or if necessary, take post behind his own archers in order to repel a charge of cavalry. The pavise, once introduced, was quickly improved upon, and soon de-

Fig. 330.—Arbalestier, *temp.* Edward IV. (Harl. MS., 4379.)

veloped into a convex shield of wood faced with leather or other protective material, and resting upon the ground.

Some of these were elaborately decorated, being painted with designs of more or less merit, some of which have been preserved to the present age and form remarkable instances of mediæval art. In the Wallace Collection is a pavise of parchment upon a foundation of wood, with a semicircular ridge down the centre, upon which occurs a representation of a castle and background. It is of German origin, and dates from about 1490; another in the same museum of about the year 1500

Fig. 331.—Arbalestier, early fifteenth century.

has a similar ridge down the centre, is of the same materials, and is painted black. The arms of Nuremberg in colours are upon the left-hand top corner. The examples are only sufficiently large to cover one man, and might therefore have been used by archers, arbalestiers, cannoniers, &c., for these were alert to seize upon the new defence, and quickly adopted it.

FIG. 332.—Chapelle-de-fer, *c.* 1490. (Tower of London.)

FIG. 333. — Chapelle-de-fer, *temp.* Edward IV. (Roy. MS. 14, E. IV.)

During the siege of a town or fortress the pavise was in constant use, and in MSS. of the fifteenth and sixteenth centuries it is common to note in the illuminations how they are employed to cover every type of combatant. In Cotton MS., Julius, E. IV., many examples are delineated, bodies of pavisiers being shown in combat with each other. Fig. 329 is a representation of a mediæval long bowman of the year 1473, in which he is shown with a hat and gorget of banded mail and a hauberk of overlapping scales of leather covered by a brigandine of leather. The only plate defence is a corselet. The quiver is slung at the back and a sword in front. The arbalestier

FIG. 334.—Archers' salades, *temp.* Edward IV. (Roy. MS. 14, E. IV.)

shown in Plate XL., p. 366, is habited in a very graceful salade, a brigandine of the fifteenth century partly covered by demi-breast and backplates, or placcates, and wears a knee-piece upon the left leg. The arbalestier of

the time of Edward IV. is represented in the Harleian
MS. No. 4379 (Fig. 330) as possessing a complete defen-

FIG. 335.—Salades, *temp.* Henry VI.

sive equipment, consisting of bascinet, camail, brigandine
of jazeraint work, tuilles of leather plates, and complete
plate for the legs. In addition he has a
corselet of plate. The peculiarly-shaped
quiver for the bolts is characteristic of
the period. That arbalestiers were as an
established rule better provided with defences we have already seen: a further
confirmation is afforded by the accompanying Fig. 331 of an arbalestier of
the earlier part of the fifteenth century,
before the dagged houppelande of Richard
II. and Henry IV.'s reign had gone out
of fashion: he is represented as being
clothed in it, whereby the defences of
the body and arms are hidden, but the
legs are in plate, with sollerets for the
feet, and a chapelle-de-fer, or plain skull-

FIG. 336.—(No.6984 Bib-
liothèque Nationale,
Paris.) Late fifteenth
century leather and
plate defences.

cap, covers the head. It is taken from Sloane MS.
2433. The chapelle-de-fer was a common headpiece
for the soldier of the fifteenth century; an example

dating from *c.* 1490 is preserved in the Tower (Fig. 332) which shows a point in front, and numerous holes round the brim for a padded lining. Another representation is from Roy. MS. 14, E. IV. (Fig. 333), which is simply a pot-de-fer with the addition of a turned-down

brim. The soldier also wears a coif-de-mailles. It must not be supposed that salades were entirely confined to the knightly orders; they are seen upon horse and foot soldiers of all grades; three are delineated here which are very common, and are represented freely in MSS. (Fig. 334), while others of different forms appear in this chapter (Fig. 335). In MS. No. 6984 of

FIG. 337.—Petardier and swordsman, fifteenth century. (Roy. MS. 18, E. V.)

the Bibliothèque Nationale, Paris, a work of the late fifteenth century, a reputed knight is shown opening a door. He is copied in Fig. 336, and is undoubtedly a leader of arquebusiers, pikemen, or arbalestiers, and not of the knightly order. The extra protection of a roundel at the side of the salade was very common upon the Continent, while leather is used for taces as in Fig. 330. The limbs are in plate, and a corselet is shown. The tabs at the neck, shoulders, and knees are of frequent occurrence in illuminations.

The petardier of the fifteenth century, who hurled small bombs, or else pots filled with Greek fire, into the ranks of the enemy, was also clothed in plate, sometimes from head to heel. He was considered of great importance, and consequently rendered as impervious as possible to the weapons with which he might be assailed. The thrower of the fire-pot represented in Fig. 337 (from Roy. MS. 18, E. V.) is protected thus, even to roundels covering the goussets, unless these are mammelières, which are of very frequent appearance. Opposing him is a foot soldier wielding a bastard sword and protecting himself with a small buckler; he wears a visored salade with

FIG. 338.—Hand-gun man, c. 1473.
(Roy. MS. 18, E. 5.)

camail and a gorget, a close-fitting brigandine over a hauberk of mail, and his arms are protected by plate. As is the case in the majority of representations of soldiers of this period, the legs are entirely undefended. From the same MS., which dates from 1473, we reproduce an interesting figure (No. 338) of a hand-gun man discharging one of the crude pieces of that period, whose picturesque appearance it would be difficult to excel. The salade is especially enriched with an enlargement of the customary roundels, while two demi-placcates reinforce his breastplate, which is probably of leather. Only genouillières appear upon his legs, a system of defence which was much in vogue at that time. A hand-gun man of 1470 is depicted in Fig. 339. Among the mercenaries introduced into England during the Wars of the Roses were "Burgundenses" or Burgundian handgun men. Warwick had a body of these at the second battle of St. Albans in 1461, and in Fig. 340 we have in all probability

FIG. 339.—Hand-gun man, 1470.   FIG. 340.—Hand-gun man, c. 1470.

a representation of their accoutrement. Upon the body the defences are a padded jacque, similar in nature of material to the gambeson, combined with chain mail and pourpointerie. The visor upon the salade is apparently fixed, while the legs are encased in mail chausses covered with demi-cuissarts and jambarts. The cannonier of the period was usually without any defensive equipment whatever. A small illustration is appended from the Sloane MS. No.

2433 of the fifteenth century, from which it will be perceived that he is dressed in ordinary civilian garments (Fig. 341). It was probably deemed unnecessary to clothe him in armour by reason of the distance which separated him from the contest.

Javelin men are represented in many MSS. of this

FIG. 341.—Cannonier, fifteenth century.
(Sloane MS. 2433.)

FIG. 342.—Javelin man, 1480.
(Harl. MS. 4374.)

period, but invariably in those of a foreign origin. The soldier delineated in Fig. 342 is taken from Harl. MS. 4374, and is remarkable for the cap-à-pie defences he wears. The size and shape of the shield is also worthy of notice.

Two brigandines as used in the fourteenth and fifteenth centuries are preserved in the Tower of London; details of their structure are given in Figs. 343 and 344, both being drawn the exact size of the originals. In Fig. 343, A is a square sheet of thin iron, rounded at the corners and with a hole in the centre. In B it is placed between two coverings of canvas and fastened by strings, three of which pass through the centre; the loose ends are continued to pass over and through four more plates which surround B and practically touch it on all sides. This is a common and inexpensive form of jazeraint.

Fig. 344 is more complicated. A represents a small plate of iron,

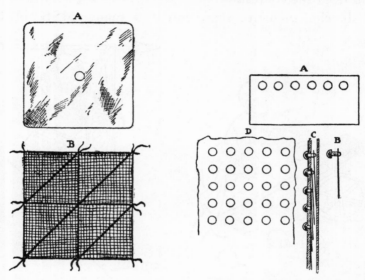

FIG. 343.—Details of brigandines, fourteenth and fifteenth centuries. (Tower of London.)

FIG. 344.—Details of studded Brigandine, fourteenth and fifteenth centuries. (Tower of London.)

thinner than that used in the preceding example. The heads of six studs, which are screwed or otherwise fastened into the plate, are shown side by side. In B the plate is shown edgewise and one of the studs also. C represents this plate and four others placed between two layers of canvas, cloth, or other material with the stud heads perforating one of the layers and the plates overlapping like slates upon a roof. D represents the appearance of the face of the brigandine when finished. It will readily be perceived that such a garment would be very pliable, and yet offer considerable resistance to an arrow, or bolt, or a sword-cut.

CHAPTER XIII

THE TRANSITION PERIOD, 1500-1525

THE salient features of the Transition Period are : —

    1. The adoption of sabbatons in the place of sollerets.
    2. The chain mail skirt.
    3. The general use of a closed helmet.

The Helmet.—This defence was invariably of the "closed" pattern, and consisted of a crown with a ridge,

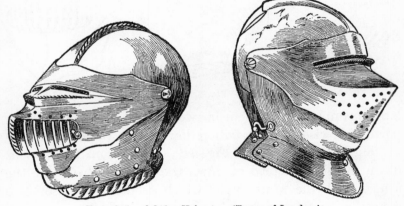

FIGS. 345 and 346.—Helmets. (Tower of London.)

generally roped, down the centre ; two cheek-pieces meeting together at the chin and fastening there ; the visor and bavière formed of one piece, pierced with oblong apertures for the occularium, and having small holes for ventilation and breathing purposes. The bavière was a relict of the mentonnière of a previous period, and the close helmet may be

265

regarded as a direct evolution from the armet; indeed it is at times difficult to differentiate between the two. The roundel at the back of the neck in the armet gave way to a plate-guard. The neck portion of the close helmet was furnished with a hollow rim, generally decorated with roping, which fitted over a corresponding solid rim upon the upper portion of the gorget and permitted the head to be rotated from side to side. The visor and bavière in the early helmets were in one piece, and very often of the bellows pattern, but

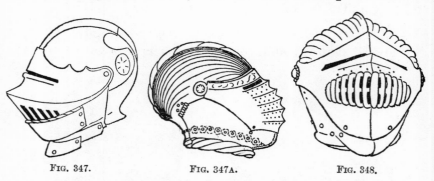

FIG. 347.   FIG. 347A.   FIG. 348.

later examples show them in two distinct pieces, the upper portion, or visor proper, falling down inside the bavière.

The helmet shown in Fig. 347, dating from 1500, opens down the sides instead of down the chin and back like the armet, and the same pivot which secures the visor also serves as a hinge for the crown and chin-piece. In Fig. 347A we have illustrated a German fluted helmet, partly engraved and gilded and of good form and workmanship. It opens down the chin. The skill shown in the forging of the crown and the fluting of the twisted comb is remarkable, and each rivet of the lining strap of the cheek-pieces forms the centre of an engraved rose. It is provided with a roped rim to fit over a solid rim on the gorget. Fig. 348 is the front view of a helmet dating from 1520 which differs chiefly from the last helmet in the form of the visor, while the example shown in Fig. 348A is of Italian origin and of the same period. It is small and of an extremely graceful form. Figs. 345, 346, are contemporary helmets from the Tower of London.

FIG. 348A.

The Gorget of the period consisted of laminated plates riveted at the sides of the neck and working freely upon each other, but covering from below upwards. These gorgets were an essential feature of the following, or Maximilian, period. It often spread over the chest and extended down the back as well; it was furnished with sliding rivets to allow of the maximum of freedom. At times this gorget was fixed to and formed part of the

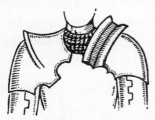

FIG. 349.—Standard of mail, William Bardwell, 1508. West Herling Church, Norfolk.

close helmet. Towards the latter part of the period the standard or collar of mail appears to have been worn very frequently to protect the neck; in these cases one or more lames forming a gorget were added to the lower part of the helmet to fit over and reinforce the standard. An example is shown in Fig. 349.

The Breastplate was globose, and as a rule furnished with one or more articulated lames (or taces) at the lower part, which permitted freedom of motion for the body at the waist. Fig. 350 represents a breastplate in the Tower which has one lame. Goussets of plate are invariably found at the junction of the arms with the body; these

were also made to slide freely upon their rivets.   At the
top a projecting collar protected the part where the
gorget was covered by the breast-
plate, and this feature is exemplified
in Figs. 350 and 351, the latter also
being an example from the Tower
of London though a little later in
date.   The apertures pierced in it
were made for the attachment of
various tilting pieces.   The ornamentation shown in Fig. 350 consists of mere sunken indentations,
and suggests flutings.

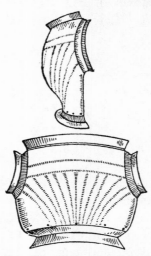

FIG. 350.—Globose breastplate,
1510. (Tower of London.)

The Pauldrons.—These became
much modified from the huge examples characteristic of the latter
part of the Tabard Period, losing
their angular appearance and be-
coming more rounded and at the same time mobile.
This was effected by making the whole pauldron of lames
of steel, generally overlapping up-
wards ; the upper lame was as a
rule moulded into a strong pike-
guard, sometimes upon the left
shoulder only, but generally upon
both.   The lames were carried
well round to the back and front
over the goussets, and were attached to the back- and breast-
plates.   If the right gousset is exposed a roundel is generally
affixed to the pauldron.   That the plate pauldrons of an

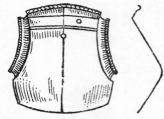

FIG. 351.—Breastplate.   (Tower
of London.)

PLATE XXIII *

Flemish Armour, 1624

earlier date were not, however, entirely superseded is shown by the monumental brass of W. Bardwell, 1508, in West Herling Church, Norfolk, where a massive pauldron furnished with two pike-guards is shown upon the left shoulder, and a dissimilar one of still larger proportions, and provided with one guard, upon the other (Fig. 349).

The Brassarts, Vambraces, Coudières, and Gauntlets all partake more or less of the laminated character, but the coudières are remarkably small when compared with those of the later Tabard Period, and furnished with large expanding guards for the inside bend of the arm.

The Cuissarts, Genouillières, and Grevières are of plate, with rounded caps for the genouillières and a few lames for reinforcements.

The Sabbatons.—These broad-toed sollerets were introduced during the later part of the previous period, those of Piers Gerard (date 1492) being illustrated on p. 232. They present many varieties of form, but are not distinguished for extraordinary size, as they were during the Maximilian period.

The Skirt of Mail was a marked feature of the period, and one by which it may generally be recognised. At times it almost reached to the knees, but as a general rule it terminated a short distance below the middle of the thigh. It was of fine mail, and in all probability only a skirt fastening round or below the waist. Occasionally it is slit up a short distance back and front, in order to give facilities for riding. The mail skirt had been growing in favour for some time: Lord Audley, 1491, upon his brass in Sheen Church, Surrey, exhibits it, and Edward Stafford,

Earl of Wiltshire, 1499, in Luffwick Church, Northants, has a similar skirt, namely to mid-thigh. Perhaps the earliest example is that of John, Lord L'Estrange, 1478, at Hillingdon, Middlesex, who has a mail skirt to the knees, one tuille in front and one on either side; sabbatons; a pike-guard upon the pauldron, and guards round the back of the knees: but all are very plain, similar to the Stanley brass.

The tuilles lying upon this skirt were generally of large proportions and suspended from the bottom tace; they did not reach, however, so low as the hem of the skirt. Wm. Bardwell's brass exhibits no tuilles whatever over the skirt of mail, and Richard Gyll, 1511, sergeant of the bakehouse under Henry VII., shows upon his brass in Shottisbrooke Church, Hants, two almost ludicrously small tuilles, affixed to the lowest of four narrow taces. John Colt, 1521, of Roydon Church, Essex, has extremely small tuilles over his deep skirt of mail similar to the Gyll brass; he is habited in a tabard.

From the foregoing it will readily be gleaned that very important alterations occurred in armour of this period, differentiating it from that of the preceding. The great pauldrons, exaggerated coudières, and general angularity, and, one might almost say prickliness, of the later Tabard Period was modified to a smoother and rounder style, while it lost entirely that remarkable beauty of form which, however much distorted by fanciful additions, characterised the Gothic armour as a whole. The beautiful flutings and ornamental curves disappeared to make way for a heavy, cumbersome style indicative of German stolidity, and in direct antagonism to the mobile quickness and agility suggested by the majority of suits dating from the latter half of the previous century. These characteristics may be readily seen in the brass to Sir Humphrey Stanley

FIG. 352.—Sir Humphrey Stanley, 1505. Westminster Abbey.

FIG. 353.—Knight, c. 1510.

in Westminster Abbey, Fig. 352; and also that to a knight, *c.* 1510, shown in Fig. 353.

That this excessive plainness was not always carried out, however, may be gleaned from a few effigies which display an almost lavish ornamentation. The genouillière

of Sir Roger le Strange, 1506, Hunstanton, is given here
(Fig. 354) as an example, where the spike and fluted
reinforcements are a special feature, and also the right
genouillière of Sir John Cheney, 1509, in Salisbury
Cathedral, where the cusped reinforcements are noteworthy (Fig. 355).

Towards the end of the period, however, we find that
although the salient points of this Transition Period in

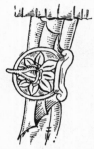

armour were retained, the
taste for ornamentation led
many knights to discard
the extreme plainness of the
mode, and to adapt a style
of decoration which in many
cases approached the graceful. Effigies of the years
1515 to 1520 show flutings
upon the breastplate, taces,
and tuilles; rosettes or other
ornaments upon the splays

Fig. 354.—Genouil-
lière and rein-
forcements, Sir
Roger le Strange,
1506, Hunstanton.

Fig. 355.—Genouil-
lière, Sir John
Cheney, c. 1509.
Salisbury Cathe-
dral.

of the genouillières and coudières, with fluted pauldrons
of artistic shape spreading over the backplate and breastplate.

A suit of armour is preserved in the Rotunda Museum
at Woolwich which is of unique interest, inasmuch as it is
attributed to, and certainly is of the date of the redoubtable Chevalier Bayard. It was brought from the Château
of St. Germain, and is an object of profound regard to Gallic
visitors. The armour is engraved, russeted, and partly gilt
(Plate VIII., p. 64), and dates from c. 1520 or earlier.
In places it is fluted, but a marked peculiarity of the

suit is the polygonal section of the cuissarts and jambarts, which may be discerned by a close inspection of the
figure. The breastplate is globose and the left epaulière
is furnished with a pike-guard, while the sabbatons are
of the bear's-paw pattern.

For tilting purposes the great heaume was still in
use, and several examples preserved in our museums date
from this period. Not the least interesting is the well-
known Wallace heaume, of English construction, and
dating from *c.* 1515 (Fig. 356). This
rare example is formed of two plates
only, the top and back part being one
piece, and the front part or bavière
being the other. The two plates are
securely riveted together at the sides
and a piece is flanged over upon the
crown, where four rivets hold it in
place. The height of the heaume is

FIG. 356.—The Wallace
heaume, *c.* 1515.

14 inches. It is much pitted, and in places broken.
Of the heaumes preserved in the Tower a great probability exists that they were made for pageant purposes
or simply for funeral achievements. One of early fifteenth
century date weighs 15 lbs.; another of the usual shape,
but furnished with a comb, is said to have belonged to
John of Gaunt. Probably the most interesting in that
collection is a globular tilting heaume fitted with a bavière
which is affixed by screws, and also gripped by the visor
pivots; it extends downwards to the breastplate, to which
it was fixed by an almayne screw (Fig. 357). In it a
square opening occurs opposite the right cheek, protected
by a small door, opening and closing upon a spring.

The visor is strongly reinforced, and works upon a central comb on the crown: the occularium is formed by the

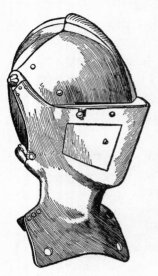

lower part of the visor and the upper edge of the bavière, and is remarkably narrow. It weighs 13 lbs. In the Rotunda at Woolwich is preserved the well-known Brocas heaume (Plate XXXIX., p. 364), dating from the time of Henry VII. and formerly in the Brocas Collection. It weighs $22\frac{1}{2}$ lbs. In Haseley Church, Oxon; Petworth Church, Sussex; Ashford Church, Kent; and in Westminster Abbey, are other heaumes of considerable interest, and a few are in private collections. A heaume which dated from c. 1510 was at one time in Rayne Church, Essex,

FIG. 357. — Globular tilting heaume. (Tower of London.)

and belonged to Sir Giles Capel, the head portion of which was almost globose, while a second example, in which, however, the visor is slightly ridged, or of the bellows variety, is in Wimborne Minster. These heaumes invariably weigh more than 20 lbs.; but the Westminster example is an exception, as it only scales 17 lbs.

CHAPTER XIV

MAXIMILIAN ARMOUR, 1525-1600

THIS style of armour, which prevailed for so long a period, and of which examples in some form or other exist in almost every museum of importance, saw its origin in the reign of the Emperor Maximilian, from whom it is named. It is essentially the late Gothic style of armour richly decorated with fluting, and reinforced by numerous extra pieces designed to afford additional security to the wearer in the tilt-yard. For the battle-field the plain, unornamental armour of the Transition Period was invariably used; the Maximilian was for tilting and pageant purposes chiefly, and for display. Its introduction, and subsequent development upon the lines followed by the civil dress, was a sign of the decadence of armour for use in the battle-field—the turning-point which eventually led to its abolition.

The invention and use of gunpowder was the death-knell of chivalry in the full sense of its meaning. The mail-clad knight and the heavily armed man-at-arms had played their part through many centuries, and were now to disappear; steel-clad squadrons in all the majestic might of the pomp and circumstance of glorious war, with levelled lance and mantling streaming in the wind, had lived their day and were now to be no more. Armour had served its purpose so long as sword and lance, javelin and bolt, were the usual weapons of war; but when it was discovered that against the deadly lead of the arquebus it was of no avail, it

FIG. 358.—The Emperor Maximilian I.

was gradually discarded as obsolete and cumbersome.

All the examples of Maximilian armour present the same broad features, and can be easily recognised. As an effective defence against lance and sword and mace they

FIG. 359.—Maximilian armour, 1535.   (Wallace Collection.)

were extremely efficacious, and the armourers of the period attained a high degree of excellence in producing suits which were, for tourney purposes, invulnerable. The general features of the armour followed the lines shown in

Fig. 358, which is taken from a drawing by Hans Burgk-mair in 1508, and represents the Emperor Maximilian I.

FIG. 360.—Helmet, Maximilian armour. (Wallace Collection.)

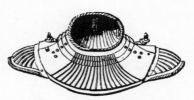

FIG. 361.—Gorget, Maximilian armour.

A suit (Fig. 359) eminently typical of Maximilian armour, having its whole surface ridged throughout in closely grouped channels, is in the Wallace Collection; it was manufactured at Nuremberg in 1535. The closed helmet

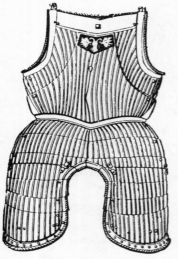

FIG. 362.—Breastplate, &c., Maximilian armour, 1535.

FIG. 363.—Backplate, Maximilian armour, 1535.

(Fig. 360) is of a very fine pattern, simple but effective, with visor and bavière in one piece, only a narrow occularium being pierced for sight. The neck articulates with the upper plate of the gorget, which consists of four plates (Fig. 361).

The breastplate (Fig. 362) is ridged with a strongly marked tapul upon the large placcate which strengthens it; the double-headed eagle appears upon the upper portion of this. In the upper centre of the breastplate proper is a hole

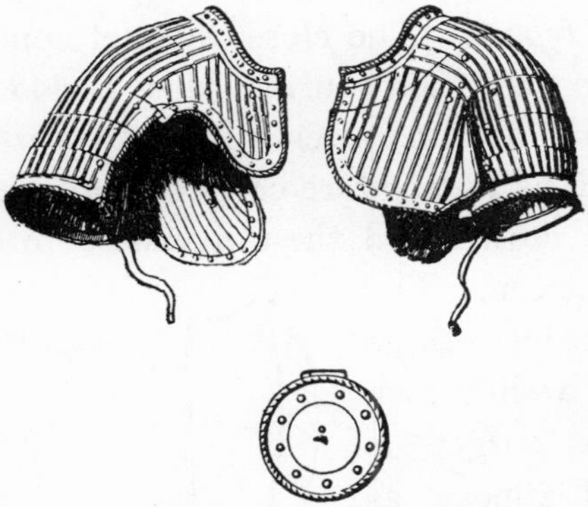

FIG. 364.—Pauldrons, Maximilian armour, 1535.

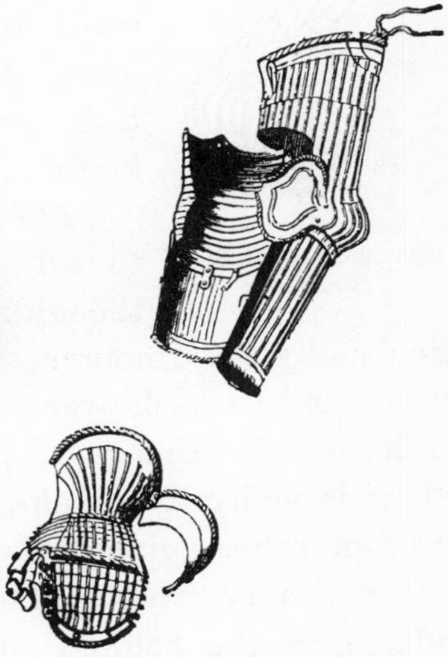

FIG. 365.—Maximilian armour, 1535.

of square section for affixing a mentonnière or bufe. To the backplate (Fig. 363), in the lower part of which occurs a fleur-de-lys, a garde-de-rein of two plates is attached.

The taces of three plates have the tassets fastened to the lower lame. The pauldrons (Fig. 364) are large and of a different pattern for each shoulder, the right being hollowed for the lance, with a roundel to protect the opening. The inside bend of the arm has fourteen splints for protection, as may be seen from the illustration (Fig. 365). Strange to say, the inner bends of the knees have the same protection (Fig. 366).

The sabbatons present a very fine example of the " bear's paw " pattern; they are attached to the jambarts, which, as usual in this style, are not fluted (Fig. 367). In many of the European collections, suits of armour of this pattern may be found.

FIG. 366.—Maximilian armour.

The Helmet.—The closed helmet continued to be used during this period, though modified and altered in many particulars by the armourers. The flutings are carried as a rule from front to back over the crown, and the universal comb is decorated with a roped pattern. The visor is generally moulded into three or four ridges, giving the well-known bellows appearance. The gorget is affixed to the helmet, and appears as three or more spreading lames of steel, the lowest being worked into a pattern; at times, however, it appears distinct, and the helmet revolves upon the expanded upper edge of the gorget.

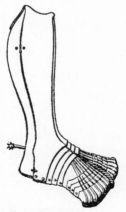

FIG. 367.—Sabbaton, Maximilian armour. (Wallace Coll.)

A very perfect type of close helmet is shown in Fig. 368, in which the comb is much larger than was the custom at an earlier date and resembles that of a morion. The visor is formed of two parts, the upper or visor proper, which falls down inside the second

part or bavière, and could be raised for vision if required
without disturbing the lower portion.   The date is *c.* 1560,
and it is probably Milanese.   The helmet engraved in Fig.

FIG. 368.—Milanese close
helmet, *c.* 1560.

FIG. 369.—English close
helmet.

369 is of English origin and partakes of the nature of a
helmet and also a burgonet.   The latter form of helmet
appeared during the Burgundian wars, hence its name, at
the beginning of the fifteenth cen-
tury, and is essentially a helmet
with cheek - pieces attached, the
protection for the face being
afforded by separate pieces, the
bufe or laminated chin-piece being
used at times.   Fig. 370 is an
Italian burgonet dating from 1540.

For war purposes the salade
was still preferred, though the
form in the Maximilian Period

FIG. 370.—Italian burgonet,
1540.

was at variance with that in the Tabard, and even in the
Transition, Period.   A fine example, dating from 1520, is
preserved in the Wallace Collection (Fig. 371).   It has a
low comb, and the neck-guard is broken up into three

lobster-tail plates. The visor is large, and contains the occularium; in the lower part it is hollowed so as to fit the chin, while a series of breathing-holes are pierced through the centre.

The Breastplate is short and furnished with goussets

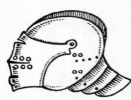

FIG. 371.—Salade, Maximilian, 1520. (Wallace Collection.)

sliding upon almayne rivets; a cable pattern appears upon the turned-over edges, and flutings radiate from the waist upwards. A placcate is often found reinforcing the breastplate after the manner of the fifteenth century Gothic suits, and this feature may be seen exemplified in Fig. 224 in the Wallace Collection. If a placcate is not used, at times a thick band of steel makes a reinforcement round the waist, forming an integral part of the breastplate. The taces are generally three or four in number, and to the lowest are affixed the *tassets,* which are laminated, and of three or more plates, taking the place of the now obsolete tuilles. To the backplate is affixed the garde-de-rein, or kidney guard, which may be of chain mail, or

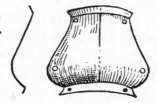

FIG. 372.—Breastplate with tapul. (Tower of London.)

laminated scales; if of plates these are placed inside each other upwards, so as to guard against the thrust of the pike from a footman. The scales, if used, are also turned in the same direction.

The breastplate of the earlier part of this period was more globular than the Gothic example; the slight ridge down the centre gradually developed into a strongly marked *tapul* (Fig. 372). In the first years of Elizabeth's reign the tapul was humped in the centre with a very marked projection, but as the reign progressed this hump descended until it was near the lower edge and produced the *peascod* form (Figs. 373, 374), which was an imitation in metal of the doublet then prevalent. For combats on foot the breastplate was often made entirely of lames of plate moving upon rivets, thus insuring great freedom of movement for the body (Fig. 375).

The Pauldrons are invariably furnished with large pikeguards; the left differs from the right, which is hollowed to

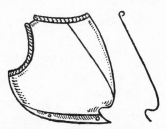
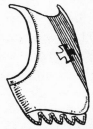

FIG. 373.—Peascod breastplate.
(Tower of London.)

FIG. 374.—Breastplate.
(Tower of London.)

receive the lance, with a roundel falling over it for protection. The arm defences are laminated where possible, and large butterfly coudières occur. In some suits the inside bend of the arms, and also the backs of the knees, are protected by a series of laminated plates affording great protection while allowing complete freedom of movement; the beautiful workmanship and accurate adjustment of these lames are especially noteworthy. An example from the Wallace Collection is given in Fig. 376; there are two examples in that museum and another in the Tower, upon a suit made for Henry VIII. for fighting on foot.

The Cuisses, &c.—These are long, and furnished with one or more laminated plates at the tops for flexibility.

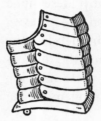

They are generally complete, covering the back of the leg as well as the front; to insure mobility the back at times is composed of lames. The genouillières are small and tight-fitting, but provided with large plates to protect the back of the knee. The jambarts are close-fitting and of fine form, and these are the only parts undecorated with fluting which appears more or less over the whole suit. Sabbatons are of the bear's paw pattern, the toes being at times of remarkably wide dimensions.

FIG. 375.—Laminated peascod breastplate. (T. of London.)

The brayette was generally composed of steel plates, although examples exist which are made of a single plate. It was designed to afford protection to the abdomen, as the breastplate only descended as far as the waist, where the brayette was affixed by means of straps. At times it was made entirely of chain mail modelled to the form, while many suits exhibit the cuisses, tassets, and brayette made in one piece. In deference to British susceptibilities these pieces are removed from contemporary suits of armour in our museums and exhibited

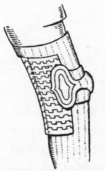

FIG. 376.—Defence for bend of arm.

separately, but on the Continent they are invariably shown in position.

The tilting reinforcements were many and varied, but a few of the most prominent may be described.

The Grande Garde.—This was a protection for the left side of the breastplate and the left shoulder; it extended from the neck to the waist, and generally covered a small portion of the right of the breastplate as well. In Fig. 377 the general shape is indicated, the left or bridle arm being incapable of a forward movement when it was affixed. The three large screws and nuts are for securing it to the breastplate, and also for engaging with the lower edge of the volante piece, which in this example is separate, and has oblong indentations for that purpose as seen at A.

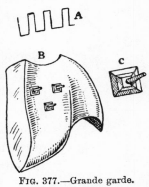

FIG. 377.—Grande garde.
(Wallace Collection.)

The Volante Piece.—This reinforcement was intended for the protection of the neck and face up to the eyes;

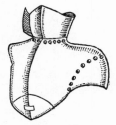

FIG. 378.—Volante piece and grande garde, *c.* 1580. (Wallace Collection.)

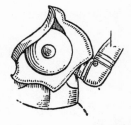

FIG. 379.—Grande garde and volante piece. (From a Missal.)

it was either separate from the grande garde, as in Fig. 377, or formed a part of it as in Fig. 378, where a series of studs are shown which permanently fix it. In this example an oblong slit is shown in the lower part of the grande garde by which an attachment to the breastplate can be effected. If no grande garde is used a volante piece similar to a large mentonnière in construction was affixed

FIG. 380.—Manteau d'armes, 16th century. (Tower of London.)

to the breastplate, generally by three screws, and while effectually protecting both sides of the helmet was also prolonged over both shoulders.

A combined grande garde and volante piece (Fig. 379) is represented upon a king engaged in combat in the field in a fifteenth century missal presented by the Duchess of Burgundy to Henry VI.,

FIG. 381.—Manteau d'armes. (Wallace Collection.)

which indicates that some of the reinforcements used in the tilting yard were at times made available for war purposes; this, however, was the exception and not the rule.

The Manteau d'Armes.—This piece consists of a large concave shield intended to protect the left side of the breastplate and

FIG. 382.—Polder mitten. (Tower of London.)

the left shoulder, and was used in the Italian or Free Course. It was firmly fixed to the breastplate by screws. The surface of the shield was usually embossed with a raised trellis-work design, either appliqué or raised from the surface by repoussé; this arrangement was intended to furnish a " grip " for the adversary's lance (Fig. 381).

The Polder Mitten, or *Epaule de Mouton,* was attached

to the right vambrace, and afforded protection against lance-thrusts to the bend of the arm and the parts immediately above and below. The example shown in Fig. 382 is from the Tower of London.

The Garde-de-Bras was essentially a protection for the left arm in tilting; it was attached to the cou-dière.

The Maximilian armour for fighting on foot in the lists was of very elaborate work-manship, but not as a rule embellished with the ornamentation which distinguished the equestrian suit. A complete suit for this purpose is preserved in the Tower; it was made for King Henry VIII., and is one of the finest in existence, containing as it does

Fig. 383.—Suit of armour for fighting on foot, King Henry VIII. (Tower of London.)

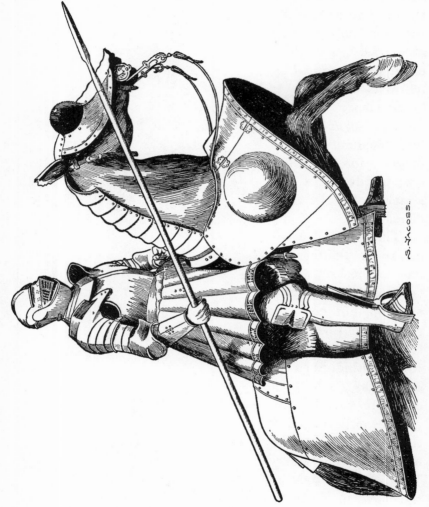

FIG. 384.

over two hundred separate pieces, most of them provided with a hollow groove which fits over a corresponding ridge upon the adjacent piece, thus presenting such a perfect interlocking system that the suit could not be taken to pieces without the greatest trouble. There are no goussets or exposed parts of the person of the wearer, the whole body being enclosed in a case of steel whose joints do not permit of the passage of a pin. It weighs nearly one hundred pounds, and has the broad-toed sabbatons of the period, and not only is the armour carried inside the legs and arms at the bends but plates

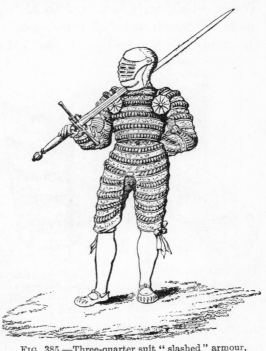

FIG. 385.—Three-quarter suit " slashed " armour, 1520.   (Wallace Collection.)

are also provided under the seat. The breastplate has a slight ridging down the centre, the precursor of the tapul or prominent projection so characteristic of the breast-plates immediately following. Upon this suit arm and knee protections are used similar to those illustrated in Fig. 376.

Lamboys or Bases.—The drapery used at this time,

depending in folds from the waist and hanging over the thighs, was occasionally imitated in steel, but examples preserved to the present age are of great rarity.

The finest in existence is probably that preserved in the Tower, which once belonged to Henry VIII.; it is a suit made by Seusenhofer of Innsbruck, and was presented to the king by Maximilian I., in 1514 (Fig. 384). It is

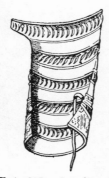

FIG. 386.—Arm defences, slashed armour, 1520. (Wallace Collection.)

FIG. 387. — Interior of tasset, slashed armour, 1520. (Wallace Collection.)

FIG. 388.—Tasset, slashed armour, 1520. (Wallace Collection.)

shown mounted in the collection, a portion of the lamboys back and front being removable for the purpose. A close helmet with gorget attached protects the head and neck; pike-guards are affixed to both pauldrons, and a tapul appears upon the breastplate. The legs are encased in close-fitting plate defences with no elaborate ornamentation; indeed, but for a beautifully-designed border in brass with the initials H and K appearing upon it, it is now practically devoid of ornamentation. This, however, was compensated for when new by being silvered.

A most interesting three-quarter suit of armour of this period, dating from 1520, was formerly in the Meyrick Collection but is now in the Wallace. It was made in imitation of the slashed and puffed dress of the early part of the sixteenth century, and these features are reproduced by repoussé from the back of the plates in steel (Fig. 385). Other suits of a similar character are in existence (a portion of one being in the

FIG. 389.—Backplate, slashed armour, 1520. (Wallace Collection.)

FIG. 390.—Culette in place of garde-de-rein, slashed armour, 1520. (Wallace Collection.)

Tower), but no other so fully exemplifies this peculiarity as the Wallace example. The helmet is of the closed type with a bellows-pattern front of five ridges, the visor and bavière being in one piece; the chin-piece is singular in being of only one plate hinged upon the left side of the helmet. The gorget is a standard collar of mail. The breastplate is globose and furnished with laminated plate goussets (Fig. 391); five plates form the taces, while tassets (Figs. 387, 388) of five plates are moulded round the thighs; the protection behind is afforded by a *culette* (Fig. 390), an arrangement of five plates, shaped to the figure, and depending from the backplate (Fig. 389), thus taking the place of the garde-de-rein. Upon these suits (*i.e.* for fighting on foot) were at times worn the grotesque helmets which many museums exhibit, showing satanic faces, and extravagant erections upon the head. One of these is the well-known ram's-horn visor in the Tower, a present from the Emperor Maximilian to Henry VIII. It was formerly gilt,

but has subsequently been painted and furnished with a pair of spectacles. Allied to these grotesque helmets were the pageant varieties, of which a number are extant at the present day. They were made solely for processions, triumphs, general obsequies, &c., of gilded leather, wood, and other materials. Examples are given in Figs. 392, 393, and 394.

FIG. 391.—Breastplate and taces, slashed armour, 1520. (Wallace Collection.)

The latter half of the Maximilian Period, or broadly speaking from about 1545 to 1600, saw a change in armour which renders it distinct from the preceding half. The rich flutings were discarded by reason of their tendency to hold the opponent's lance and to direct its head towards vulnerable spots. As a substitute for the ornamental fluting the plain surface of the steel became covered with rich artistic designs, some of them being of exquisite beauty and marvellous workmanship, while occasionally repoussé work was added to heighten the effect.

Aqua fortis was freely used for etching in combination with hand engraving, while damascening in gold and silver was also resorted to, the resulting suit presenting the absolute

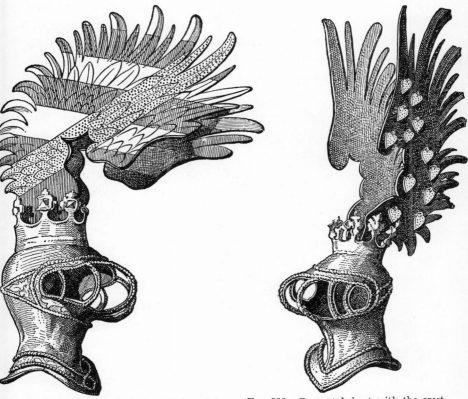

FIG. 392.—Pageant helmet with the crest of Burgau.

FIG. 393.—Pageant helmet with the crest of Austria (ancient) or Tyrol.

perfection of ornamentation of that particular character. But it is only in the surface decoration that we can admire the armour of the period, for in other respects it falls far short of that which preceded it. The outline was in most cases grotesque, or bordering upon it ; the metal was thinner and lighter than before, while the devices for permitting it to cover the bombasted breeches, so fashionable at the period, effectually mars its beauty of outline. So similar in contour and general configuration of the several parts is the armour of this time (which may be termed the Decorative Period) that a description of one suit is to all intents and purposes a description of the whole, and the suits severally preserved at the Armourers' Hall

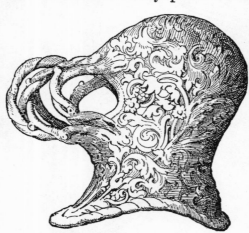

and the Wallace Collection will answer the purpose. These were made by the celebrated English armourer, Jacobi, whose illustrated album of twenty-nine suits, made by him between 1560 and 1590, is now in the South Kensington Museum. The album was sold at the Spitzer sale

FIG. 394.—Pageant helm, second half of the 15th century (Sigmaringen).

to M. Stein and was acquired by the nation; it is of extreme value to the student of armour, and a reproduction of the work has been issued. The suits were made for the Duke of Norfolk, the Earls of Rutland, Bedford, Leicester, Sussex, Worcester, Pembroke, and Cumberland, Sir Henry Lee, Master of the Armoury, Sir Christopher Hatton, &c., and a number have been preserved and identified by the details in the album. The suit in the Armourers' Hall is one of the three made for Sir

Henry Lee, while that in the Wallace Collection was made for Sir Thomas Sackville, created Baron of Buckhurst in 1567, and subsequently Earl of Dorset. This suit came from the Château Coulommiers en Brie, and was taken thence

FIG. 395.—Jacobi armour, 1575.   (Wallace Collection.)

when the château was dismantled during the first French Revolution (Fig. 395).

The Helmets are of the closed pattern, of the burgonet type, with an umbril or shade for the eyes, made after the style of a visor and coming well forward, while a falling bavière (Fig. 398) is hinged at the sides and projects well to the front, forming an occularium with the umbril (Fig. 396). A deep comb passes over the top of the helmet.   The

Sackville suit has a triple-barred face-guard as well (Fig. 397).

FIG. 396.—Helmet,
Jacobi suit.

A morion could be worn with these suits; it was an oval helmet with a high crest like a comb, and a brim which was peaked both before and behind (Fig. 415).

The Gorget consisted of four lames of plate.

Breastplates.—These are all of the peascod form with roped turnover borders and the goussets laminated with one plate. The backplates are secured to the breastplates by steel straps over the shoulders and under the arms (Figs. 397 and 398).

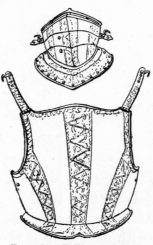

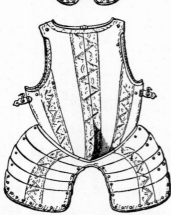

FIG. 397.—Face-guard, breastplate, tace, and tassets, Jacobi armour, 1575.

FIG. 398.—Falling bufe and backplate, Jacobi suit.

Taces are of four plates adapted to cover the bombasted breeches. In the Wallace suit the taces are of one plate only, to which are permanently affixed the *Tassets* of four plates, and these may be detached from the lower edge of the breastplate if required, so as to permit of the bombasted breeches being worn with no covering, the breastplate being finished at the lower edge to allow of it. In other suits, however, the lobster-tail tassets descend to the knees in a dozen or more lames of plate, where they are covered by the genouillières.

Genouillières are of a close-fitting pattern, with small plates defending the outside bends of the legs, and two or more reinforcing plates above and below.

Jambarts. — These are splinted and laminated at the ankles.

Sabbatons are

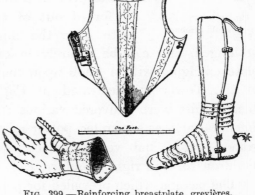

FIG. 399.—Reinforcing breastplate, grevières, sabbatons, and gauntlet, Jacobi armour, 1575. (Wallace Collection.)

round-toed, closely fitting, and composed of about ten plates (Fig. 399).

Pauldrons.—These are of about five plates coming well forward in order to protect the goussets (Fig. 400).

Brassarts cover the upper arms and are provided with *Turners*, a device for allowing the arm protections to revolve. The brassarts were made generally in two plates, one having a hollow roped border which fitted over a solid rim provided for it upon the adjoining plate, thus allowing a complete revolution of half the brassart. In addition the arms are protected by coudières and vambraces.

The Gauntlets are of the usual description, but one supplied with the Lea suit is in the Armourers' Hall, and is of the locking pattern, an invention of the latter part of the sixteenth century. It was often termed the "Forbidden Gauntlet." Its object was to prevent a weapon being wrenched or forced out of the hand; the extra plate over the fingers is considerably

FIG. 400.—Pauldron, Jacobi armour.

prolonged, and can be securely locked by a hole in the plate engaging with a knob upon the wrist. An example in the Tower is illustrated in Fig. 401. With these Jacobi suits were delivered various extra defences, such as a manifer, polder mitten, grande garde and volante piece, extra pauldron for the right shoulder, &c.

The passion which prevailed for parade armour during the reign of Queen Elizabeth, led, as we have seen, to a high degree of ornamentation being bestowed upon many suits, but perhaps the greatest amount of intricate workmanship was

FIG. 401.—"Forbidden" gauntlet. (Tower of London.)

lavished upon the *rondaches*, or shields, which were made to accompany the armour. In the Wallace Collection there is one of the most beautiful examples in existence, a rondache magnificently embossed and damascened, made for Diane de Poitiers and bearing her monogram and insignia. It dates from *c.* 1530, and is of Milanese manufacture, probably by the Negrolis. About a century and a half ago it was purchased in Italy for five hundred pounds. There are excellent examples in the Tower, Windsor Castle, and the British Museum, while those at Madrid are renowned for the wealth of orna-mentation bestowed upon them. Plate I.*, p. 16, is of Italian make and composed of different pieces screwed together; the four ovals contain representations of classical scenes, and four heads among other decora-tions are upon the border. A shield which once be-longed to Philip II. is shown in Plate II.*, p. 24; while in Plate III.*, p. 32, a German masterpiece by Desiderius Colman, finished in 1552, is shown. This was executed at the time when the fiercest rivalry existed between the Colmans of Augsburg and the Negrolis

FIG. 402.—The Ferrara half-suit, 1570.
(Wallace Collection.)

of Milan. The subjects depicted are War, Peace, Wisdom, and Strength. Another rondache of Augsburg make is given in Plate IV.*, p. 40, whilst Plate V.*, p. 48, and Plate VI.*, p. 56, exhibit two beautiful designs from Italy.

One of the most splendid examples of armour of the Decorative Period in Europe, or, as has been asserted, *the* most splendid example, is the Ferrara demi-suit once belonging to Alfonso II., Duke of Ferrara, &c. *b.* 1553, *d.* 1597 (Fig. 402). The armour dates from *c.* 1570, and is probably the work of Lucio Picinino ; it occupies a prominent position in the Wallace Collection, and asserts pre-eminence even in that wonderful aggregation of examples of beautiful workmanship. The pieces consist of a breastplate of the peascod variety with laminated goussets, and a back-plate ; a gorget of five lames and a tace of one plate, which could be removed if required from the breast-plate ; tassets, laminated pauldrons, brassarts, vambraces, and coudières. The entire design of this grand example of the armourer's art is worked out by embossing from the back to surfaces of different levels, chasing and enriching with fine gold damascening,

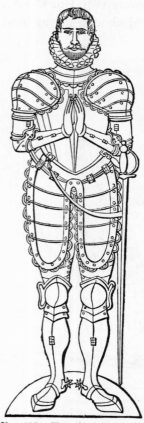

FIG. 403.—Humphrey Brewster 1593. Wrentham Church, Suffolk.

FIG. 404.—Close helmet, Hatfield House, late sixteenth century.

plating, and overlaying. The work is of remarkably even quality, and is at the present time in an excellent state of preservation. Examples of some of the decorations are given in the beginning of this work, where (to the number of four) they are inserted as ornamental head- and tail-pieces.

A half-suit of armour dating from about the close of the sixteenth century is to be seen in the Wallace Collection. It is of North Italian manufacture and is adorned with

FIG. 405.—Italian armour, late sixteenth century.   (Wallace Collection.)

vertical bands containing panels of classical figures, interlaced designs, trophies of arms and armour, &c.

The closed helmet (Fig. 406) has a skull-piece with a comb, and the chin-piece opens down the side; the very deep visor strengthens the front of the helmet and is pierced for sight, while the lower edge of the helmet articulates with the upper edge of the gorget (Fig. 407), which consists of

three plates.   The breastplate (Fig. 408) is slightly peascod
in form, and is furnished with a massive lance-rest.   The
tace of one plate has tassets of three plates depending

(Fig. 410), while the
pauldrons (Fig. 411)
consist of seven lames
each.   The suit was
evidently intended for
tilting purposes, as there
are holes for the adjust-

FIG. 406.　　　　FIG. 407.

ment of various reinforcements, while the lance-rest of such
strong proportions and the deep flange upon the inner side
of the tassets only confirm the supposition.

During the later years of the reign of Elizabeth the

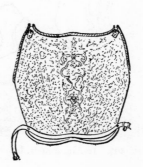

FIG. 408.　　　　FIG. 409.

ordinary armour for fighting purposes assumed a character
which is very familiar, inasmuch as it is depicted upon scores
of brasses and modelled upon hundreds of effigies in all parts
of the kingdom.   Fig. 403, from the brass of Humphrey
Brewster, 1593, at Wrentham, illustrates the style.

The infantry of the Maximilian and Decorative Periods consisted of pikemen (who we glean from contemporary documents formed the greater part of the army at that time), arquebusiers, cannoniers, and archers.

The Pikeman was furnished in the early portion of the period with a plain pot-de-fer having a turned-down brim, but later with a crested helmet based upon the classic style, and later still, the cabasset helmet. Very little armour is represented upon the pikemen in contemporary drawings of the early part of the century, but

FIG. 410.   FIG. 411.   FIG. 412.

it is probable that a breast- and backplate with occasionally armour for the arms and thighs, were in general use. A tunic, slashed breeches, and long hose are as a rule shown, but no attempt at uniformity. Henry VIII.'s army is delineated in Aug. III. in the British Museum upon a somewhat large scale, and the pikemen are represented in every variety of costume prevalent at the time. Their weapons are a pike or spear of considerable length and a sword, while a circular buckler is apparently the only means of defence; the lower class of officers carry the halberd.

During the reigns of Edward VI. and Mary the morion and the cabasset helmet became almost universal for the pikemen, being in many cases richly etched in vertical bands or covered with arabesques. When first adopted the cabasset helmet was comparatively small (Fig. 413); about 1560 the small projecting spike at the apex became curved, and as the century progressed the brim grew narrow at the sides, and projected to a considerable distance before and behind, while the height of the headpiece increased (Fig. 414). The morion, which is distinguished from

FIG. 413.—Cabasset helmet.

FIG. 414.—Cabasset helmet, Hatfield House, c. 1580.

FIG. 415.—Morion.

the cabasset helmet by having a comb (Fig. 415), developed an exceedingly large one, at times 6 inches in height, about the years 1570–80, while the brim took on a very strong curve and was generally roped at the edge. By the end of the century the comb had lessened in height, and the brim became wider—it was still very lavishly decorated.

The pikemen during the reigns of Edward VI., Mary, and Elizabeth were defended by back- and breast-plates with tassets, gorgets, gauntlets, and steel hats or cabasset morions (Plate XXVI., p. 318). The breastplates were made much thicker than formerly in order to be bullet-proof, or at least pistol-bullet-proof, while the tassets were generally of one plate, though marked in imitation of several. The point of the tapul gradually descended upon the breastplate until it assumed the peascod variety and eventually disappeared.

The Arquebusier in the early part of the sixteenth century carried little body armour; he is usually represented in the slashed and ribbed dress of Henry VIII.'s time, with a bonnet bearing a feather upon his head. He was provided with a matchlock arquebus and a rest, with a sword at the left side, while hanging from a cord which crossed the body from the left shoulder were the circular powder-flasks and bullet - bag. The arquebusiers opened the battle, being in the van with the artillery.

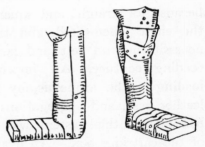

FIG. 416.—Sabbatons, Hatfield House.

About the year 1550 we find the arquebusiers clad in the armour termed almayne rivets, a name which was first applied to the system of sliding rivets invented in Germany, whereby lames and plates were given a considerable amount of play by the longitudinal slots in which the head of the rivet worked, but subsequently was applied loosely to suits of armour in which these rivets were used. Henry VIII., for example, sent to Milan for 5000 suits of " almayne rivets," and in 1561, when an inventory was made of armour in the Tower of London, 3752 " almayne rivets " are catalogued, besides 350 " almayne corselets " (Harl. MS. 7457). The armour thus designated embraced a back- and breast-plate with espalier pauldrons to the elbows; three taces with pendent tassets of eight plates to the knees, fastened to the thighs by straps. A rigid gorget of plate and the headpiece completed the defence. This armour for the arquebusiers lasted during the century with but little variation; towards the end the tassets were much widened to accommodate them to the breeches then worn, and the breastplate was made so high in the neck that occasionally a gorget was dispensed with. Among the firearms used by the arquebusiers the *carabine*, *petronel*, and *caliver* may be mentioned; the petronel was so called because its straight and square butt-end was held against the chest when fired, and the caliver was a light piece necessitating no rest and largely in use during the succeeding century. An improvement was made in the loading of the arquebus, by having a single charge in a leather case, and aggregations of these cases were termed bandoliers; this system was in use until the invention of the cartridge-box. An example of the armour worn by arquebusiers and footmen toward the close of Elizabeth's reign is given in Plate XXIV., taken from Edinburgh Castle, where the high breastplate is seen, covered, however, in this case, with a gorget. The pauldrons are large, and below them occur complete protection for the arms, the turners being very prominent. A similar suit is in the same museum which is furnished with the long breastplate strengthened with a placcate at the bottom; it exhibits a little more ornamentation and is better finished (Plate XXIV.).

The Cannonier had no particular uniform allotted to him, and his only distinction was an apron. His cannon commenced the battle, as is generally the case in modern times, but with this difference, that he was placed in the forefront of the fray instead of the rear. To afford him some kind of protection a large mantlet was part of the equipment, and in a combat a mantlet and a gun were placed alternately. The artillery used was the falcon and serpentin, and we have also mention of bombards, while in the waggons were carried the powder and stone balls, together with bows and arrows, for archers were in use at this period and for some decades of the succeeding century.

The Cavalry consisted chiefly of demi-lancers clad in half-armour, and many suits of this character are preserved in museums. It was, as a rule, of better quality and finish than that served out to the footmen, the defences for the arms being complete, and lobster-tail tassets reaching to and covering the knees. The head was pro-tected by the close helmet or open casque, which is furnished as a rule with

FIG. 417.—Close helmet, Hatfield House, show-ing umbril.

a comb, an umbril over the eyes, hinged ear-pieces, and a neckplate at the back where a holder was affixed for a plume (Fig. 417). A light armour, especially adapted for infantry and light cavalry, consisting of a breastplate and tassets which reached either to the middle of the thigh or to below the knee, was much in use during the six-teenth century and known as the *Allecret*. During the Maximilian period the officers were furnished with allecrets as a rule, while the Swiss soldiers especially were partial to this system, which defended only the vital parts of the body, and did not hamper the free movement of the limbs.

For light cavalry it was of great advantage, as it gave much less trouble to the horses when the legs of the wearer were only partially defended, as with tassets. To the lance and sword which were always carried the pistol was added, this being generally a wheel-lock dag with a long barrel, the charges or cartridges being enclosed in a steel case called a patron. Troops called Dragoons came into being, who dispensed with the lance and used as their chief weapon a long wheel-lock pistol termed a dragon from the shape of its muzzle, which was modelled similarly to the head of that mythical monster. The barrel of the dragon was approximately of the same length as the modern carbine. The mounted arquebusier either discharged his piece when on horseback, resting it in a fork which projected upwards from the front of the saddle, or else dismounted to fire in the same manner as the footman.

There were a number of Courses or methods of combat in tournaments during the Middle Ages, but the three chief were the Das Deutsche Stechen, the Sharfrennen, and the Italian Course or Über die Pallia.

1. The Das Deutsche Stechen. This is generally known as the German Course, and was in use in the early mediæval period. The chief object of the knight was to splinter his lance, or unhorse his opponent, and with that end in view the saddles were unprovided with the usual high plate at the back. The lance possessed a sharp point, and the small shield upon the left side of the rider, which simply depended from straps and was not borne by the left arm, was the part aimed at by the opponents. The shield in the Wallace suit (Fig. 418) is 14 inches wide, and made of oak over an inch in thickness. This form of tilting was run with lances having a rebated coronal head in the later mediæval period. The suit mentioned has no leg armour except the tuilles, and the right hand no gauntlet, according to custom. About the middle of the fifteenth century a salade was used instead of the heaume, but a special kind of heaume like a truncated cone was used in the sixteenth century.

2. Sharfrennen. The main idea in running this course was to un-horse the opponent, and with this end in view the armour and appurtenances were different in many essentials to those used in other courses. The saddle, for example, was unfurnished with any support either in front

Fig. 418.—Suit for the Das Deutsche Stechen Course, *c.* 1485.
(Wallace Collection.)

or behind, and no armour was worn upon the lower limbs, which could thus maintain the maximum " grip " of the horse without any encum-brance. To protect the thighs and knees of the riders large steel pieces called *cuishes* were attached to the saddle ; these were necessary because the horses often collided in running this course, no central barrier being used. A pair of cuishes are preserved in the Tower which date

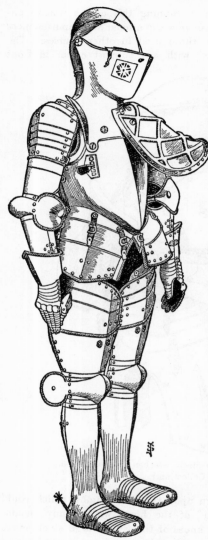

FIG. 419. Tilting armour for the Über die Pallia Course, *c.* 1580. (Wallace Collection.)

from *c.* 1480; the edges are decorated with a roped border. The lance used was thick and heavy and provided with a steel point; upon impact it was customary to drop it in order to avoid the risk of injury to the right arm by splinters in the event of the lance shivering. The vamplate used in this course was of unusual proportions, covering the whole of the right side of the body; an example may be seen in the Rotunda at Woolwich, No. XVI. 102, which is of much larger size than the one illustrated from the Tower Collection (Fig. 312). The body armour was of a ponderous nature, nearly every piece being duplicated. In this course, if one of the combatants was not unhorsed immediately upon impact, it was customary for his attendants to rush forward and aid him in recovering his seat.

3. The Italian Course, or Über die Pallia. This course was of later origin than the Stechen or Sharfrennen, and originated in Italy, as the name implies. It was introduced into Germany during the first decade of the sixteenth century, and became immensely popular. A wooden barrier with a height of about five feet separated the combatants, who rode on either side of it, left hand inwards. The suits of armour for the course are, strange to say, invariably provided with armour for the lower limbs, and

a typical example is one preserved in the Wallace Collection dating from *c.* 1580, which has a closed helmet, breastplate of the peascod form with a lance-rest, tassets of two wide plates, and a backplate (Fig. 419). The pauldrons are of the espalier pattern with brassarts, vambraces, coudières, and fingered gauntlets. The cuisses are wide, a peculiarity noticeable in the armour of the latter end of the sixteenth century. Reinforced genouillières, jambarts, and sabbatons complete the suit. Additional defences are the large *manteau d'armes* with the lower edge turned outwards from the body and decorated with a trellis pattern to engage the lance of the opponent, and also a tilting reinforcement for the elbow on the left-hand side. A second suit of much interest is provided with a tilting helmet of great weight, the back of which is affixed in a peculiar manner to the backplate (Fig. 420 was similarly fastened), which rises high in order to receive it, while the bavière is of the form of a mentonnière, being affixed by bolts to the breastplate. There is a manifere for the left hand as well as manteau d'armes and elbow reinforcement (Fig. 421). A third suit for this course has no sabbatons, the stirrups being made to protect the feet.

FIG. 420.—Tilting-helmet of Sir John Gostwick, 1541.

The lance used was tipped with a coronal head; it was held upon the left side of the horse's head, and the main idea at first was to unhorse an adversary, which was a matter of great difficulty, as the riders sat in a deep well-saddle with high projections both back and front. Subsequently, however, the shivering of lances became the chief object, and they were made light and hollow (the bourdonass) for that purpose, and riders very seldom lost their seats in consequence. The armour also began to lose that ponderous character it formerly possessed, and light Italian suits were in favour. These also were adapted for running the various courses prevailing, screw holes and adjustments allowing of the reinforcements being attached for each.

Arising out of the three chief courses were various subsidiary ones, the Free Course being probably the chief. It was the Italian Course used without the central barrier, and therein resembling the Stechen.

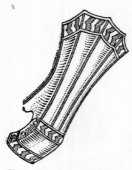

A cap-à-pie suit in the Wallace Collection dating from about 1580 resembles that for the Italian Course, but has an addition to the manteau d'armes protecting the left side of the breastplate and the top of the left espalier, a small extra plate to fasten on this and the left-hand part of the breastplate, together with a reinforcing plate to fix to the right espalier. This course dates from the second half of the sixteenth century. The Foot Tournament was fought with lance and sword, and no leg armour was used—striking below the belt being forbidden. There was also a Club Tournament, in which a short wooden mace, the baston, was used by the combatants, and this caused a peculiar type of helmet to be evolved termed the "grid-iron," which is shown in Fig. 422,

FIG. 421.—Manifere, left-hand tilting gauntlet, c. 1560. (Wallace Collection.)

dating from the fifteenth century. A later variety (Fig. 423) is furnished with a latticed visor.

In connection with tournaments generally, the saddles preserved in

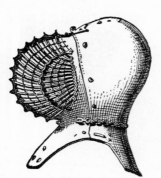

FIG. 422.—"Grid-iron" helmet, 15th century.

FIG. 423.—Helmet, with latticed visor, end of 15th century.

many museums are of interest, the one dating from 1470, in the Tower of London, being exceptionally so from its enormous dimensions, inasmuch as when seated in it nearly the whole body of the tilter was protected.

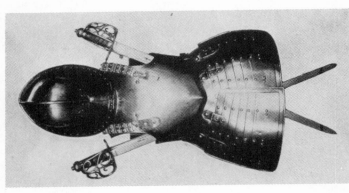

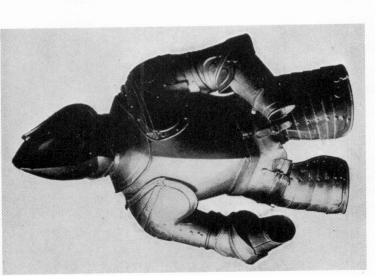

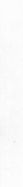

PLATE XXIV

Pikeman's Armour, end of Sixteenth Century. (Edinburgh Castle)

Cromwellian Armour, c. 1644. (Edinburgh Castle)

Footman's Armour, late Sixteenth Century. (Edinburgh Castle)

CHAPTER XV

THE HALF-ARMOUR PERIOD AFTER 1600

ALTHOUGH to the average student the armour prevailing after the sixteenth century possesses absolutely no interest whatever, yet as a certain amount continued to be worn, and it possessed characteristics entirely its own, it is necessary to be acquainted with these features in order to possess a comprehensive knowledge of the entire subject. Of cap-à-pie suits it may be broadly stated that none exist ; of three-quarter and half-suits there are many to be found, but extremely few of these are of workmanship which can in any way compare in wealth of decoration with that of the

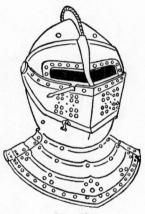

Fig. 424.

latter half of the sixteenth century, or vie in elegance of form with the Maximilian or Gothic armour. The period exhibits a brutal strength and crudity in armour which forcibly suggests boiler-plate work. The defences are simply made to cover the vital parts of the body with the maximum amount of efficiency, without any consideration whatever for gracefulness of outline or beauty of surface. The helmet continued to be of the same pattern as that of the end of the Maximilian Period ; variations, however, may be found; that, for example, delineated in Fig. 424, and dating from *c.* 1605, is more of the nature of a close-helmet than a burgonet, being entirely self-contained.

A typical three-quarter suit of English manufacture is that shown in Fig. 425, dating from about 1630 and forming a part of the Wallace Collection. It is shown in the Museum as a cap-à-pie suit, but the sabbatons and jambarts do not belong to it and date from *c.* 1580. The close helmet is fitted with an umbril to which is riveted the face-guard, pierced with sight and breathing apertures; a gorget plate is affixed bearing the number 10 upon it. Under

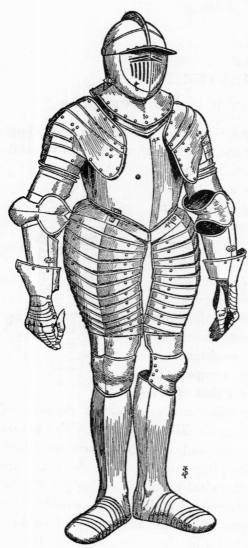

FIG. 425.—Three-quarter suit, 1630. (Wallace Collection.)

this plate is the gorget proper, consisting of three plates. The breastplate has a slight tapul and is marked 42. Upon the right-hand side an indentation has been caused by a musket ball. There is a backplate, and also a garde-de-rein of three plates. The espalier pauldrons have brassarts attached fitted with turners. The tassets of thirteen plates have the genouillières depending from them.

Cavalry.—During the early years of the reign of James I. the cavalryman had his name altered from lancer or demi-lancer to cavalier, probably owing to Spanish intercourse. The general tendency to discard armour as being cumbrous and ineffective led to many noblemen and officers of regiments contenting themselves with a cuirass worn over a buff coat, and subsequently, in Charles I.'s reign, whole regiments were thus accoutred, and received the name of cuirassiers in consequence. The dragoons also, who were introduced into the army during the latter years of the preceding century, only wore as a defence a buff coat made long and full and a burgonet. Apart from these, however, we find that the regiments using the lance were equipped with a close helmet, gorget, back- and breast-plate, pauldrons, vambraces, gauntlets, tassets, and garde-de-rein, while a good buff coat with long skirts was worn beneath the armour. The weapons comprised a sword which was stiff, cutting, and sharp-pointed; a lance of the usual pattern or pike-shaped, 18 feet long and provided with a leather thong to fasten round the right arm, and one or two pistols, with the necessary flask, cartouch box, and appurtenances.

The cuirassier was armed with two pistols carried at the saddle, and a sword similar to the lancers.

The arquebusier wore a good buff coat, a back- and

breast-plate, and armour generally resembling the lancer; he carried an arquebus 30 inches in length, two pistols, and the usual necessaries.

The carbineer had similar defences, but carried a carbine or petronel (Plate XLI.*, p. 368), instead of the arquebus, and a sword in place of the pistols.

The dragoons carried a pike and also a musket.

In 1645 the arquebusiers wore triple-barred helmets, cuirasses with garde-de-rein, pauldrons, and vambraces; at the same time the dragoons changed their muskets for the shorter piece termed the dragon, and four years afterwards again changed it for the caliver. The triple-barred helmet of the arquebusiers and dragoons is shown in Plate XXVI., from Edinburgh Castle, and Plate XXV., from the same source, illustrates a three-quarter suit of an officer of arquebusiers or lancers of the time of Charles I. A second suit, No. 32, is furnished with palettes over the goussets and an open-faced helmet called a casquetel (Plate XXV.).

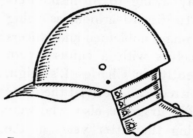

FIG. 426.—Casquetel (British Museum.)

The Pikeman of the time of James I. was accoutred in a morion-shaped helmet with a comb of moderate size and a flat brim, not curved, but pointed back and front. It was provided with a holder at the back, in which four or five large feathers were inserted. A back- and breast-plate reached to the waist, to which were affixed two broad tassets meeting in front of six plates each (Plate XXIV.), which spread over the well-padded breeches, reaching to the

PLATE XXV

Three-quarter Suits, *temp*. Charles I. (Edinburgh Castle)

knee and covering the front part of the limbs only. No gorget or defences for the arms are shown. His arms are a pike and a sword. Grose in his "Military Antiquities" illustrates thirty-two different positions in the exercise of the pike. The pikeman of the Cromwellian period had a similar accoutrement, but his morion may better be termed an iron hat, inasmuch as the crown is low with a small comb, the brim wide and drooping and coming well over the eyes and the back of the neck, and it is without plumes (Fig.

FIG. 427.—Pikeman's pot, 1620. (British Museum.)

427). Two cheek-guards are added. A back- and breast-plate with pendent tassets consisting of many plates formed with a leather coat and the helmet the sole protection. In Charles I.'s reign a rondache was served out to pikemen, but after a few years was discarded.

The Musketeer wore a morion in James I.'s reign similar to the pikeman but with no feathers, and this with a back- and breast-plate completed his metal defences. In 1625, the morion was discarded in favour of a jaunty felt hat with feathers, but subsequently the morion was again worn with the addition of cheek-pieces. No tassets are shown upon a musketeer's uniform. Grose illustrates forty-five separate orders for the discharge of one bullet from the musket. In 1637 an elaborate drill-book was issued by a Colonel Munro, in which he states that musketeers should be formed in companies with a front of thirty-two men, but six ranks deep; the first firing at once and casting about and reloading; the second rank passing to the front between the files to give fire next; then the third rank, and so on until the whole ranks have discharged. Directions for handling the matchlock published in 1620 contain quaint directions to the musketeer: "He must first learn to hold the piece, to accommodate the match between the two foremost fingers and his thumb, and to plant the great end on his breast with a gallant soldier-like grace, and if ignorant let him acquaint himself first with the firing of touchpowder in his pan, to bow and bear up his body, and to attain to the level and practice of an assured and serviceable shot, ready to charge and, with a comely touch, discharge, making sure at the same instant of his mark with a quick and vigilant eye."

In the reign of James I. a long rapier blade was added to the equipment of the musketeer for protection after he had discharged his piece. It was variously called the "swine's feather," "hog's bristle," and "Swedish feather," the latter probably indicating the country of its origin. The swine's feather and also the musket rest were abandoned during the Civil War.

Archers.—The persistence of archers in the ranks of the English forces long after the introduction of firearms and cannon is a noteworthy feature. During the sixteenth century they formed a numerous force, and were the subjects of especial care by the military commanders in the time of Queen Elizabeth. In Harl. MS. 7457, being an inventory of the Tower arms in 1561, there are accounts of many hundred brigandines, jacks, salades (salletts), and skull-caps for furnishing the defences of archers, while

PLATE XXVI

Triple-barred Helmet, *temp.* 1689.
(Edinburgh Castle)

Cabasset Helmet, Footman, *temp.*
James VI. (Edinburgh Castle)

regulations are extant of the same period which provide that: "Captains and officers should be skilful of that noble weapon, and to see that their soldiers according to their draught and strength have good bows, well nocked, well stringed, every string whip in their nock and in the middle rubbed with wax; a bracer and shooting glove and some spare strings; every man a sheaf of arrows in a leather case which contains twenty-four arrows, whereof eight should be lighter than the rest to gall the enemy with a hailshot of light arrows before they shall come within the danger of their harquebus shot. Let every man have a brigandine or a little coat of plate, a skull or huskyn, a maule of lead of five foot in length, and a pike, the same hanging by his girdle with a hook and a dagger; being thus furnished teach them to march, shoot, and retire, for these men can neither be spared in battle nor in skirmish. No other weapon can compare with the same noble weapon." Even as late as the time of Charles I. special commissions were issued under the Great Seal for enforcing the use and practice of the long-bow, and the Earl of Essex at the commencement of the Civil War issued a precept in 1643 directing the raising of a company of archers for special service.

In the time of Charles II., James II., and William and Mary officers still wore breastplates, but armour for the ordinary soldier was as a rule altogether discarded. As late as the commencement of the last century the officers of some regiments wore a small steel gorget, but all that remains to us at the present day to remind us of the days of chivalry and the steel-clad forces of bygone times, is the Life Guard with his back- and breast-plate and steel helmet.

CHAPTER XVI

WEAPONS OF THE EARLY AND MIDDLE AGES

The Guisarme.—This may be claimed with all confidence to be one of the most ancient of weapons, as its first inception

occurred in the Bronze Period, and from that remote age down to the seventeenth century it was more or less in evidence (Fig. 428). It terminated generally in an extremely strong and sharp point; the two sides were approximately parallel, and both brought to a keen and almost razor-like edge, while a short way down the blade a hook was

FIG. 428.—1. Halberd, 1470. 2. Bill. 3. Two-handed sword.

fashioned. During the Mediæval Period, when it was known by the name of the fauchard, an agitation for its abolition occurred in consequence of the deadly and ghastly nature of the wounds inflicted by this weapon. There are many forms, and additions of various hooks and spikes occur in varieties of the guisarme; the point also was at times modified, and instead of being straight partook more of the form of the curved bill-hook of modern times. The blade lent itself to elaborate ornamentation, and many examples of the sixteenth and seventeenth centuries exhibit splendid

FIG. 429.—1. Pole-axe.   2. Fauchard (guisarme).   3. Halberd.
4. Glaive, 1550.

specimens of the work of the engraver. It was used in England as late as the battle of Flodden (Fig. 429).

The Pole-Axe.—The battle-axe and the pole-axe may be claimed as one and the same weapon, simply differing in the length of the shaft, which necessitated the use of both hands in the case of the pole-axe, whereas one was sufficient for the other. It is essentially a weapon of the northern nations of Europe, and in its primitive form was

the flint axe of the Stone Age, subsequently fashioned
in bronze in the succeeding period. The form was as
a rule very simple from the Saxon Period to the fourteenth
century, consisting merely of an axe-blade upon one side
balanced by a spike upon the other; in that century and
also in the following it became one of the most important
weapons of war, and saw many alterations and modifications.
The blade, for example, became enormously lengthened,
broadened, and flattened, and the spike occasionally became
lance-shaped, or falcon-beaked, like a military pick, while
the head of the shaft developed into a spike or a short,
double-edged sword-blade.   In the fifteenth century it
became the favourite weapon for encounters on foot, when
the pole was furnished with one or two guards for the
hands, and was strengthened with iron splints; the lateral
spike developed into the shape of a war-hammer having
a broad head furnished with rows of pyramidal studs or
spikes, the vertical blade at the head being retained.   The
earliest preserved in the Wallace Collection dates from
c. 1350, and is similar in form to a pole-axe delineated in
Roy. MS. 16, G. VI., which shows a straight cutting
blade rectangular at the base, and with the top edge
forming an acute angle with the cutting edge.   Another,
of date c. 1420, has a strong semi-circular axe-blade
balanced by a hammer with pyramidal projections upon
the face, the head terminating in a strong spike.   Two
iron pieces almost cover the shaft for a distance of nearly
three feet.   In Edinburgh an axe is preserved dating
from the Maximilian Period (Plate XXVII.) which
shows an axe-blade with a circular cutting edge balanced
by a spike, the head being furnished with a pike-blade.

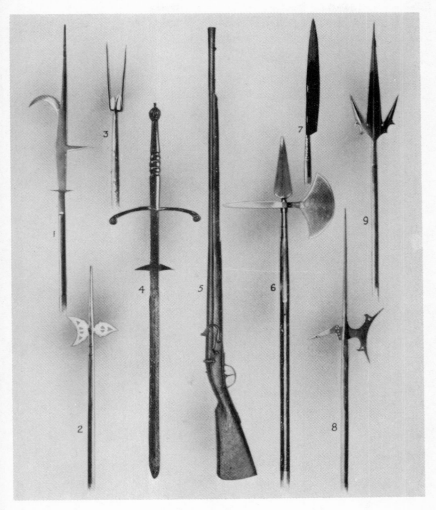

PLATE XXVII

Arms from Edinburgh Castle

1. Bill.
2. Halberd.
3. Military Fork.

4. Two-handed Sword.
5. Arquebus.
6. Pole-Axe.

7. Glaive.
8. Halberd.
9. Ranseur.

The shaft is protected for some distance from the axe-head.

The Halberd.—This weapon consists essentially of an axe-blade balanced by a pick, the head of the shaft being prolonged in the form of a spike. In the northern part of Europe the weapon had been in use from an exceedingly early period, but was not introduced into France and England until the end of the fourteenth century. The forms are many and varied, the blade developing from a crescent shape to that of a square, which prevailed in the fifteenth century and preceded the curved form. The spike also underwent changes, broadening and flattening at times until it presented a blade-like aspect, which was often curved downwards towards the shaft. It was essentially a weapon for the foot soldier, and although it is occasionally seen with a very long shaft, these are for pageant purposes, the war weapon seldom exceeding five or six feet in length. The form of the halberd probably lent itself more to ornamentation than any other weapon of the age, and those made for parade purposes exhibit at times a remarkable wealth of decoration. The halberd became obsolete when the pike came into favour. A beautiful example of a halberd of the date *c.* 1470 from Edinburgh Castle is shown in Plate XXVII., which exhibits a singularly long and formidable spike, with a concave cutting edge to the axe-blade balanced by a drooping pick. The shaft is ironed for a good distance from the head. Fig. 428 exhibits a halberd of the date 1470 where the axe-blade is crescent-shaped and the beak slightly drooping, as in the Edinburgh example; the spike, however, is not so long, but has a stronger section of diamond shape. The oldest specimen in the Wallace Collection dates from about 1430, in which the axe-blade possesses a straight cutting edge, and the spike is superseded by a strong tapering blade. A later example, dating from *c.* 1550, from the Edinburgh collection is shown in Plate XXVII.

The Partisan.—This weapon was introduced into England in the middle of the fourteenth century, and from the fifteenth to the seventeenth centuries was used extensively on the Continent, but especially in France. It consists of a long double-edged blade, wide at the base, where it is provided with projections of various forms, hooked, crescent, &c., and tapering to a point. It is always symmetrical, both sides balancing in form. The Ranseur and the Spetum are modifications of the partisan. In Plate XXVII. a ranseur is shown from the Edinburgh Collection, dating from the early sixteenth century: here the two points on the lateral projections give a graceful outline to the weapon, while at the same time increasing its efficiency. A spetum from the Wallace Collection is shown in Fig. 430 ; it dates from *c.* 1490.

The Pike.—The pike was the "bayonet" of the mediæval and later periods, and only disappeared at a comparatively recent date. It was one of the simplest of weapons, being merely a long, narrow, lance-like head of steel strengthened by lengthy strips of metal, which ran for a considerable distance down the pole, rendering it almost immune from sword-cuts. The length of the weapon varied very considerably, from over twenty feet to less than ten, but the latter was the usual length. For resisting a cavalry charge the base of the pike was fixed into the ground, an iron shoe or point being provided to protect that part. The

FIG. 430.—1 Spetum (partisan), 1490.   2. Partisan, 1570.
3. Partisan, 1580.

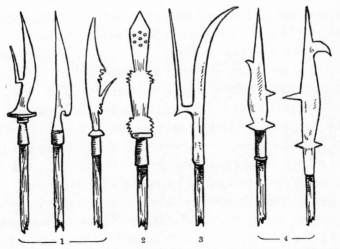

FIG. 431.—1. Glaives.   2. Ox-tongue partisan.   3. Guisarme.   4. Bills, 1540.

long strips of steel down the shaft may be considered one of its special features, as it could not be put out of action by any ordinary cuts of the sword, axe, &c.

During the eighteenth century a half-pike was carried by infantry officers which was known as the Spontoon. It had a long shaft with a leaf-shaped head, the latter having as a rule a cross-guard beneath it.

The Voulge.—This weapon may be regarded as a cousin to the guisarme, from which at times it differed but little. In its simplest form it consists of a broad blade fixed at the side of a shaft, and attached to it by two or more rings which spring from the back of the blade. The latter is invariably carried up to a sharp point over the axis of the shaft, and some examples show a spike upon the side opposite to the blade. The voulge is a Swiss weapon, and was in use by that nation at a very early period; it did not become popular among the Continental nations, although the French seem to have used it in the fifteenth century, when the arbalestiers were armed with it.

The Fork.—The military fork undoubtedly owed its conception to the agricultural implement, and in its earlier forms was of equally simple construction. The two prongs were eventually made of unequal length, and examples are to be found having three prongs, all unequal. As usual with shaft weapons, hooks were added with which a horseman might be dismounted from his charger, and barbs were occasionally added to give effect to side blows. During the fourteenth century it was much used; it appeared as early as the eleventh century, and was not entirely discarded until the end of the seventeenth. Plate XXVII. from the Edinburgh Collection is a scaling-fork with a particu-

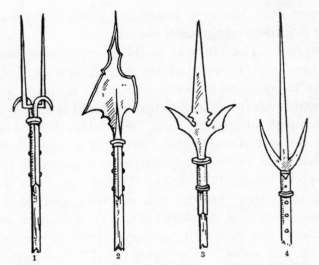

FIG 432.—1. Military fork.   2. Halberd.   3. Corseque (partisan).
4. Spetum

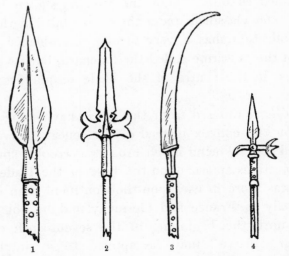

FIG. 433.—1. Spontoon (partisan).   2. Partisan.   3. Glaive.   4. Halberd.

larly long shaft, the very prominent hooks being designed
to drag defenders off the battlements.

The Bill.—The bill was in its incipient condition the
agricultural scythe mounted on a staff, and as such was
used for many years following the ninth century, but developments took place in its structure, and it subsequently
became much altered in form, invariably, however, pre-
serving the one characteristic feature of a crescent-shaped
blade with the inside edge sharpened.   A small portion
of the point was double-edged.   This weapon was usually
referred to as the "brown" bill, which suggests that their
usual condition was a rusty one.   It remained in use
until about the fifteenth century, when it was superseded by the pike.   The term "bill" is essentially a
generic one, and all shafted weapons of peculiar form
which do not fall readily under any particular heading
are classified as bills.   Thus the weapon shown in Plate
XXVII., and classified under the term "bill" in the Edinburgh Collection, has a very strong resemblance to that
variety of the guisarme called the fauchard, but its extreme
narrowness in the centre of the blade disqualifies it.   It
dates from *c.* 1470.

The Glaive differed from the bill in having the cutting
edge upon the convex instead of the concave curve of the
blade, and also in being much broader.   Hooks, spurs, and
other projections appear upon the base of the blade.   This
weapon was more in use upon the Continent than in England, chiefly in France and Germany, and did not become
obsolete until the beginning of the seventeenth century.
The term "glaive" may be applied to a simple shaft
weapon bearing any resemblance to a knife blade: thus

No. 7, Plate XXVII., from the Edinburgh Castle Museum, would fall under that category.

The Morning Star.—This was a mace with a spiked head, in great use upon the Continent, especially among the German nations; both cavalry and infantry were armed with it, the long-shafted weapon being appropriated by the foot soldier. Doubtless one of its advantages was the facility with which it could be made, a skilled armourer not being necessary. The short weapons of the cavalry were generally made of iron.

The Military Flail, or Holy Water Sprinkler.— The Military Flail is akin to the Morning Star and the Morgenstern. It consists of a shaft to which is affixed a staple having a chain depending, and to

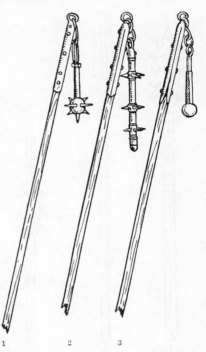

FIG. 434.—1. Holy water sprinkler. 2. Military flail. 3. Holy water sprinkler.

the end of this a ball of iron usually covered with spikes. At times a flail of iron or wood, garnished with spikes, is substituted for the chain and ball (Fig. 434).

The Mace.—The mace has probably a more remote antiquity than any other weapon. Commencing in the Stone Age, it has come down through the Bronze Period to that of Iron, and was in general use by Egyptians, Assyrians, and throughout the East. The Normans and Saxons both used it at Hastings, and, as a weapon, it did not disappear until the sixteenth century. It has under-

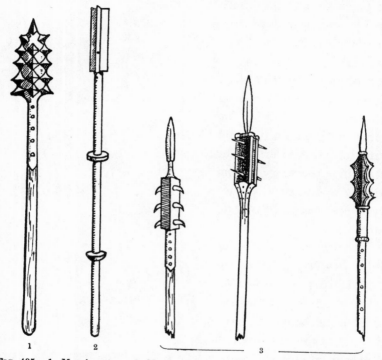

FIG. 435.—1. Morning star. 2. Mace. 3. Maces (or goedendags, or morgensterns).

gone many changes of form, being at times of cog-wheel shape, oval, globular, dentated, &c., but the general form was that of radiating flanges surrounding a central head. The knob was at times of lead, and some maces are furnished with a spike, as a prolongation of the shaft (Fig. 435). As early as the fourteenth century, the mace was in use as a sign of authority among the law officers, and in the sixteenth century was the characteristic weapon of the sergeant-at-arms. The royal arms were stamped upon the shaft at the termination of the grip: this end became in consequence the important part of the weapon; the ornaments and guards augmented and developed, while the end furnished with the knob shrank into insignificance. Finally the mace was reversed; the arms now appear upon the upper end of the shaft in all corporation and other maces. The mace was the weapon of militant churchmen, who sought thus to avoid the denunciation against those "who smite with the sword"; they argued that although the Scripture forbade the shedding of blood there was no restriction respecting the dashing out of brains.

The Martel-de-Fer.—Under the mace variety the martel-de-fer may be classified. It is of very ancient origin, and has at all periods been a favourite weapon of both horse and foot soldiers, but probably more so during the fourteenth and fifteenth centuries than at other periods. The mediæval archer is often represented with this weapon, and apparently preferred it to the sword. The general shape was a plain hammer-head projection, often serrated to prevent glancing off plate, balanced by a pick or blade upon the opposite side; in only a few examples is the shaft prolonged into a spike. In the Chain Mail Period it was often made with a heavy falcon beak without the hammer-head, while some examples dating from the Tabard Period have two sharp beaks of pick-axe form for penetrating the joints of armour, which are probably the same weapons mentioned by writers of the fourteenth century and termed bisacutas.

The Lance.—The spear, javelin, and lance of the Bronze and Iron Periods down to the time of the Saxons and Normans have been treated under their different headings. For three centuries after the Norman Conquest the spear does not exhibit any remarkable change; it was of uniform size and thickness from end to end, with a lozenge or leaf-shaped head, rarely barbed, the lozenge being the commoner form. For tournament purposes the heads were blunted, but as jousting became more popular special points or coronals were introduced, of which examples are shown in most museums. These were not intended to pierce, but only to give a grip upon plate armour.

During the Splinted and Camail Periods the men-at-arms invariably dismounted and fought upon foot, and in order to adapt the lance to these altered conditions it was cut down to about five feet in length. Later in the Camail Period a small circular plate was fixed upon the lance to protect the hand, and this subsequently developed into the vamplate of varied form and dimensions. At this time also the shaft of the lance became much enlarged for tilting purposes, and was made hollow, with longitudinal grooves upon the exterior; in this form it splintered in the encounter; when the tilting had for its object the unhorsing of combatants the lance was made stronger and heavier. During the reign of Elizabeth the lance ceased to hold the important position it had hitherto maintained among weapons, and became obsolete, but in later times it has been revived for the use of cavalry.

The Sword.—The various parts of a sword should perhaps be mentioned before proceeding to a chronological description of the varieties. The two essential parts are the blade and the hilt. The prolongation of the blade which fits into the handle is the tang; the upper portion near the hilt the ricasso. The essential portions of the hilt are the quillons, which cross at right angles between the blade and the handle to protect the hand; the grip, which is self-explanatory, and the pommel, the expanded piece at the end of the grip.

Pre-Norman Period.—The swords of this age generally in use throughout Europe were of the Scandinavian type, and may be divided into three classes: (1) those having the character of a broadsword, with parallel sharp edges and an acute point, and the tang only for a grip; (2) a similar variety having a cross guard; and (3) a sword with the blade slightly curved. The grip was usually of wood covered with skin, but some-

FIG. 436.—Sword, *c.* 1340; blade 33 in. long, 2 in. wide at hilt. (Wallace Collection.)

times of bone: the pommels were of varying shapes, as round, triangular, trefoil, and quatrefoil. The cross-guards began in a simple projection, but increased as time went on; they, together with the pommel, were at times very highly ornamented. The sheaths were usually of leather, stiffened with a wood framing. As will be seen by referring to the plates, the sword did not vary much in form from the twelfth to the end of the fifteenth century (Fig. 436). The blade was always two-edged, and about forty inches in length; the quillons at times drooped towards the blade, but were generally straight; the grip varied perhaps more than any other part, being at times almost double handed, and at others — the later Tabard Period, for instance—was so short and swollen as to appear unserviceable.   The shape of the pommel takes many forms, varying almost with the individual taste of the owner; occasionally the pommel and other parts were subjected to a high degree of ornamentation, with precious stones and inlaid work of all descriptions.   During the thirteenth century the curved sabre was used, but very rarely; it is shown in Fig. 154, p. 125, a group from the Painted Chamber.   Other varieties were the falchion, cultellus, anelace, and scimitar.

The Falchion was chiefly used by archers and men-at-arms.   It had a blade wide at the point; the edge was curved and convex, the back concave.

The Cultellus was a short sword, and is not often mentioned or represented.   It was designed especially for the use of foot soldiers when rushing upon knights who had been dismounted in a cavalry charge, or for the close encounter of infantry against infantry.

The Anelace was a long dagger which was secured to the person by a chain.   It is often represented upon effigies and brasses of civilians in the fourteenth and fifteenth centuries, and at times assumed very large proportions.   The handle is as a rule made in the fashion of that of the cinquedea, from which it was probably derived.   The latter is a dagger or short sword which had its origin in Italy; the blade is generally of the width of five fingers at the hilt (whence the name); the quillons

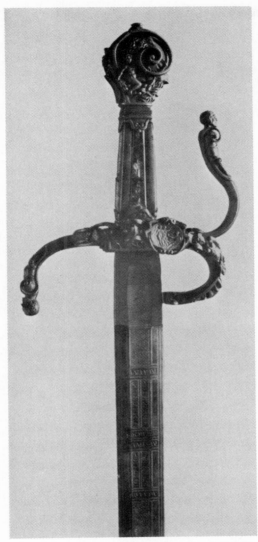

Plate XXVIII*

Sword of Philip II., with the Mark of Clement
Horn of Solingen

always bend towards the blade, and the latter, which is two-edged, averages from eighteen to twenty inches in length. The representation given here is from a beautiful specimen in the Wallace Collection dating from 1470 (Fig. 437), the blade of which is nearly four inches wide and nineteen inches long; the quillons are of latten and the handle of ivory, studded with filigree work.

The Scimitar became a favourite weapon with the infantry during the greater part of the Tabard Period, the blade being curved at the back with a cusp at the point, which distinguished it from the falchion. A finger-guard was often added by prolonging one side of the cross-piece, whereby it ran parallel to the grip, and then either curved outwards or, later in the period, turned inwards to join the pommel.

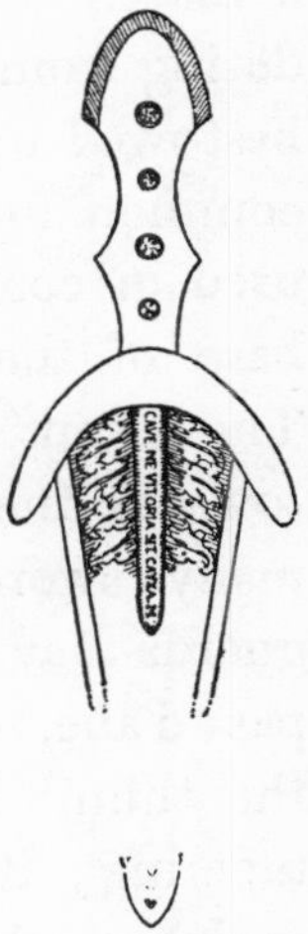

In the Transition and Maximilian Periods the sword underwent many changes, chiefly in the hilt, which presented a bewildering variety of additional pieces, all intended for the protection of the hand and the entanglement or breaking of the sword-blade of the opponent. Four examples are given here from the Royal Armoury at Madrid which exhibit these extra guards (Plates XXVIII.* and XXIX.*). The old cross-piece did not die out, but became bent in another form as a capital **S**; rings appeared on either side of the cross-piece and at right angles to it; back-guards were introduced, and also the basket-hilt. The quillons, by being curved as indicated above, developed the knuckle-guard on one side of the grip

Fig. 437.

which eventually reached the pommel, while the other, circling towards the blade, developed counter-guards for protecting the back of the hand. Thus the rapier-guard was developed, the varieties and modifications of which are almost numberless. The Wallace Collection contains a matchless array of these beautiful weapons, the earliest dating from 1540 : some of these have lavish ornamentation bestowed upon them. Broadly speaking, cup-hilts were a common form where long, straight, or curved quillons were used in conjunction with a cup-shaped finger-guard at the base of the blade, which was as a rule highly decorated. The swept hilt had a broad back-guard which narrowed towards the pommel, together with curved quillons. Upon many swords of the sixteenth century and later curved guards may be seen extending round the ricasso ; this is the pas d'ane, while rings may also be observed for passing the thumb through. The rapier blade was long, thin, and tapering ; it was essentially a thrusting sword, but not exclusively so. These weapons were for parade and the duel, a two-edged rapier of special design being used in war. During the eighteenth century the general tendency of the hilt was to become less complicated and to develop the simple basket form.

The Two-handed Sword was an invention of the fourteenth century, and formed one of the ordinary weapons of the foot soldier. To wield it both hands were employed in making cutting sweeps, and consequently very open order was necessary for troops thus armed ; at first it did not find favour in England, except for use in the lists, being chiefly carried at the saddle-bow by knights as a reserve weapon in case of being dismounted, when they trusted to its use against foot soldiers. In Scotland, however, it appears to have been in great favour, and its practice much resorted to. An excellent example and of an early date (*c.* 1490) is preserved in the Banqueting Hall of Edinburgh Castle, which is remarkable for its exceptional length, being exactly six feet,—four feet three inches in the blade, and the handle twenty-one inches (Plate XXVII.). The grip is of the usual character and the pommel is small; the quillons droop slightly towards the blade and terminate in two spirals, small engaging-guards being furnished on both sides. There is a strong ricasso of oblong section giving great strength to the blade, and the usual two lateral projections of rather large proportions. During the Maximilian Period it was a favourite weapon in England, and its value for the defence of a narrow pass, and against stormers at a beleaguered town, was fully recognised. The Scottish claymore is really the two-handed sword, and the application of the name to the basket-hilted broadsword of the eighteenth century is a mistake. The two-handed sword with waved blade is called a flamberge (Fig. 438); the example is from the Wallace Collection (date about 1630); the blade measures fifty inches and the

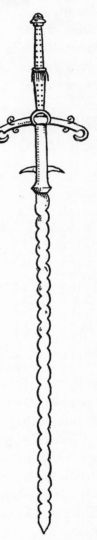

Fig. 438.—Flamberge, c. 1630. (Wallace Collection.)

handle over twelve. A ring-guard is furnished on either side of the quillons; there are the two usual projections from the ricasso, which is covered in leather. An earlier example, c. 1530, has a grip of no less than twenty-two inches; the blade is fifty inches long, and it has ring-guards and diagonally curved quillons (Fig. 428). The ricasso is covered with leather, as in the former example.

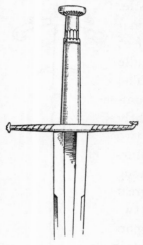

The Hand-and-half, or Bastard Sword, illustrated in Fig. 439, dates from 1490, and may be claimed as belonging to the two-handed variety. It came into vogue in England during the Camail and Jupon Period, but was used much earlier in Germany; the blade is forty inches long, but in some examples it is nearly fifty. It could be wielded with one hand, but to give extra effect to a blow, if desired, the left hand could be brought into action near the pommel, where the grip is smaller. This type of sword was in use during the whole of the fifteenth century.

FIG. 439.—Hand - and - half sword, 1490. (Wallace Collection.)

The Dagger.—This weapon has been described where necessary in preceding chapters up to and including the Camail and Jupon Period, when the misericorde with its triangular blade was so much in evidence. In the reign of Richard II. the wearing of a dagger of some kind was universal, even the ladies having a small baselard attached to their girdles. Shortly afterwards a long poniard of Continental origin superseded the previous weapon, which,

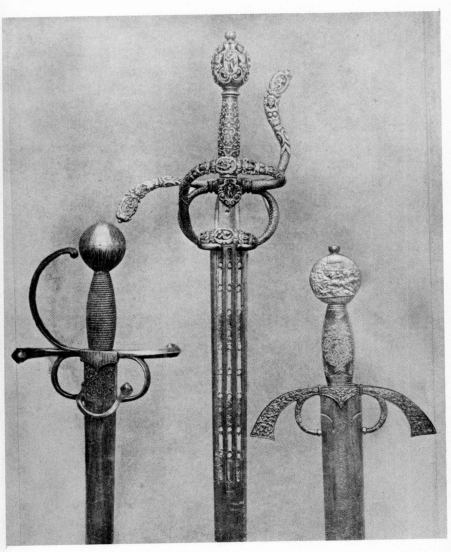

A. F. Calvert

PLATE XXIX *

1. Sword of Hernando Cortes.
2. Sword of Philip II.
3. Sword of Gonsalvo de Cordoba, late Fifteenth Century.

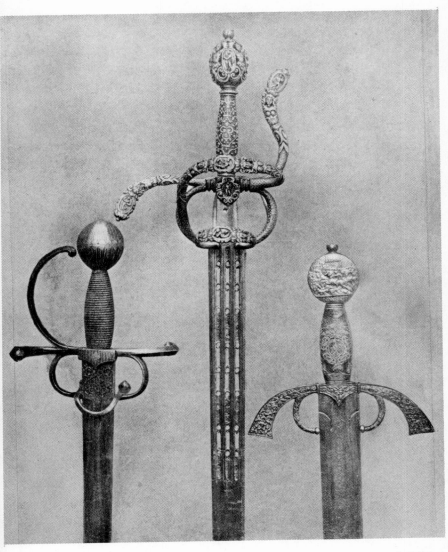

A. F. Calvert

PLATE XXIX *

1. Sword of Hernando Cortes.
2. Sword of Philip II.
3. Sword of Gonsalvo de Cordoba, late Fifteenth Century.

like the sword, had a thumb-guard attached in the form of a ring. The cinquedea, which may be looked upon as a dagger, has been dealt with on p. 334. An example of the military dagger of the fourteenth century is in the Wallace Collection, dating from 1440, with a fifteen-inch blade, and is of the greatest rarity, although illustrations in missals, &c., are numerous. A specimen of the "Kidney" dagger, so called from the shape of the base of the grip, is also preserved there, dating from 1480; it was in common use in England until the time of Charles I.

The main-gauche, or left-handed dagger, was of Continental origin, and enjoyed an immense popularity in England during the sixteenth century. It was held in the left hand to ward off blows and entangle the point of the adversary's weapon, while the long rapier was being used in the right hand.

CHAPTER XVII

PROJECTILE-THROWING ENGINES

No evidence is extant respecting the inventor of the first machine for missile throwing, but we know that they have existed from the earliest ages, and have been used by all the great nations of antiquity. Under the Greeks and Romans, but especially the former, they attained a remarkable degree of excellence, and many accounts of their extraordinary efficiency have come down to us. The Romans took their ideas from the Greeks as a basis to work upon; among their best authorities Vitruvius may be classed. The principles involved in these engines were not altogether lost, but descended to the mediæval ages, and probably during that period more elaborate, powerful, and gigantic machines were constructed than at any previous time.

The complicated methods by which a fortress was captured or a town carried during the Middle Ages are not generally known, and the means adopted at the present time are as a general rule credited with being the outcome of the skill and science of the past few centuries. This, however, will not bear the test of investigation, for we find that almost every device has had its prototype in past ages, and nearly every idea has been forestalled. It comes almost with a shock to some, and produces feelings of incredulity, to be told that huge missiles vieing in destructive effect with the modern shell, and as a rule many times larger,

PLATE XXX *

Armour of Charles V., from Augsburg or Nuremberg

were sent with unerring aim into the heart of a besieged town, levelling houses to the ground and dealing destruction far and wide. The idea of a siege in mediæval times is generally that of a tree to batter down a door, archers to shoot down the defenders on the walls, desperate charges of cavalry against sallies of the garrison, and forlorn hopes of men carrying scaling-ladders with which to surmount the walls. These are, however, only a few concomitants of the complicated methods by which a siege was accomplished.

The Greeks and Romans constructed their engines upon the principle of the bow, whereas the mediæval engineers adopted that of the sling. The latter was by far the more clumsy of the two, but probably just as effective. Had the methods by which the Greeks were enabled to construct their splendid engines been handed down, the possibility is that mediæval machines would have been far less cumbersome and much smaller. Probably the greatest living authority upon projectile-throwing machines is Sir Ralph Payne-Gallwey, Bart., who has constructed models of ancient and mediæval machines with most successful results. He says, " My engines are by no means perfect in their mechanism, and are always liable to give way under the strain of working. One reason of this is that all modern engines of the kind require to be worked to their utmost capacity, *i.e.* to the verge of their breaking-point, to obtain from them results that at all equal those of their prototypes. The ancient engines did their work easily and well within their strength. Although my largest catapult will throw a stone to a great distance it cannot throw one of nearly the weight it should be able to do, considering the size of its frame, skein of cord, and mechanism. In this respect it is decidedly inferior to the ancient engine."[1] The author of the above has, however, been able to construct a catapult which throws a stone of 8 lbs. to a distance of between four hundred and fifty and five hundred yards.

The Catapult.—The " Tormentum " of the Romans was a generic name for military engines, and so named from the twisting of the hair, thongs, sinews, &c., of which the propelling mechanism was made. What were the exact materials used, and in what proportions, is entirely unknown, and probably the knowledge did not extend beyond a century or so after the fall of the empire. There can be no doubt but that the sinews of animals played an important part in the construction of the skein. The method of making the catapult was as follows, omitting unnecessary details. A quadrangular wooden frame of great strength was fitted near one end with the skein, which was made in the form of a circle and of very considerable thickness, the rubber tyre of a large motor-car wheel approximating both in size and shape. This was folded into two parallel straight lines and passed through holes in the frame on either side, where a simple mechanism grasped it which could revolve the ends, cogs preventing them from turning in any direction but that desired. Between the parallel parts of the skein the end of the arm was placed, and by twisting the ends of the skein the arm was made to press with considerable force against a horizontal beam supported by uprights at the two sides. The arm was provided with a hollow in the

[1] From "Projectile-throwing Engines of the Ancients," by Sir Ralph Payne-Gallwey, Bart., by kind permission of the author, to whose work I am indebted for several particulars in this chapter.

upper part for holding the stone. If now the arm were
drawn back by means of levers, ropes, and pulleys, the
distortion upon the skein was increased enormously, and
if when loaded with a projectile the arm were released, it
sprang back against the beam with great velocity and
force, throwing the stone to a distance during the action.
This propulsive force was considerably augmented in some
machines by the addition of a sling to the end of the arm,
which practically lengthened the arm and consequently
hurled the projectile to a greater distance. Ancient writers

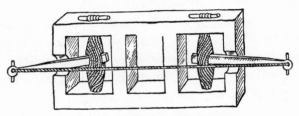

Fig. 440.—Principle of the balista.

assert that the range was sometimes as much as from seven
hundred to eight hundred yards.

The Balista.—This machine was used by the Romans
for discharging the Falarica or ponderous spear, which had
an iron head of over a foot in length at one end, with a
ball of lead at the other end, and was at times used to carry
incendiary material. It was projected upon the same
principle as the stone in the catapult, namely by means
of twisted skeins, but in the case of the balista two were
in use. They were fitted vertically in a frame open to the
front: an arm was passed through each skein, and when
the skeins were twisted, the arms sought to diverge from
one another. A rope acted like the string of a bow, and

was wound back by a suitable apparatus, thus tending to draw the arms to a parallel position; upon its release the falarica was propelled in exactly the same manner as an arrow is discharged. It rested in a directing hollow trough until the trigger was pulled. These heavy missiles travelled at times to a distance of between three hundred and four hundred yards and it will thus be seen that practically the two ends of a bow are used for the propulsive force. The balista could also be used for discharging stones if required by a simple alteration of the bow-string, and the addition of another trough for directing the missile.

The Trebuchet.—The Trebuchet was a mediæval weapon derived from the classical engines of previous ages, but depending entirely upon the principle of the sling in contradistinction to that of torsion. It was a gigantic arm of wood, lengthened considerably by a sling; the arm was pivoted near one end remote from the sling, and this beam being actuated by the fall of an extremely heavy weight caused it to describe the quarter of a circle and discharge the missile. It superseded the catapult, chiefly for the reason that the making of the skeins of the latter had become a lost art, and also that a trebuchet could be quickly constructed on the spot required with materials generally found ready to hand, whereas the catapult necessarily had to be transported. Consequently trebuchets were invariably dismantled after a siege and not carried from place to place, the ponderous nature of the machine presenting an obstacle to such a course. There is no doubt that the addition of the sling was an idea obtained from the East at a very early date, as a MS. of the thirteenth century contains a representation showing it. In Add.

MS. 10,292, British Museum, a trebuchet is shown in use against a castle which is being attacked by knights of the Ailette Period clad in banded mail. This shows the sling affixed to the arm, but no comparison of size is possible, as the machine is shown smaller than a horse, and the horse is nearly the size of the castle. In Roy. MS. 16, G. VI., dating from c. 1330, two trebuchets are shown in action against a castle. They are much out of drawing, as the arm bearing the counterpoise of one is actually shown longer than the arm bearing the sling, whereas it was probably only a small fraction of the length. Hewitt quotes from a work written by Gilles Colonne (d. 1316) for his pupil, Philip the Fair of France, in which he says, " Of perriers (a general name for stone-projecting machines) there are four kinds, and in all these machines there is a beam which is raised and lowered by means of a counterpoise, a sling being attached to the end of the beam to discharge the stone. Sometimes the counterpoise is not sufficient, and then they attach ropes to it in order to move the beam. The counterpoise may either be fixed or movable, or both at once. In the fixed counterpoise a box is fastened to the end of the beam, and filled with stones or sand or any heavy body. These machines cast their missiles with most exactness, because the weight acts in a uniform manner. Their aim is so sure that one may, so to say, hit a needle. If the gyn carries too far it may be drawn back or loaded with a heavier stone; if the contrary, then it must be advanced or a smaller stone supplied. Others of these machines have a movable counterpoise attached to the beam, turning upon an axis. The third kind has two weights, one fixed to the beam and the other movable round it; by this means it throws with more exactness. The fourth sort, in lieu of weights attached to the beam, has a number of ropes, and is discharged by a number of men pulling simultaneously at the cords. This last kind does not cast such large stones as the others, but it has the advantage that it may be more rapidly loaded and discharged than they. In using the perriers by night it is necessary to attach a lighted body to the projectile; by this means one may discover the force of the machine and regulate the weights of the stone accordingly." This very valuable description of four varieties of the trebuchet at such an early date gives us an idea of the state of perfection to which they had then arrived, and from other sources may be obtained particulars relating to the size and weight of the missiles employed. They were not always of stone, but barrels of Greek fire, pitch, naphtha, and other inflammable substance were used; also occasionally the bodies of dead horses and other animals, often in a state of decomposition, barrels of offensive or putrid matter, and other missiles of a similar nature designed to cause pestilence, were thrown into towns or fortresses when the defence was obstinately prolonged. In the account left to us by Guillaume des Ormes of Carcassone in 1240, we read: "Afterwards they set up a mangonel before our barbican, when we lost no time in opposing to it from within an excellent Turkish petrary, which played upon the mangonel and those about it; so that, when they essayed to cast upon us, and saw the beam of our petrary in motion, they fled, utterly abandoning their mangonel. And in that place they made ditches and palisades, yet as often as we discharged our

PLATE XXXI*

Burgundy Cross Armour of Philip II.

petrary we drove them from it." At the siege of Bedford Castle in 1224, the garrison of which were followers of Faukes de Breauté, a leader of mercenaries in the time of King John, seven mangonels were in use in the besieging force. Matthew Paris mentions the terrible effects of the trebuchets in 1246 at the siege of the castle of Cappacio, when seven well-ordered machines discharged day and night such an uninterrupted storm of missiles upon the ill-fated fortress that it was battered into a helpless condition, and had perforce to surrender. He also states that in 1253 the Gascons hurled stones and darts of such wonderful size that many of them were carried into England to be exhibited as curiosities. In the defence of castles the garrison naturally set up missile-throwing weapons, and these were as a rule built upon the ground within the encircling walls, and threw their projectiles high in the air over the battlements into the enemy's camp. Smaller ones were also built upon the walls and towers. Where large towns were besieged it was no unusual thing to have from one to three hundred projectile-throwing engines in action. The mangonel, petrary, mangonella, biblia, and many other names used by mediæval writers, all refer to the trebuchet and its many modifications.

Various machines were invented during the Middle Ages, in which the principle of propulsion was the steel bow mounted upon a frame partaking of the nature of the arbalest. These bows were at times of considerable size, and threw javelins, spears, and weapons of a similar nature. Being mounted upon wheels, they served all the purposes fulfilled by modern field artillery. In the same category may be mentioned one which threw one or two stones at a single discharge: it consisted of a vertical spring of steel which was pulled backwards by ropes and pulleys. and upon being released threw one missile from a sling attached to its extremity and another from a cup fixed to the steel.

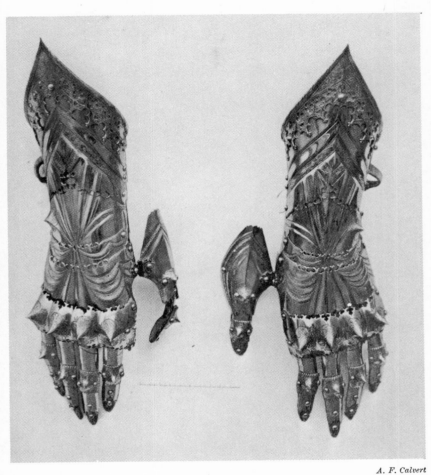

PLATE XXXII *

Gauntlets of Charles V.

CHAPTER XVIII

GERMAN, ITALIAN, AND OTHER INFLUENCES UPON EUROPEAN ARMOUR

It may come somewhat in the nature of a shock to the self-complacency of the average Englishman to learn that in the great stores of armour in the public and private collections of Great Britain and Ireland only an infinitesimal portion is of English origin, and also that England was never celebrated in any age for the output of reliable suits. The excellent quality of English steel is, at the present time, accepted throughout the world, while the care and finish bestowed upon articles fabricated from it is proverbial, and in marked contrast to that of many other nations. This fact is so well known that the average inhabitant of our isles unconsciously places armour in the same category, and believes as a matter of course that it was pre-eminent in the Middle Ages. But the superiority of British iron is a matter of the last two or three centuries, and only sprang into existence when armour was becoming obsolete, whereas upon the Continent the manufacture in some places dates back almost to remote antiquity. This is especially the case with regard to Germany, whence has emanated the great majority of the armour seen in our museums. If we take the Wallace Collection, for instance, we find that sixteen cap-à-pie suits are contained in it, of which thirteen are German, two

Italian, and one English. Of this number the eight earliest, dating from 1460 to 1560, are of German manufacture. Of the three three-quarter suits dating from 1520 to 1540 the whole are German, while of the nine half-suits only one is Italian, the remainder coming from Germany A similar comparison taken in other museums would probably give a like result. If, however, a collection has no suits of armour previous to the year 1605, a probability exists that English armour might occupy the second if not the first place, inasmuch as the half and three-quarter suits in use during the Civil Wars were largely made in England. It must not be supposed, however, that the English armourers of the Middle Ages were incapable of manufacturing defensive or offensive equipments, for it is almost certain that the greater part used from the time of the War of the Barons to the Wars of the Roses was fabricated at home, always excepting that worn by royalty and the most prominent nobles. English armour was, however, heavy and cumbrous, the inferior quality of the metal necessitating great thickness in order to secure efficiency; consequently those who could afford it procured the foreign article, where the superior temper gave a minimum of weight with the same or even better protection. It may be compared to the modern Harveyised steel plate for battleships, of six or eight inches in thickness, which affords greater security than the eighteen inches of iron formerly in use. A large amount of foreign armour has found its way into our country owing to the law of tournaments, whereby the equipment of the vanquished became the lawful spoil of the victor; while the prolonged wars waged upon the Continent by English armies—invariably with some degree of success—must have furnished both the knight and the common soldier with means of defence superior to that of home manufacture.

It is curious to note how in the early part of the Middle Ages the same general outline of military equipment prevailed over the civilised portion of the continent of Europe, and this is exemplified in Fig. 441, taken from Add. MS. 11,695, a Spanish parchment of the eleventh century. If the warriors delineated in it are compared with those represented upon the Bayeux Tapestry, the only essential differences to be discovered are the excessive lengths of the hauberk and gambeson, and also the circular shield. The trilobed pommels of the swords and the cross

FIG. 441.—Spanish soldiers, eleventh century. (Add. MS. 11,695.)

guards of the lances suggest a Scandinavian origin, but the hauberk, nasal helmet, and leg defences are almost exact counterparts of the Norman equipment. Again, in Fig. 442, which represents a continental warrior of the year 1100, the general appearance is similar to our own knights of the Chain Mail Period, if we except the peculiar helmet

and the deep indentations in the skirt of the surcoat.   The
coif-de-mailles, hauberk, chausses, shield, and sword are

almost precisely the same.   In the year 1330
the continental equipment was the same in
its broad character as in England, which
may be seen from Fig. 443, taken from
Add. MS. 12,228 in the British Museum,
where the only differences are the trefoil
coudière and the laminated brassarts, which
were not general in our country, although
isolated instances occur of both.   During
the Camail and Jupon Period the plate
armour was precisely similar all over the
Continent, the only variations being in the
shape of the jupon, which was sleeveless

FIG.   442.—Conti-
nental   warrior.
(From a foreign
MS., *c.* 1100.)

in England, but was often provided with
baggy sleeves ornamented with rows of
buttons in other countries,

chiefly Spain and Italy, while tight sleeves
were worn in Germany.   The frequent
intercourse between the Continent and
ourselves in the fifteenth and sixteenth
centuries led to the free introduction of
foreign supplies, and English armour lost
what little insular character it formerly
possessed.

It may be stated as a general fact that
no authentic suits anterior to the year
1400 are in existence, although many

FIG.443.—Frenchknight,
c. 1330.

separate pieces are preserved which were made before that
year, chiefly helmets, mail, gauntlets, and a few pieces of

PLATE XXXIII*

Armour of Charles V., made by Colman

plate. The same may be said of the armour prevailing from 1400 to 1440, though larger and more numerous portions of it exist, but of the Gothic armour which came into being after that date a number of complete suits are extant. Germany was almost the sole maker of this description of defence, and not only are the majority of suits of this period of German make, but Germany itself has for long been the happy hunting-ground of collectors, and was at one time deemed almost inexhaustible. There are many German armourers whose names have been handed down upon the roll of fame, but the most honoured bore the name of Colman. This family had settled in Augsburg in the latter part of the fourteenth century, and gradually established a reputation; the most famous and best known being Lorenz Colman, who began work in 1467. He was patronised by Maximilian, King of the Romans, a few years later, and appointed Court Armourer in 1490. In conjunction with the emperor there can be no doubt that the Maximilian style was evolved in the first decade of the sixteenth century. Lorenz died in 1516, and an example of his workmanship dating from 1515 may be seen in a cap-à-pie suit in the Wallace Collection. His successor, Koloman Colman, surnamed Helmschmied, produced many wonderful examples of skilled workmanship, such as are exemplified in his suits constructed for the Emperor Charles V. (Plate XXXIII.*), and preserved in the Royal Armoury at Madrid.[1]

[1] The Royal Armoury at Madrid is undoubtedly the finest collection of its kind in the world. It was founded by King Charles V., 1516–1568, and in addition to Spanish armour and arms contains magnificent examples of the works of the greatest armourers of Europe. By the kindness and courtesy of Mr. Albert F. Calvert, author of "Spanish Arms and Armour, being a Historical and Descriptive Account of the Royal Armoury at Madrid," we are enabled to produce illustrations of many of the exhibits from photographs supplied by him. These illustrations are distinguished by an asterisk (Plate I.*, &c.).

In Plate XXX.*, the large tilting-piece, comprising grande garde, volante piece, and pauldron in one defence, is remarkable, while the pair of gauntlets belonging to the same monarch and illustrated in Plate XXXII.*, are admittedly the most superb examples in existence. The magnificent flutes, together with the delicate enrichments of the gadlings, have probably never been equalled. The style of ornamentation agrees exactly with that of Colman Helmschmied.

FIG. 444.—Complete plate : head and neck, *c.* 1400. (Roy. MS., 20, c. 7.)

The equestrian suit shown in Plate XXX.*, p. 340, is of Augsburg or Nuremberg make, and is also of the time of Charles V. It is of considerable interest in exhibiting the various kinds of extra defences such as the grande garde, garde-de-bras, and manifere, the last differing from the Wallace specimen in having separate fingers. The subject of horse armour, or bardings, has not been treated in this work owing to the exigencies of space ; it is a matter of considerable interest, and the horse shown in this plate exhibits it in very nearly its highest development. The error is very prevalent that horse defences were of comparatively late introduction (*i.e.* of the fifteenth and sixteenth centuries); the accompanying Fig. 444 from Roy. MS. 20, c. 7, *temp.* Henry IV. or earlier, shows defence of a very high order, inasmuch as the chanfron covers the whole of the head, and the crinet, of lames of plate, encircles the neck completely. In England horse-armour originated in the twelfth century. Plate XXXIV.*, exemplifies the wealth of elaborate decora-

PLATE XXXIV *

1. Moorish Chanfron.
2. Chanfron and Mainfaire, Sixteenth Century.
3. Chanfron, with Imperial Arms.

tion bestowed upon horse furniture in the sixteenth century; the chanfron in the centre has been worked into the semblance of a dragon with which the mainfaire is in harmony. The chanfron on the left is of Moorish workmanship.

During the fourteenth century the Italian armourers had been making steady progress towards fame, and in no city more so than Milan, where, towards the end of the century, armourers came to the front whose names are famous. A Milanese salade, c. 1480, is represented in Plate VII.*, p. 60, and was produced by one of the Negroli family, who made their home in the city. The salade is cast in one piece, except the visor, and the ornamentation is a pleasing combination of the Italian and Oriental styles. The delicacy, vigour, and force of its execution may readily be perceived upon inspection of the illustration. Another example of the work of the Negrolis is given in Plate X.*, p. 80, which represents a three-quarter suit made for Charles V. The Milanese were among the first to feel and acknowledge the influence of the Renaissance in their work, and the decorations upon the pauldrons, coudières, &c., of this suit exemplifies it.

Among the armourers who were entrusted with work for King Philip II. of Spain, the successor of Charles V., were the Wolf family of Landshut, and an example of their skill is shown in Plate XXXI.*, p. 346, upon the suit known as the Burgundy Cross armour. It was made in 1551 by Sigmund Wolf, and is richly decorated with bands of the natural colour of the steel, on which are etched alternately the Cross of Burgundy (the St. Andrew's Cross), and the emblems of the Golden Fleece, all gilded. The high pike-guard upon the *right* shoulder is a structural feature of this suit. An example of German armour dating from 1549, when Philip was heir-apparent (Plate XXI.*, p. 236), is an excellent example of the Decorative Period of the sixteenth century; it shows a mitten gauntlet upon the left hand, and unequal tassets. An earlier suit, made by Desiderius Colman in 1545, is adapted for jousting on foot, and has lamboys or bases (Plate XII.*, p. 128). The espalier pauldrons and roundels, the peascod breastplate, and the lames of plate over the knee in the cuisses, are features of the suit. Wolf of Landshut in 1554 made a suit for Philip II. (Plate XV.*, p. 146), for the Über die Pallia, or Welsches Gestech Course, which exhibits the manteau d'armes affixed and a small reinforcing piece attached to the right espalier, forming a pike-guard. To this suit a forbidden or locking gauntlet for the right hand is attached. The tassets are of unequal length. A helmet supplied at the same time as the above suit is a veritable triumph of the armourer's craft (Plate XVI.*, p. 166). The details may readily be seen in the illustration, and the volante piece, fixed to the helmet by a strap round the gorget, and so moving with it, is of special interest. Sigismund Wolf in 1550 made a suit for Philip which is represented in Plate XIII.*, p. 132. " Many of the extra pieces for this suit are now at Brussels. The ornamentation is chaste, consisting of narrow bands, etched with graceful scrolls and volutes on white burnished steel."

The year 1554, which saw the production of some of the above suits, probably witnessed the delivery of another to King Sebastian of Portugal, which is preserved in the Royal Armoury at Madrid, and is perhaps the most magnificent in the whole collection. The details of the back-

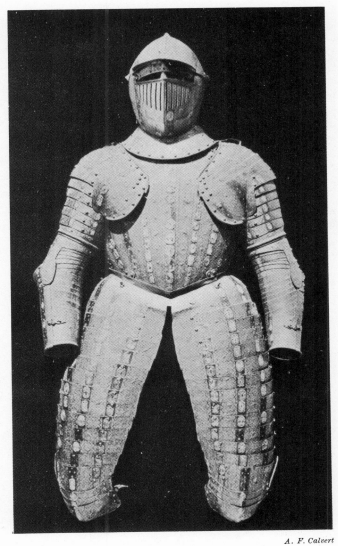

PLATE XXXV *

Milanese Armour of King Philip IV.

plate, pauldrons, and arm defences are shown in Plate XX.*, p. 232. It is the work of Anton Pfeffenhauser of Augsburg, and undoubtedly his masterpiece; as an example of repoussé work it places him upon an equality with the best German masters of his time. " Mythological figures are embossed upon the bands traversing the backplate; designs symbolical of Power, Victory, Peace, and Navigation are represented on the pauldrons, back and front, while the coudières display the four figures of the cardinal virtues." It is essentially a pageant suit, as is also the one presented to Philip III., when prince, at the age of seven. It is a half-suit of Italian workmanship, formed in gilded iron and decorated with figures, masks, &c., all embossed and damascened (Plate XVIII.*, p. 196). Another, presented to the same monarch in his childhood, is represented in Plate XIX.*, p. 212, and is believed to be the work of Lucio Picinino of Milan. The decoration is less profuse but quite as beautiful as in the preceding example. A piece of Spanish armour made at Pamplona in Navarre in 1620 is shown in Plate XXII.*, p. 240. Mr. Calvert states: " It is of steel-plated iron and of extraordinary thickness. . . . A curious feature is the seven indentations made by the bullets of an arquebus, and each set with silver pearls. These marks do not say much for the quality of the metal, which is 10 millimetres thick. The backplate, which is only 3 millimetres thick, has been perforated by a bullet. The arms are defended by espaliers reaching to the elbow, where they meet the cuffs of the gauntlets."

Plate XXI.*, p. 236, is a suit of Milanese make, early seventeenth century, intended for war purposes, and absolutely devoid of ornamentation. An example of Flemish

armour of 1624 is represented in Plate XXIII.*, p. 268 ; it
was sent by the Infanta Isabel Clara Eugenia to Philip IV.
The ugliness of the breastplate and the huge rivet-heads upon
the pauldrons are strongly suggestive of the " boiler plate "
armour prevailing in England at the same period.　Plate
XXXV.* is a suit presented by the Cardinal Infante
Ferdinand to Philip IV., and exhibits the lames of plate
inserted in the gousset of the coudière, similar to the Henry

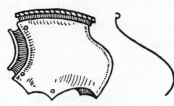

VIII. foot armour in the Tower.
It is of Milanese make, and
decorated with vertical bands of
medal-lions, &c.

　A second example of armour
of Spanish make is given in
Plate XXXVI.* ; it was fabricated at Pamplona for the Duke

FIG. 445.—Globose breastplate (Burgundian).　(Tower of London.)

of Savoy in 1620, and is decidedly an improvement upon the
suit shown in Plate XXII.*, p. 240, which came from the
same locality.　It is worthy of remark that Spain, with all its
vast resources of the finest iron ores in the world, did not
become a centre for arms and armour.　She was undoubtedly
able to supply her own requirements, and in the wars
against the Moors these were of no mean order, but no
distinct Spanish " School " was evolved similar to the
German or Italian.　The excellent quality of her swords
attained world-wide reputation, and the blades of Toledo,
Bilbao, and Seville are justly famous.　No town in France
achieved special success in armour or arms, although many
were active in the production.　Burgundy was chiefly noted
for its eccentricities, the breastplate illustrated in Fig. 445
furnishing an example, though many inventions, such as

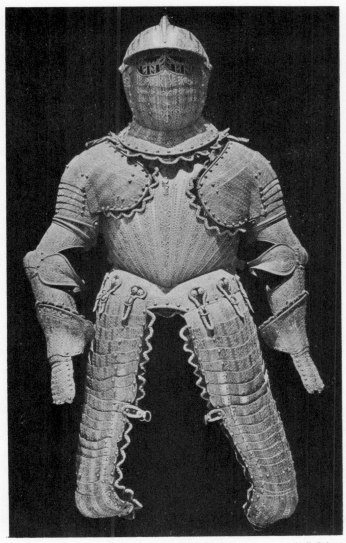

PLATE XXXVI *

Armour of Duke of Savoy, 1620.   Made at Pamplona

the burgonet, emanated from that warlike district, while
its hand-gun men of the fifteenth century were the best
in the world. Holland and Belgium have always enjoyed a
reputation for arms, and Netherlandish weapons and defences were in great demand. The overwhelming superiority
of Italian products must not be ascribed solely to one
town, Milan, for many others were famous, such as Pisa,
Verona, Lucca, Mantua, and Brescia, while Florence became
a serious rival to Milan in the latter part of the sixteenth
century. In Germany, Augsburg and Nuremberg probably
were the most renowned for armour, but Cologne bore
pre-eminence for weapons.

CHAPTER XIX

THE INTRODUCTION OF GUNPOWDER AND ITS INFLUENCE UPON ARMOUR

THE invention of gunpowder and its use in propelling missiles from tubes was the signal for the abolition of armour, as we have indicated, though the struggle for supremacy between the two lasted for considerably more than a century. The Eastern nations are generally credited with the discovery of the properties of a mixture of salt-petre, carbon, and sulphur so far as their use in fireworks is concerned, but it was undoubtedly to the Western nations that the knowledge and application of the propelling nature of the mixture were due. The first authentic account of its use for military purposes must be ascribed to the seventh century, when, under the name of Greek fire, it was used at the defence of Constantinople by the Byzantine emperors against the invading Saracens. The true Greek fire, how-ever, is supposed to have contained more ingredients than the three which constitute gunpowder proper, viz. resin and naphtha, the latter being in excess, and this mixture appears to have been so inflammable and so difficult to extinguish that the terror excited by its use was out of all proportion to the destruction that it wrought. It was propelled from balistæ, projected from tubes, and carried by means of arrows which bore tow steeped in the composition, while its use in a besieged town to pour down upon assailants was

PLATE XXXVII *

Double Breech-loading Cannon, in Bronze, used in Spain from the end
of the Fifteenth Century

probably the most efficacious. Its composition was for a long time kept secret, but the knowledge gradually spread, and during the later mediæval period its use was not unknown in England (Fig. 337). Gunpowder proper was used for the first time in the Spanish wars with the Moors in the twelfth century by both combatants; and the secret of its composition was discovered by Roger Bacon in the thirteenth century, probably from the translation of manuscripts. Schwartz, a German Frank, perfected it about a century later, and its first use in England occurred in the wars against the Scots by Edward III. in 1327, when the cannon were denominated "crakeys," a diminutive from "crake," the first name of the composition, which may be a corruption of "grec." At the siege of Cambrai in 1339 cannon were in use, and they are specifically mentioned by Froissart. After that time their use became general, and in 1346 many were in operation at the battle of Creçy, the gunpowder being imported from abroad until the reign of Elizabeth, when English powder-mills were established in the country. The word artillery had been in use to denote projectile-throwing weapons anterior to the use of gunpowder, and became eventually the term by which the larger kind of firearms was designated. The construction of the first cannon was, as might be inferred, of the rudest possible description. Pieces or bars of iron were arranged longitudinally so as to form a rough tube, around which iron hoops were placed to hold them together. The powder and ball were in a separate case, open at one end to allow of the exit of the ball; this case was inserted in one end of the tube and secured by a stirrup arrangement pivoting upon two projections on either side of the tube, which fell over the open end and prevented the case from being blown out when the discharge occurred. The powder was fired by the insertion of a red-hot wire. The cannon was fixed down to a piece of timber which rested upon a similar piece : at the breech end of the cannon the two planks were hinged together, and by the insertion of wedges in the front between the timbers the piece could be elevated. Other contrivances almost as crude as that described were introduced in order to overcome the difficulties of taking aim. The projectiles were at first made of stone, and subsequently of lead or iron, or stone coated with lead. It must not be supposed that the introduction of such weapons created the profound consternation which a few contemporary writers have led us to suppose; the general impression produced was, in fact, one of contemptuous indifference, and it was only after many improvements had been effected that cannon began to be taken seriously. The earliest were only used in sieges, as the transport of such cumbrous pieces was nearly an impossibility, and when they were subsequently adopted for use in the field it was but seldom they were used after the first discharge. During the fifteenth century fresh developments took place; trunnions were invented, whereby the recoil was transferred directly to the carriage; the weapon was cast in one piece which tapered towards the muzzle, and many improvements in loading and discharging were made. Bombards were introduced, being short pieces with a large bore which were fired at a considerable elevation and discharged balls of stone to a small distance; they were the prototypes of our modern mortars and howitzers. One of the earliest examples of mediæval ordnance preserved in this country may be seen at the

PLATE XXXVIII

The Dardanelles Bronze Gun, A.D. 1468. (Rotunda, Woolwich)

Rotunda, Woolwich (Plate XL., p. 366). It is known as the Crecy Bombard, and may possibly date back to the time of Edward III. It is said to have been found in the moat of Bodiham Castle, Sussex, and is known to have been in Battle Abbey for many years. Its interior is of cast iron, one of the earliest known specimens of the metal in that form, and iron hoops have been shrunk upon this inner core. The chamber in the smaller portion of the breech will hold about three or four pounds of powder; the stone shot discharged weighed about a hundred and sixty pounds and was fifteen inches in diameter. The carriage is modern. The cannonier wears a capacious salade and is defended by a hauberk of mail and a thick leather apron; he is discharging the bombard with a hot iron and protects his face with his hand from the inferior powder blown off the touchhole by the explosion.

Very large cannon were in use at times. Mons Meg at Edinburgh is an example of a fifteenth century production; it weighs nearly four tons, has a calibre of 20 inches, and threw a stone projectile of 300 lbs. The powder-chamber is considerably smaller in bore than the cannon, in order to withstand the force of the discharge. This piece is reputed to have been made in 1455 for the siege of Thrieve Castle by James II.; this latter monarch was killed five years later by the bursting of a similar cannon, the Lion. Another example is preserved at Ghent, where a foundry existed for their manufacture: the piece has a calibre of 26 inches, while English guns are to be seen at Mont St. Michael of 15 inches and 19 inches bore respectively. A remarkable example of fifteenth century monster ordnance is the Dardanelles bronze gun preserved at the Rotunda, Woolwich, and illustrated in Plate XXXVIII.). It was cast during the reign of Sultan Mahomed II., A.D. 1468, and presented to Queen Victoria by the Sultan of Turkey in 1867. It weighs 18 tons 14 cwt., the calibre is 25 inches, and the total length equals 17 feet. It is made in two parts, which are screwed together, and the breech portion which forms the powder chamber has a bore of only ten inches. The stone shot weighed 6 cwt. each. The names applied to ancient ordnance were many and various, and at the same time confusing, inasmuch as the calibre of the various pieces was constantly changing. The following is an approximate list of some of the pieces ordinarily in use :—

Cannon Royal, weight of shot, 66 lbs.; Carthorun, 48 lbs.; Cannon, 34 lbs.; Bastard Cannon; Great Culverin, 15 lbs.; Bastard Culverin, 7 lbs.; Demi-Culverin, 2 lbs.; Basilisk, Serpentin, Aspik, Dragon, Syren. For field service : Falcon, 1 lb.; Falconet, 14 ozs.; Saker.

Cannon have been made of various materials apart from iron and bronze, such as wood, paper, and rope, the outside covering being of leather. All the early guns used in England were obtained from abroad; the first foundry in England was that of Hugget of Uckfield, Sussex, in 1521, who cast cannon in brass and iron, using the Sussex iron smelted with charcoal. There are some pieces of ordnance preserved in the Rotunda at Woolwich which are of this age, and may possibly have come from the Sussex foundry. Examples of early cannon are rare in England, but on the Continent many may be found, especially in Belgium. The Rotunda and the Tower of London probably contain the finest specimens in the

PLATE XXXIX

1. Peterara, time of Edward IV.   2. Wall Arquebus. (Rotunda, Woolwich.)
3. The Brocas Heaume.   4. Heaume from Rotunda.

British Isles. In the Royal Arsenal at Madrid is preserved a small piece of ordnance dating from late fifteenth century. It is double-barrelled and breech-loading, and exhibits a wealth of ornamentation upon almost every part (Plate XXXVII.*). A breech-loading peterara of forged iron of the time of Edward IV. is in the Rotunda, and is illustrated in Plate XXXIX. It is made of longitudinal bars of iron hooped together with iron rings; the powder-chamber with its lifting handle is seen in position, and a simple locking arrangement prevented its blowing out upon the discharge. Trunnions are affixed to the piece, and the metal by which it was attached to the long-decayed wooden gun-carriage is still preserved. The length of the gun is 3 feet and the calibre 2½ inches, while the name implies that the shot was of stone. This very rare piece of ordnance is in excellent condition.

The progress in artillery was very slow, but gradually cannon became mounted upon wheels and rude carriages, an advance upon the logs and cumbrous beds of the preceding period, while iron was substituted for stone in the projectile. The engagement of trained professional gunners in place of the civilians who had managed the artillery in the fourteenth century, was another step which led to improvement, Dutch artillerymen being employed by Henry VIII. Charles VIII. and subsequent French monarchs undoubtedly did much for the improvement of the weapon; they adopted light guns for field artillery, and introduced the system of rapidly taking up different positions from which to assail the enemy. The Civil War in England found a great scarcity of cannon, and more particularly of efficient gunners, and generally it may be stated that the English use of artillery was much behind that existing upon the Continent until the middle of the eighteenth century.

The existence of cannon in the mediæval period would naturally suggest a weapon that might be used in the hand, and from a very early period hand-guns have been in evidence. They are rarely mentioned by writers of the time, and very few illuminations are extant showing the weapons then employed, which would tend to show that their use was restricted, and their efficacy valued but little. The earliest were simply tubes affixed to a stick and fired by means of a lighted match; some of them were ignited from the muzzle, thus indicating that they were shotless and only used to frighten horses in a cavalry charge. The long-bow and arbalest were of infinitely greater efficacy than the early hand-gun, and it is a matter for wonder that the latter held a place at all in the armies of the period. It was made in various shapes, but that generally shown in contemporary illustrations is depicted in Fig. 339, the piece being discharged by means of a touch-hole on the top of the barrel near the breech. The earliest use of a hand-gun is involved in obscurity; there can be no doubt that many attempts were made to introduce such a weapon, but the first mention that occurs is in the reign of Edward III., when they were brought into England from Flanders. They were in use by both horse and foot soldiers, the stock in the first case being shortened so that it could be placed against the chest, while in the second it passed under the right arm, the left hand being used to grasp it and the right to hold the discharging match. The gun was

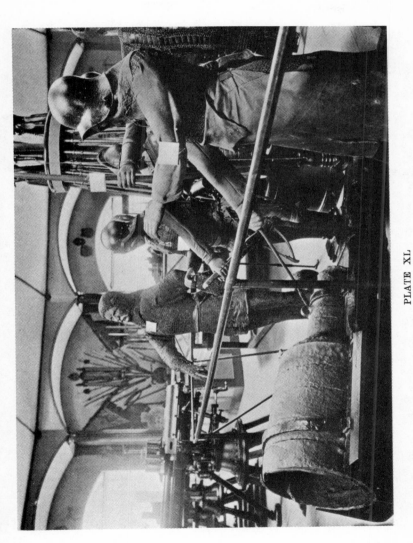

PLATE XL.

The "Crecy" Bombard, *temp.* Edward III. Arbalestier, Fifteenth Century. (Rotunda, Woolwich)

supported in the case of cavalry by a forked rest which projected from the saddle. In all these guns the powder-chamber was smaller than the calibre of the barrel. In some cases the hand-gun was used as a mace after being discharged.

Hand Culverin.—A larger hand-gun was subsequently evolved, which was much in use during the second half of the fifteenth century, and necessitated the presence of two men for its manipulation. It was called the hand culverin, and had a bore of about three-quarters of an inch; it was constructed of forged iron, and was attached by bands to a straight stock of wood. This weapon was fired from a rest. It was subsequently improved by the addition of a pan and touch-hole at the side and a modification of the stock, while the barrels were often of brass or bronze, and polygonal in section. Their weight varied from ten to sixteen pounds, and a variety which was carried on horseback at times weighed nearly sixty pounds. Warwick the King-maker employed " Burgundenses " or Burgundian hand-gun men in the Second Battle of St. Albans, 1461, and culveriners formed a part of the forces under Edward IV. in the later battles of the Wars of the Roses.

The Serpentin, Matchlock, or Arquebus.—An improvement was made about the year 1500, whereby the slow match, hitherto held in the hand, was affixed to a lever bent into the form of a serpent and fastened by the centre to the stock on a pivot; by pulling the lower portion the upper end carrying the match was made to descend upon the priming powder. Subsequent innovations consisted of a sliding cover over the flash-pan, and the jointing of the serpentin to increase the leverage. The matchlock was in use for about two centuries, in spite of the cumbersome nature of the weapon, the slow rate of its discharge, the trouble involved in keeping the match alight during boisterous or rainy weather, and the heavy rest for holding it when loading and taking aim. The greatest merit was undoubtedly its simplicity and cheapness. The arquebus shown in Plate XXVII., p. 322, is of the sixteenth century, time of James VI., and is in the Edinburgh Museum. The figure of an arquebusier may be discerned in Plate VIII., p. 64, under the horse's head of the Bayard figure. The arquebus is seen poised upon its rest with a piece of loose tow hanging from the barrel; the arquebusier is in the act of taking aim, and is accoutred in seventeenth century military dress. In Plate XXXIX. a wall arquebus is shown from the Rotunda, which is nearly 9 feet in length and weighs 87 lbs. It is fitted with a tube sight and an arrangement for pivoting in an iron socket upon a wall or in an embrasure. Its calibre is 1·3 inches. These pieces were at times carried into the field and required three men to manipulate them.

The Wheel-lock.—The great difficulty experienced in keeping the match alight resulted in the invention of the wheel-lock in the earlier part of the sixteenth century at Nuremberg, and its introduction into England about 1540. The mechanism consisted of a wheel serrated at the edge which protruded into the priming pan, and was fixed by its axle to the lock plate (Plate XLI.*). This axle was made square upon the outside for a key, while at the other end a strong spring engaged with it; by winding it the spring was compressed and held in place by a catch. The lock

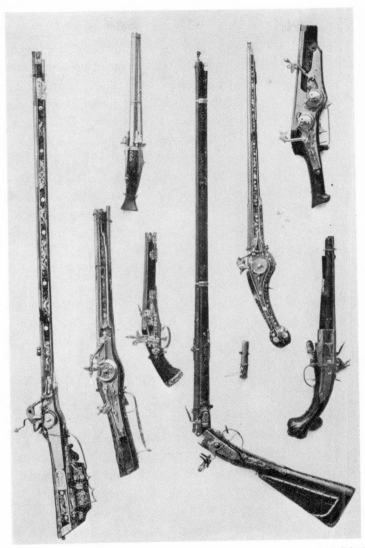

A. F. Calvert

PLATE XLI *

Left to Right.—1. Spanish Arquebus, Wheel-lock.
　　　　　2. Petronel, 1547, Wheel-lock.
　　　　　3. Three-barrelled Pistol.
　　　　　4. Pistol with Rifled Barrel.
　　　　　5. Breech-loading Flint-lock Hunting Gun of Philip V.
　　　　　6. Wheel-lock Petronel, Sixteenth Century.
　　　　　7. Revolver, Eighteenth Century.
　　　　　8. Wheel-lock Pistol, two Barrels, Sixteenth Century.

held a piece of pyrites, and when it was depressed rested in the priming pan, which had a removable cover; upon the trigger being pulled the spring caused the wheel to revolve quickly, whereby its file-like edges struck sparks of fire from the pyrites with which it was in contact and thus ignited the powder. For the cavalry and also for sporting purposes the wheel-lock was in use for many years, but its cost precluded a general introduction among the infantry. A · high degree of ornamentation was lavished upon many of these weapons; examples may be readily found in all museums of importance.

The Snap-hance.—This variety of lock was invented in Holland or Germany about 1550, and from the simplicity and ease with which it was made and the consequent cheapness of production, rapidly came into favour in England and on the Continent. It is said to have been evolved by a body of Dutch poultry stealers (Snaphans), who could not use the match-lock because of the light entailed, or the wheel-lock because of the expense, and thereupon devised the snap-hance, little dreaming that the invention would become so popular. The wheel-lock was superseded by a hammer which struck upon a piece of sulphurous pyrites; the flash-pan was the same, but the cover was actuated by a spring and flew back when the hammer descended, thus allowing a free passage for the shower of sparks.

The Flint-lock.—The snap-hance was undoubtedly the intermediate weapon between the wheel-lock and flint-lock. The latter may be claimed as an English invention, as a specimen occurs in the Tower having the date 1614 upon it, the date generally assigned for its introduction being 1630 according to continental records. The knowledge that fire could be produced by striking flint upon steel was well known to the ancients. In the flint-lock the fall of the hammer containing the flint was made to open the flash-pan and at the same time to strike sparks from its cover. The earlier kinds had all the mechanism upon the outside of the lock, but subsequently it was hidden, and a tumbler connected the mainspring with the hammer. Highly decorated examples of the flint-lock are common, especially those of Italian and Spanish origin (Plate XLI.*). The weapon did not come into extensive use in England until the second half of the seventeenth century, but it eventually superseded all others, and was adapted for every kind of firearm, both military and civil, and remained in use until the advent of the percussion cap about 1830.

Pistols underwent the same variations as the larger weapon, but these were often combined, being fixed in shields, battle-axes, pole-axes, daggers, halberds, &c.

The subject of this chapter is an extremely wide one, and an attempt to cover it completely in the pages of this work has not been attempted; the broad facts given here may, however, be acceptable to the general reader.

INDEX

INDEX

Rivets, almayne, 305
Roman armour, Republican, 36
   „   „   Imperial Period, 37
   „   engines, 341
Rondache, Augsburg (Plate 4, p. 40), 299
   „   Desiderius Colman (Plate 3, p. 32), 299
   „   Italian (Plate 1, p. 16) 299
   „   „   (Plate 5, p. 48), 299
   „   „   (Plate 6, p. 56), 299
   „   Philip II. (Plate 2, p. 24), 299
Rondaches, 298
Rotunda, 253
   „   cannon at, 364
   „   heaume, 185
Roundels, 118
Royal Armoury, Madrid, 353

Sabbaton, 232
Sabbatons, bear's-paw, 280
   „   of Piers Gerard, 232
   „   Hatfield House, 305
   „   Jacobi, 297
   „   Transition Period, 269
Sabre, 334
Salade, 217, 260
   „   on brasses, 248
   „   of Duke Ludvig of Bavaria, 220
   „   of German pattern, 220
   „   Maximilian Period, 281
   „   Milanese (Plate 7, p. 60), 355
   „   Tower of London, 219
   „   Wallace Collection, 219
Salletts, 218
Saxon arrow-head, 55
   „   axe, 53
   „   byrnie, 58
   „   chain mail, 60
   „   dagger, 54
   „   helmet, 56
   „   long-bow, 55
   „   pole-axe, 54
   „   shield, 57
   „   sling, 55
   „   spear-heads, 49
   „   swords, 50

Saxon umbo, 57
Saxons and Danes, 47
Say, Sir John, brass of, 252
   „   „   „   tabard of, 215
Scaling fork, 326
Scarisbrick Tabard, 216
Scimitar, 209, 335
Sebastian, King, armour of (Plate 20, p. 232), 356
Septvans, Sir Robert de, brass of, 117
Serpentin, 307, 367
Sharfrennen, 309
Shell gauntlets, 253
Shelton, Sir Ralph, tabard of, 215
Shield, Assyrian, 21
   „   Bronze Age, 17
   „   (British Museum MS.), 203
   „   Camail and Jupon Period, 92
   „   Danish, 64
   „   Egyptian, 23
   „   Etruscan, 35
   „   Greek, 25, 28
   „   Norman, 77
   „   Roman, Imperial Period, 39
   „   Saxon, 57
   „   Sir Richard Pembridge, 183
   „   Studded and Splinted Period, 157
   „   Surcoatless Period, 203
   „   of Robert Wyvill, 183
Shields or rondaches, 298
Shurland, Sir Robert, effigy of, 141
Sieges, 340
Sir John de Bitton, 87
Sir Oliver d'Ingham, stone effigy, 100
Sir Roger de Kerdeston, stone effigy, 100
Sir Robert de Trumpington, brass of, 99
Sir William de Staunton, heaume, 101
Skirt of mail, Transition Period, 269
Slab, Sir John de Bitton, 87
Slashed armour, 291
Sling, Saxon, 55
Sling-stones, 7
Snap-hance, 369
Snout-faced visor, 171
Soldier, Cyclas Period, 144
   „   Chain Mail Period, 93

A CATALOGUE OF SELECTED DOVER BOOKS
IN ALL FIELDS OF INTEREST

A CATALOGUE OF SELECTED DOVER BOOKS
IN ALL FIELDS OF INTEREST

AMERICA'S OLD MASTERS, James T. Flexner. Four men emerged unexpectedly from provincial 18th century America to leadership in European art: Benjamin West, J. S. Copley, C. R. Peale, Gilbert Stuart. Brilliant coverage of lives and contributions. Revised, 1967 edition. 69 plates. 365pp. of text.

21806-6 Paperbound $3.00

FIRST FLOWERS OF OUR WILDERNESS: AMERICAN PAINTING, THE COLONIAL PERIOD, James T. Flexner. Painters, and regional painting traditions from earliest Colonial times up to the emergence of Copley, West and Peale Sr., Foster, Gustavus Hesselius, Feke, John Smibert and many anonymous painters in the primitive manner. Engaging presentation, with 162 illustrations. xxii + 368pp.

22180-6 Paperbound $3.50

THE LIGHT OF DISTANT SKIES: AMERICAN PAINTING, 1760-1835, James T. Flexner. The great generation of early American painters goes to Europe to learn and to teach: West, Copley, Gilbert Stuart and others. Allston, Trumbull, Morse; also contemporary American painters—primitives, derivatives, academics—who remained in America. 102 illustrations. xiii + 306pp. 22179-2 Paperbound $3.50

A HISTORY OF THE RISE AND PROGRESS OF THE ARTS OF DESIGN IN THE UNITED STATES, William Dunlap. Much the richest mine of information on early American painters, sculptors, architects, engravers, miniaturists, etc. The only source of information for scores of artists, the major primary source for many others. Unabridged reprint of rare original 1834 edition, with new introduction by James T. Flexner, and 394 new illustrations. Edited by Rita Weiss. 6⅝ x 9⅝.

21695-0, 21696-9, 21697-7 Three volumes, Paperbound $13.50

EPOCHS OF CHINESE AND JAPANESE ART, Ernest F. Fenollosa. From primitive Chinese art to the 20th century, thorough history, explanation of every important art period and form, including Japanese woodcuts; main stress on China and Japan, but Tibet, Korea also included. Still unexcelled for its detailed, rich coverage of cultural background, aesthetic elements, diffusion studies, particularly of the historical period. 2nd, 1913 edition. 242 illustrations. lii + 439pp. of text.

20364-6, 20365-4 Two volumes, Paperbound $6.00

THE GENTLE ART OF MAKING ENEMIES, James A. M. Whistler. Greatest wit of his day deflates Oscar Wilde, Ruskin, Swinburne; strikes back at inane critics, exhibitions, art journalism; aesthetics of impressionist revolution in most striking form. Highly readable classic by great painter. Reproduction of edition designed by Whistler. Introduction by Alfred Werner. xxxvi + 334pp.

21875-9 Paperbound $2.50